Canadian Cataloguing in Publication Data
Bruce, Harry, 1934–
  Down home
ISBN 1-55013-098-6
1. Maritime Provinces — Description and travel —
1981–   .* 2. Maritime Provinces — Social life and
customs. 3. Maritime Provinces — Biography.
4. Bruce, Harry, 1934–   . I. Title.
FC2025.5.B78 1988   971.5'04   C88-094277-0
F1035.8.B78 1988

Key Porter Books Limited
70 The Esplanade
Toronto, Ontario
M5E 1R2

The publisher gratefully acknowledges the assistance of the Ontario Arts Council.

Design: Marie Bartholomew
Illustrations: Renée Mansfield
Typesetting: Vellum Print & Graphic Services Inc.
Printed and bound in Canada

88 89 90 91 92   6 5 4 3 2 1

Christmas 1988,

Dear Mother.

May this novel help to preserve
the memories that you cherish of
your home in Nova Scotia.

Love,
Stephen.

DOWN HOME

NOTES OF A MARITIME SON

HARRY BRUCE

KEY PORTER·BOOKS

CONTENTS

1

WON'T YOU COME BACK HOME?

I am writing this in longhand in the house where my father was born, and where, if he'd had his choice, he'd have died. It is often as silent here as the dark corridors of a locked cathedral. A mongrel may bark at furtive deer on the MacIntosh farm to our west. Dogs of white men have been yelping and baying around here for a couple of centuries. And a chain-saw may buzz for a while on the Grady property to our east. All through my father's boyhood, and for decades both before and after, a saw mill kept on humming over there, and young Floyd Grady, who just came home from away, yearns to start up another one by the same old Mill Brook that still roars in the springtime as it tumbles from McPherson Lake to join salt water. My father Charles would have applauded Floyd's dream. Now and then a truck whines along the paved highway that slices through the Bruce, MacIntosh, and Grady land, and the land of others whose Scottish and Irish forebears found themselves on this mean soil, among these tough trees, long before Wellington whupped Napoleon.

So there are some noises here at Port Shoreham, Nova Scotia. Port Shoreham is not a port, nor a town, nor even a village. It is a shore. It is a handful of old farms, scattered over the low hills as loosely as their own sheep. Some maps pretend there's no such spot, and even its name is variable, like the wind. At times, the postal address of Port Shoreham has been Clam Harbour, Ragged Head, and Rural Route 1, Mulgrave. Most Nova Scotians have never heard of Port Shoreham, much less seen it.

In bed, I can hear my ears ring and the doomed tide of my blood. The air outside is often so still I hear something else. It's the whisper of Chedabucto Bay as it obeys the moon. It's the sound of gentle swells as they lap on the beach and suck at a billion smooth little stones all along the perfect three-mile curve to Ragged Head. The gravel beach is a third of a mile south of what my ancient Bruce aunts still call the homestead, but those rhythmic sighs float all the way up over the balsam fir and wire birch on the humpbacked peninsula known as Bruce's Island; across Clam Harbour, a seaweed-matted pond that no longer shelters schooners but still boasts rich clam beds; farther inland to the subarctic jungle at the foot of our field; then up the field and in the window of the northwest bedroom where Penny and I sleep.

The echo of the surf comes to us like the breathing of a distant giant who slumbers well, and in the early fall the air that ferries the sound northward over our land smells not only of the clean sea but also of hay, and spruce and fir needles, and wild roses. "Will you smell that air?" Penny says. "God, you could almost eat it." We are not used to the silence and the perfume. We are city people. "The nights are those a man remembers, looking upward through the murk of cities, his instinct looking back," my father wrote from Toronto, a quarter-century after he left the house where I now write. "There are nights in the full moon of October when darkness is a kind of silver daylight, when the sea is a sheet of twinkling light, the shadows of barn and fence and apple tree black and incredible, the air vibrant and alive but still as a dreamless sleep."

But I set these words down on a morning in March, when the air is bursting with explosions and violent tinkles. Sometimes the noise in the woods sounds as though a drunk in an antique shop has toppled a cabinet full of crystal wine goblets. Sometimes it's as though a madman were hurling bone china at a cement wall. And beyond all this we can hear sharp reports, like rifle fire. *Crack! Crack! Crack!* Something is ripping branches off trees as easily as a child rips petals from a daisy. And all this unearthly din is the aftermath of an ice storm like none I have ever seen before, or may ever see again.

Overnight, ice encased every twig, cone, bud, branch, and trunk for tens of miles in every direction. God alone knows how many million spruce and fir needles wore their own glistening sheaths this morning. Glassy cylinders hugged every wire, fencepost, and clothesline pole. Doorsteps, woodpiles, rocks, pebbles, cars, trucks, tractors, roadside garbage drums, and letterboxes—they all shone under this new, hard, gleaming, and transparent skin. Before breakfast, the light of the low sun struck the white hills and turned the whole infinitely intricate maze of ice into an impossible razzle-dazzle of sparkle and flash and golden magic, and beyond it all lay the royal blue of the implacable bay.

We left the kitchen, with its wood stove burning, and went outside to examine the miracle. From our Toyota's radio aerial, I lifted a fragile straw of ice. A mould of one of the exterior mirrors fell apart in my hands. Even the outhouse was beautiful in its jacket of ice. Everywhere, the light in the sun-fired ice made the world's most elegant Christmas decorations look as tawdry as a bargain-basement sale on Boxing Day; but already, somewhere beyond our vision, we heard the first goblets shatter, the first platters smash, and the dreadful cracking of limbs.

It's 9:30 now, and I've had my breakfast: grapefruit juice, blueberry muffins, toast with neighbour Jean Grady's homemade crab-apple jelly, three salt-cod cakes, and three cups of Irish tea. I am sitting at my desk in the northwest room on the ground floor of the house my great-great-grandfather, Richard Bruce, built 140 years ago. The room is not big. No room in this house is big, and most college basketball players would have to stoop to pass through any of our doorways or mount our skinny stairs. Early Bruces in these parts were short physically and short financially.

But certain features of the room where I've planted my desk and books suggest it has always been special. The framing around the three windows is eight inches wide and ornate, and it's only in this room that wood panels decorate the wall beneath each window. Pine planks, some fifteen inches wide, cover the bedroom floors upstairs, but the floor in here is hardwood. This is the room where the nineteenth-century pump organ once stood. Labelled "mouseproof," it came by rail in the age of steam, and then by horse-drawn wagon over dirt roads, from the Dominion Organ Company up in Bowmanville, Ontario; in the hands of my grandmother, Sarah Tory Bruce (who lived almost long enough to celebrate her hundredth birthday along with

Canada's), it sometimes sounded like the introductory music for a vampire movie starring Vincent Price.

This room was The Parlour, and both the primitive lock on the door and the memory of my Bruce aunts suggest it was open only on Sundays, only for visits by clergy, for occasional hymn-singing gatherings among the more respectable women of the shore, and for Special Occasions. One special occasion in The Parlour occurred only a few years ago. In August 1982, precisely 109 years after a notorious gale hurled local schooners into the upper branches of trees, my aunts summoned me to The Parlour to propose one of the most important deals of my life. In order of seniority, "the Bruce girls" were Bessie Willena Bruce, a spinster, born October 4, 1891, the year the world's first old-age pension went into effect in Prince von Bismarck's Germany; Mrs. Anna May MacKeen, a widow, born July 17, 1893, the year Detroit machinist Henry Ford road-tested his first "gasoline buggy"; Mrs. Carrie Louise MacMillan, a widow, born July 12, 1895, the year Zanzibar abolished slavery; and Mrs. Zoe Ella Josephine Shulze, a widow, born July 22, 1898, during the sixty-first year of Queen Victoria's reign over the Empire.

The title to the Bruce homestead, which my father often called The Place, lay in Bess's name. She grew feebler by the hour, and the 1982 conference in The Parlour of The Place was a response to my proposal that I buy the property from her. They were waiting for me in there, all four of them. They were tiny, white-haired, bespectacled, smiling, and suddenly decisive. As a group, they'd spent 351 years on earth, and their manner reminded me that they'd spent a fair number of those years in their mother's profession. They were all ex-schoolmarms. They would brook no argument from a mere nephew, a whippersnapper barely forty-eight years old. Bess was a tough bargainer. She bargained my price *downward* and insisted she'd accept not a nickel of interest on the mortgage she took back.

She died in June of 1986. Her body is five miles from here, in the graveyard at Boylston United Church, and so are my father's ashes, and the headstones of our forebears right back to the fellow who built our farmhouse when Dickens was young and Disraeli was thought promising. One day I'll be in that graveyard myself, but right now Carrie's in Maryland, Zoe's in California, Anna's just along the road in Boylston, the organ's in the kitchen, and I am in The Parlour. I may be the first Bruce ever to report to The Parlour to do a day's work.

I am looking through the west window. Thirteen hundred miles over the horizon sits Toronto, the city where I was born— son of a bluenose expatriate and a Vancouver woman whose father was another bluenose expatriate—and where I first heard talk of a far-off zone called Down Home. Just down the slope from my window some scaly apple trees, planted by heaven only knows what Bruce in what year, utter arthritic groans as the ice once again tortures their joints. This is as good a day as any to begin the story of what Down Home has meant, not only to my own family, but to hundreds of thousands of Maritimers who could not help leaving and could never stop remembering. The story is also about those who refused to leave Down Home, about those who stuck like rockweed to the seaside provinces that, too often, richer and more politically powerful inlanders have dismissed as the shag end of Canada.

* * *

Wave after wave after wave of Maritimers have left their beloved homeland, rolling westward again and again to seek jobs up and down the Atlantic seaboard, in the American midwest and far west, in Quebec, Ontario, the Prairies, British Columbia, and the northern territories. For generations of Maritimers, the streets paved with gold were supposed to lie in "the Boston states." Later, they were in the Canadian west, then Toronto, and later still the west again. Maritimers, more than other Canadians, have had to keep their eyes on horizons, and Leaving Home has long outlasted the golden age of sail as part of their heritage. It is as Down-Home as a clambake at dusk, complete with Moosehead ale.

Settled by wanderers who sought a better life than they could ever hope to build among the poverty and persecution of rural France, the German Rhineland, the potato fields of Ireland, the sheep slopes of Scotland, the regiments of the British Army, or, in the case of the Loyalists, the hatreds of revolutionary America, the Maritimes spawned whole new generations of wanderers who, in turn, sought a better life than they could ever hope to build among the big families on small farms in Prince Edward Island and the Annapolis Valley, the fishing ports of Acadian New Brunswick, or the murdering mines of Cape Breton, Springhill, and Stellarton, Nova Scotia. No living Maritimer can remember a time when at least parts of the region were not desperate for jobs. Necessity still fuels the ceaseless exodus as surely as it inspired the first European settlers to take a trans-Atlantic voyage far more gruelling and dangerous than an astronaut's ride to the moon.

The exodus began right after the plotters of Confederation had seduced the Maritimes. By 1870 more than 6,200 Nova Scotians had already settled in Boston alone, where they routinely greeted fresh loads of hopeful Maritimers who came by scheduled steamships directly from Halifax, Yarmouth, and Saint John. In the next thirty years, a quarter-million Maritimers, 40 per cent of all those in the region in 1870, moved away, mostly to the United States; and in the half-century between 1881 and 1931, more than 600,000 people left the region. Most of them were the young, unmarried sons and daughters of farmers, fishermen, carpenters, blacksmiths, shipwrights, coopers, carriage-makers, and merchants. By the 1960s, hundreds of thousands of Maritimers were living in central and western Canada, and the human tide from Down Home to the United States still flowed strong.

As the exodus continued, immigration did little to take up the population slack. Though Canada welcomed more than four million immigrants between 1901 and 1931, the Maritimes were not their destination. Those who disembarked at Halifax quickly boarded trains and shot through the dark evergreen forests of Nova Scotia and New Brunswick *en route* to Ontario and the Prairies. The story was the same during and after World War Two. More than two and a half million immigrants entered Canada between 1941 and 1971, but few ended up in the Maritimes.

The result of the exodus, and the feebleness of the immigration flow, was that in the first eight decades of this century the population of those who stayed Down Home did little better than double (from 894,000 in 1901 to 1,666,000 in 1981), while the population in Canada as a whole almost quintupled (from 5,371,000 to 24,343,000). People have talked for generations about the virtues of Maritime Union—which is fine on paper and impossible in politics—but even if the Maritimes were one province, Ontario would outnumber it by seven million people, Quebec by almost six million, and British Columbia by more than one million.

*   *   *

"Its people are intensely loyal," wrote Miriam Chapin, describing Nova Scotia in *Atlantic Canada*, "and they leave as fast as they can. . . . Though they leave they stay bound." My father knew what she was talking about. He'd been in Toronto for two decades when, in 1952, his book *The Mulgrave Road* won the Governor General's Award for poetry; but that's a book in which all the important things occur Down Home. For decades his muse was simple homesickness. "I haven't seen Queensport Light over the loom of Ragged Head in Years," he complained in one poem. "And never a smell of rollers coming up the bay from Canso." (From our kitchen windows here at The Place, we can see the far and rhythmic blink of the Queensport Light every clear night of the year, and whenever an easterly blows I have only to saunter down to the beach to smell the rollers coming up the bay from Canso.) In the same poem, my father also referred to "A few homesick men, walking an alien street; / A few women remembering misty stars / And the long grumbling sigh of the bay at night."

The first homesick Maritimers were the Acadians. In an act Acadian scholars still see as attempted genocide, the British in 1755 began to deport Acadians by the thousands, burning their houses and barns up and down the hay-sweet Annapolis Valley and across the sweeping marshlands at the head of the Bay of Fundy, nabbing those who'd fled into the woods, breaking up families while shoving the French willy-nilly aboard waiting vessels, and shipping them all off to British colonies far to the south, to France, and even to England. But the Acadians yearned so powerfully for the country they'd cultivated for a century and more that within a few years they returned by the gangload. They came back home on foot, by ox-cart, by ship, by whatever means would get them there. Some spent years on this amazingly stubborn expedition. Heroic yarns about the Great Disruption and the greater pilgrimage were passed down by word of mouth, with increasingly dramatic embellishments as the generations passed, until they became the cultural glue of the Acadian people. Acadians today, Down Home and far away, still know these tales as well as Americans know what Lincoln said at Gettysburg, and as well as the English know what Nelson achieved off Cape Trafalgar.

Antonine Maillet took the old legends and wove them into an epic novel, *Pélagie-la-Charrette*, which appeared in 1979, during the 375th anniversary of the founding of Acadia, and promptly won the highest literary honour France offers, the Prix Goncourt. *Pélagie* is about an Acadian widow who, after surviving in Georgia for fifteen years, leads fellow exiles on an ox-cart caravan from Acadie-in-the-South to Acadie-in-the-North. When someone suggests Pélagie abandon her mad mission and join the happy Acadian exiles in Louisiana, she reflects that Louisiana may indeed be tempting but it has no graves to tend nor roots to delve. (Even today, the Acadians are champion root-delvers in Canada's foremost region of root-delving.) Louisiana was rich. It was warm. But, Pélagie says, try to remember the lost Acadie: "Try to remember the harvest season with the apple trees so loaded the branches are cracking at the joints; and the sugar season with the maple sap dripping in the cans; and the season of the little wild strawberries. . . . Have they got wild strawberries and maple syrup in your Louisiana?"

That is the voice of homesickness, and if the Acadians are now a kind of nation within a nation, they are perhaps the only one in the world that owes its national identity to Homeric legends about how their ancestors conquered homesickness: by going home. They are the only people who so loved what is now the Maritimes that they chose to pioneer here not once, but twice.

For other Down Home pioneers, homesickness for the motherland may sometimes have been scarcely bearable. We don't know for sure. We know so little about them. "I once asked a neighbor why that was," my father wrote. "He simply said, 'They left no writing.' They were too busy, the implication was, to leave anything but a patch of cleared land and a new generation of flesh and blood."

For the run-of-the-mill immigrant to Canada in the eighteenth and nineteenth centuries, there'd be no summer vacations in the homeland to hug parents, explore childhood haunts, banter with old chums in the village pub, or look up the girl he left behind. There was no going home again. As a physical break with the past, braving a trans-Atlantic voyage to settle here was final, like death. The Scottish settlers remembered faces on the shore, the hills of home. Their heartbreak inspired a plaintive branch of literature, a poetry of homesickness that so mourned a lost land of gloom that it struck those from sunnier cultures as perverse, like the love of haggis.

The Lone Shieling (a shepherd's hut), one of the more famous examples of this strain of lament, appeared in *Blackwood's* magazine in 1829. It expressed the longing of Hebridean exiles for the "hoary woods" of Canada. In part, it went like this:

From the lone shieling of the misty island
    Mountains divide us, and the waste of seas—

Yet still the blood is strong, the heart is Highland
And we in dreams behold the Hebrides:
Fair these broad meads—the hoary woods are grand;
But we are exiles from our father's land.

"These few words," James Roy wrote in *The Scot and Canada*, "express much of the sorrow and suffering on which Canada has been built."

Now skip a century or two. Try to imagine the power and mournful passion of Rita MacNeil, the singer-laureate of Cape Breton Island. She is a stout woman with a wide face under a floppy hat. To the near-hysterical applause that has greeted her performances from Tokyo to Expo '86 in Vancouver, she has murmured a shy, tiny "Thenk you very much." But her singing voice sails like the bald eagles that still cruise Cape Breton skies, and then dives to a soft, growling lullabye. She writes her own songs, and no Rita MacNeil concert is complete without at least one surging lament from an expatriate Cape Breton Islander for a lost and heavenly homeland.

Nor is she the only singer to express the misery of the uprooted Islander. In the 1970s and early 1980s, a troupe staged a series of shows called *The Rise and Follies of Cape Breton Island*. These included sad and happy songs, comic routines, and much spoofing, not only of mainlanders but also of Cape Breton Islanders and their dreams, flaws, and quirks. The shows often offered political jibes set to music, as calypso does in the West Indies. The messages (if not always the roots of the music) were pure Cape Breton, and not a production went by without references to leaving home, yearning for home, or coming home.

Many descendants of Cape Breton Scots, out of whose ranks came stars of *The Rise and Follies*, feel not one but two homesicknesses. The first is pleasant. It springs from a stubborn love of their ancestral homeland and its seemingly deathless cultural heritage, even though most Cape Bretoners die without ever having visited Scotland. This is a homesickness not only for a far-off place but also for a far-off time, and it inspires a continuing passion for Highland games, Highland dance contests, the kilt, bagpipes, strathspeys, reels, hornpipes, and Gaelic lessons. It was not so long ago that the island boasted more speakers of Gaelic than anywhere else in the world: its people complained as bitterly about the Canadian Broadcasting Corporation cancelling a local Gaelic-language radio show as other Maritimers did about the corporation's killing the nationally televised "Don Messer Show."

Aroused by real memories rather than nostalgia for a legendary culture, the second homesickness is the one that hurts, and it's common not only among expatriate Cape Breton Islanders but among Maritimers just about everywhere in the world. An Acadian *coiffeur* in Montreal studies a client's hair, but her mind turns to a vision of her father's fishing boat coming in off Baie des Chaleurs at Caraquet. A Calgary lawyer ponders a brief, then thinks about his boyhood home in Woodstock and the glory of the Saint John River Valley at Thanksgiving. A racetrack groom in Toronto remembers the pretty horses his parents keep near Summerside. Born in Wolfville and trained in Halifax, a librarian in Papua New Guinea wonders if the apple blossoms are early or late this year in the Annapolis Valley. Grant MacIntosh, an Oshawa bricklayer, puts aside enough money to get home to Port Shoreham for Christmas. So does his brother Stewart, a hand on a freighter that's bouncing her way across the North Atlantic toward England. Their parents and kid sisters await them at the MacIntosh spread, which is just across a gully from The Place of the Bruces.

* * *

Unlike the pioneers, expatriate Maritimers can return to the land of their roots whenever they can scrape together the fare, and like hummingbirds, they come back Down Home each summer. J. Angus MacLean knows about hummingbirds. He used to be premier of Prince Edward Island, and he's now content to live on the homestead his grandfather hacked out of the bush in the 1860s and grow blueberries for profit on two thirty-five-acre fields. It was there at the MacLean spread, in a rangy white farmhouse with a green roof, that he told me about the ruby-throated hummingbird. I'd phoned earlier from Charlotte-town to say I'd like to meet him but knew he was busy harvesting blueberries. He'd drawled, "Come ahead. All the time there is goes by here, you know." When I got there, the harvesting was just over. Rain was falling, Mrs. MacLean was settling up with young blueberry-rakers in the homey heat from the wood stove in the kitchen, and the Honourable J. Angus MacLean, fit and braw at seventy-three, was telling me, "Hummingbirds are a marvel of creation."

Each bird, he said, weighed only as much as a one-cent piece, and yet they flew all the way down to the Gulf of Mexico and Cuba in the fall, and some flew nonstop for more than three hundred miles over the Caribbean Sea to reach South America. But each spring they returned, and certain hummingbirds zoomed all the way back to the same spot on MacLean's farm. "Now that's a miracle of navigation. Some of my best friends can't find this place." One springtime, MacLean forgot to put out his hummingbird feeders. Then, on a Sunday afternoon in late May, he heard frantic squeaks. He looked out a window and saw two hummingbirds with metal-red throats, white breasts, and backs of glossy, Robin-Hood green. They'd flown thousands of miles, and now they desperately hovered exactly where the feeders had stood in past summers. "I don't think this homing instinct is just something that's learned, or just force of habit," MacLean said. "It's deeper than that. It's an instinct in the genes of fish and birds, and probably in our own genes, too."

*   *   *

Visits by relatives are so important to Islanders that the older ones see Old Home Week not only as a time to welcome chil-dren and grandchildren but also as a signal from Nature. It marks the end of summer. No matter that Old Home Week occurs in the second week of August and that the Island always enjoys weeks more of summer weather. When Old Home Week's over, summer's over, and that's that. It's appropriate, then, that the strangest homecoming story I know of occurred on the Island. I found it in 1975 in the *Eastern Graphic*, published in Montague, P.E.I., and it goes like this: When Charles Coghlan, son of poor Irish parents on the Island, defied them by becoming an actor, they banned him from the family homestead. Late in the nineteenth century, the exile made money as an actor all over the United States. He often told his friends about a gypsy fortune-teller who'd warned him he'd never be at rest till he returned to his birthplace. While playing Hamlet in Galveston, Texas, in 1898, he died. He was buried there, but in 1900 a hurricane washed the sandy cemetery into the Gulf of Mexico. Eight years and three thousand miles later, his coffin bumped ashore on Prince Edward Island. Charles Coghlan had come home with a vengeance, and Island folk buried him beside the church where, sixty-seven years before, he'd been baptized.

Polls by provincial governments reveal that more than 700,000 of the tourists who enter the Maritimes each year come primarily to visit friends and relatives. The pilgrimage is one of the oldest annual migrations of people in North America. Some come back to stay. Thirty-odd years ago, at bars and house parties in Toronto, I used to find myself among Maritimers who, like my father, had settled up there as newspapermen. They didn't weep in their beer, but they talked over their rum-and-cokes, and eventually they got around to describing a dream. Some day, they would escape all this Hog Town crap and set themselves up Down Home, maybe to do a little writing in their last years.

Hundreds of Maritime sea captains commanded sailing vessels on voyage after voyage in the nineteenth century, and then came home with their heads full of wild memories and their houses full of souvenirs. And some of those Toronto newspapermen will realize their dream, too. They'll come back for more than a visit, with their own stories to tell. Some have already made the jump. The return of the native is an old story Down Home, and it'll continue into the next millennium.

* * *

My father was born to be homesick. His boyhood was too good to forget. He was the last child of William Henry Bruce and Sarah Jane Tory Bruce, and the first boy to survive. His four older sisters had all been born in the 1890s, and early in 1900 Sarah had given birth to William Henry Marshall Bruce. But Willie was not yet two when, after chewing on raw cabbage, he suffered convulsions that killed him. Nearly five years passed before Charles Tory Bruce came along. He was born at The Place on May 11, 1906, the year an earthquake destroyed two thirds of San Francisco and the *London Daily Mail* coined the term "suffragette." Sarah, pushing forty when Charlie arrived, was a devout Methodist and saw her new son as God's signal that He had forgiven her for her terrible failure with Willie. Bess was fourteen, Anna twelve, Carrie nine, and Zoe seven. Charlie was their darling. "We all adored him, of course," Zoe recalled eighty years later. "He was just a little prince."

He was born into a community riddled with relatives. His prolific Scottish forebears had arrived in the neighbourhood well over a century before. On his mother's side, a Scot named James Torrey (one *r* and the *e* disappeared later) came to Nova Scotia from New York in 1783, after the revolutionary war. Torrey was with the Associated Departments of the Army and Navy, a catch-all of disbanded British regiments and civilian Loyalists whom the successful patriots had bounced from the new United States. He was one of my great-great-great-grandfathers. So was James Bruce, who probably came straight from somewhere near Aberdeen and settled close to Port Shoreham around 1790. He married Catherine Cadel in 1798. Before a falling tree killed him in 1805—during a chopping bee to build a log schoolhouse—they had four children. The oldest was Richard Samuel Bruce, who built The Place where I now work in The Parlour. Richard's wife was born Margaret Morgan, and they had seven children.

Their first was James Christopher Bruce, a great-great-uncle of mine. Clam Harbour is so shallow and languid now that it's hard to imagine anything bigger than great blue herons messing about on it. Nothing in print tells us about a deeper Clam Harbour, but my father heard it from his father that there was once so much water down there that James Christopher Bruce built and launched his first trading schooner, the *J.J. Marshall*, right at the foot of our pasture. James later had a brigantine, the *Princess Dagmar*, and still later the *Commerce*, probably a 150-ton brig. Sometime between the end of the American Civil War and the birth of Canada, he sailed the *Commerce* toward Sierra Leone on the west coast of Africa, where he may have intended to sell her. But Captain Bruce, his crew, and ship all vanished. Similar stories began at countless beaches, coves, inlets, guts, and tickles throughout the Maritimes.

Richard's second child was Charles Joseph Bruce, the first to survive in modern memories. My father wrote about "Charles, my grandfather, whom I remember, barely, as a wiry little old man with forked whiskers and a remarkable reputation for piety and ability in a blow." Anna, at ninety-four, says he was cheerful, kindly, and "a great provider." He went on frequent fishing excursions with other men from our bay shore and invested his take in staples for his family. In a cardboard box at The Place, I found family documents dating back almost to the Crimean War. Among them were statements of old Charles's account—toted up in pounds, shillings, and pence, and written in a fine, flowing, ornate hand—with Halifax merchant P. Power & Co. Charles was trading barrels of herring and mackerel for flour, molasses, tea, salt, rope, and tar. His goods arrived regularly in Guysborough, nine miles from The Place by land, aboard the seventy-two-ton schooner *Isabella*—just another seagoing workhorse among the hundreds of small sailing vessels that routinely nipped along the intricate coasts of the Maritimes.

One thing Charles did *not* spend money on was booze. The box also contained his card of membership in the local Temperance Reform Club. Though dated March 1878, the card is as stiff and legible as it was on the day club officers George and John McMaster endorsed it. (Their descendants are neighbours of ours.) Believing booze "destroys health, promotes vice and poverty, and imperils the welfare of the soul," Charles did "hereby solemnly PLEDGE and BIND myself, that, by God's assistance I will abstain entirely from all intoxicating liquors and that I will endeavour to persuade others to do the same." He was forty-five, but since he was a good Methodist it's doubtful if he'd ever had a drop of liquor before he formally renounced it.

The box held a still more important document: the marriage licence, dated January 9, 1860, of Charles Joseph Bruce and Lydia Simpson McKeough. It's a skinny blue sheet of limp rag paper, wearing thin only at the folds, and signed by Charles Tupper, then the thirty-eight-year-old provincial secretary. (Tupper would later become a Father of Confederation, prime minister of Canada, baronet of the United Kingdom, and among irreverent Maritimers who knew rumours of his private life, "The Ram of Cumberland County.") "The Bruce girls" saw their grandmother Bruce as a fussy, severe woman, a meticulous housekeeper whose only memorable habit of generosity was to allow them to pore over her books and magazines. Almost all the Bruces and Torys were voracious readers of religious publications, romantic novels, travel books, verse, *The Family Herald*, and, indeed, just about any reading matter they could lay their hands on.

Most families on the bay shore were hard-up, and they endured cradle-to-the-grave frugality. By subsistence farming, a spot of fishing, cutting their own firewood, doing their own carpentry and some of their own blacksmithing, by spinning their own yarn, and helping one another out, they managed to scratch out a living. Still, as Aunt Zoe put it in her ninetieth year, "Of course, we didn't *know* we were underprivileged." Charles and Lydia were doubtless as cash-poor as just about everyone else in the district, but they carved out a bit of stature for themselves. James Tory, brother of Sarah (and, in time, lieutenant-governor of Nova Scotia), once told Zoe's sister Anna that their Bruce grandparents had been "the aristocrats of the shore."

They had a handsome horse and a spiffy open carriage. When they drove into Guysborough town, where schooners still bobbed in the harbour, Lydia wore a black silk dress and a bonnet. Charles's suit was dark, and his beard neat. Among the small, dusty treasures that still lurk in the cupboards of The Place are a stovepipe hat of the kind Abraham Lincoln wore and a black bowler that's stiff enough to use as a weapon. Neither fits me. A century has swelled Bruce heads.

Lydia was one of eight McKeough sisters. The shore's spindly economy couldn't accommodate them all, and most moved away, leaving me countless Yankee cousins I'll never know. My grandfather, William Henry Bruce, sole son of Charles and Lydia, married Sarah Tory in the mid-1880s, and then they, too, joined the long parade of Maritimers to "the Boston states."

They endured no border hassles. Free of immigration barriers and passport requirements, Maritimers and New Englanders moved back and forth as if they were all citizens of the same nation. Will was in his early twenties, and Sarah just nineteen or twenty. They may well have intended to settle in the U.S. for good, but things didn't turn out that way, and I'm glad they didn't. Will's misfortunes in Somerville, Massachusetts, brought him back home; though they occurred nearly ninety years ago, they are one reason why The Place remains the place of Bruces.

Between the time the Canadian Pacific Railway reached Vancouver and Theodore Roosevelt succeeded the assassinated William McKinley as president of the United States, Will and Sarah spent a dozen years in Somerville. Will, a cabinetmaker, landed his first job at a desk factory. Then, he and Fred

Cummings, a neighbour from Down Home, formed Bruce & Cummings, a grocery business. By 1898, when Will and Sarah had four tiny girls to raise, the grocery store was already gasping for air. Cummings bailed out to join the Klondike Gold Rush, while Will hung on in Somerville.

As a shopkeeper, he was a fine carpenter. He extended credit to bad risks, and a hired boy gradually stole $900 from under his nose. By 1900 the grocery business was dead, and at thirty-seven Will was back in the desk factory where he'd started his American career. Sarah and the girls were living with her parents at the Tory farm, "up the back road" at Port Shoreham. On September 17 Will somehow managed to send her two dollars. Two weeks later, he told her by mail he hoped that some day he'd find a way to take over The Place, where his parents still lived.

When Will followed his family back home, he was not well. His ailment may have been physical, or else the long, bootless Somerville adventure had simply depressed him. Anna believes he suffered "sort of a nervous breakdown." Following his return, he had no choice but to let his own and his wife's parents help care for his family. The girls lived off and on at the homes of both sets of grandparents, and though such arrangements were routine all over the Maritimes, these years must have been hard on Will's pride. Almost twenty years before, Sarah had been a schoolteacher. In her mid-thirties now, she returned to the classrooms of the bay shore and beyond. Every nickel of her meagre wages counted.

But in 1905 Will's seventy-six-year-old father built a new house for himself and Lydia in nearby Boylston, and the old couple sold The Place to Will for $400. He was forty-two then, and he would never again move away. The Place had a downstairs bedroom for him and Sarah and an upstairs bedroom for each of their daughters. The following May, only six months after Will had bought The Place, my father arrived. He entered a family that was together under the same roof for the first time in years, and the roof covered the ancestral home. If he came along as what he once told me was "an afterthought," this springtime baby also came along as part of the launching of the best period of his parents' lives.

*　*　*

The hefty, black, two-level wood stove made the kitchen the cosiest room in a cosy house, and my father, with his sisters egging him on, was still only two when he began to learn the alphabet by reciting the letters on the stove's name: W-A-T-E-R-L-O-O. When he started school, his oldest sister, Bess, was already the teacher at Port Shoreham's one-room schoolhouse. She once reported his classroom naughtiness to Will and Sarah, but when they scolded him he simply protested, "Well, it's only Bess!" His sisters remember him mostly as a shy, studious boy. "Now I'm not putting him in an Abe Lincoln category," says Zoe, who's lived in the United States for nearly six decades, "but I can still see him at the kitchen table, studying by the kerosene lamp. We had an old calico cat that just loved Charlie, and I can still see him studying there with the calico cat draped over his shoulders."

When Charlie was twelve, his sisters were women, and they'd left him behind with his middle-aged parents. They had not yet quit Nova Scotia, but they'd sailed away from The Place. One by one, they would join the classic exodus, moving on to Montreal, Detroit, Saskatchewan, California, Alberta, and British Columbia. But in March 1919, when Charlie relieved his loneliness by founding his handwritten weekly, *The Shoreham Searchlight*, his sister Zoe was working as a stenographer in North Sydney. At twenty, she was the closest to him in age, and for the next year and a half he concocted *The Shoreham Searchlight* exclusively for her. So far as she knew, he never showed it to anyone else, not even his parents. Thanks to Zoe, two dozen *Shoreham Searchlight*s still survive. They reveal more about my father's boyhood than he ever told me, and also offer a rare boy's-eye view of life nearly seventy years ago on one of the colder, more remote, and most intimate shores of the old British Empire.

"You know you are reading the best when you are reading *The Searchlight*," editor Bruce guaranteed his readership of one. His editorial policy was that no tidbit of shore news was too puny to intrigue Zoe. There was no character she didn't know Down Home. So he gave her the scoop that "Alexander MacMaster was unfortunate enough to lose his purse and $8.00 while smelting on the harbour. He has hopes of finding it when the snow goes off." Then he gave her the better scoop that "Alex Mac-Master, who 'lost' his purse two weeks ago, found it in his spare pants pocket. Quite a laugh is going the rounds about the incident." And surely Zoe would want to hear the astounding news under the heading "PROMINENT LADY HAS WEDDING." The story said: "What will be the next true report? Truth is stranger than fiction. 'Of course it is,' thinks Mrs. Richardson, 'or I wouldn't have married Mr. Whitman (Fred Whitman).' And this report is true! Every bit of it! Every single word of it! Oh, ain't it a queer world?" Editor Bruce, at twelve, found the marriage so miraculous that he celebrated it in verse:

> Where do we go from here, girls?
> Where do we go from here?
> All the way from Whitmans
> To Richardsons business square.
>
> All the girls, they say to me,
> "Can't I walk with you?
> If Naomi R. can get a man,
> Surely, I can, too."

Social news dominated some editions of *The Shoreham Search-light*. When Miss Grady of the Post Office married Mr. Mattie of Tracadie in St. Francis, "six sleighs accompanied the couple to the house of the groom." Former Port Shoreham resident Alfred Hart was "now visiting the home of his son, William Hart. Mr. Hart arrived yesterday, and will leave for Canso shortly. In the meantime, he's visiting some old friends. (He's downstairs now.)" Alex MacMaster, the fellow who "lost" his purse, was "one of the best known men in the Western Hemisphere and manager of the Chedabucto Mutual Telephone Company." But he refused to change "the system of running the company," and it somehow followed from this that Chedabucto Mutual planned "a Pie Social at the home of David MacMaster." Few pie socials escaped mention in the *Searchlight*. Nor did tea parties to raise money for such objectives as buying shingles for the Methodist church. Nor did the return of soldiers from the Great War.

When Private Fred Sullivan attended a reception at the home of Mr. and Mrs. W. Sceles, Bruce neighbours, he was given "a genuine diamond tie clip. He tells some wonderful stories." (Fred Sullivan was ninety-three in 1988, and still telling wonderful stories.) Another vet, Curtis Monroe, was visiting his uncle, Captain Fred MacKay, in April 1919, and the *Searchlight* reported, "Mr. Monroe is a keen hunter and spends a good deal of his time on the beach after ducks, but not very successfully. He was gassed on September third, 1918. His return was celebrated with foghorns."

When a school of pollock ran ashore on the Port Shoreham beach and Joseph McKay got forty of them with a gaff while barely wetting his feet, Zoe got the news in the *Searchlight*. When the mackerel were scarce and the herring plentiful, when James "Trout Charmer" Ferguson got sixteen big trout at the mouth of Clam Harbour River, Zoe got the news in the *Searchlight*. When skating on the lake was good and coasting on the hills "exceptionally fine," when the bay was "full of ice cakes, as big as houses, that drifted from somewhere unknown," when the flour mill at Boylston was booming and the Richardson saw mill across the stream from The Place was "full up with lumber of all descriptions," when Charlie Bruce built a drawbridge with his Gilbert Erector set, when Charlie and his father took a trip to Boylston with a cowhide, when Charlie's uncle, James Tory, won a seat for the Liberals in the provincial legislature, when Charlie's mother stumbled out into a terrific blizzard to drive her hens from the barn and back into the henhouse, when Charlie and Sarah and Will welcomed to the world "five little lambs, one of them a black one, the other four all white" . . . well, Zoe knew it all. The *Searchlight* told her so.

Editor Bruce sometimes used Bingo as a pen-name: "Bingo is carrying to 'the press' a short, dull stub of pencil and a very sick 'stummick.' Also a very doubtful opinion of persons who read OUT LOUD while we are getting *The Searchlight* ready." News of his success as a boy poet was too important to ham up in the *Searchlight*, and in a separate letter he confided to Zoe: "I won first prize in a contest in the Evening Echo Sunshine Club. There was a choice of prizes. I took a baseball glove. Certain persons think I'm foolish, but *youth is golden* and I might as well use it. . . . I got two poems in last week's *Family Herald*. Yours as of yore. C.T.B."

Mail mattered to everyone along the bay shore, and especially to a kid waiting to see if periodicals had printed his verse. It was delivered along the dirt road that wound its way through every farmyard. Remnants of the path still snake around the paved highway, and a piece of it serves as our driveway at The Place. In the winter and spring of 1919, the *Searchlight* found it vile. Rain, thaw, and sleet had turned it into "mountains of slobbery, mushy, squishy porridge." Later, mud made pedestrians "suffer large feet. From Mill Brook to Clam Harbour River Bridge is a ten-foot ribbon of the stickiest mixture ever invented, two inches thick. . . . Guysborough County's worst disgrace (she has a good many) is the five-mile ribbon of mud, sometimes called a road, and sometimes sundry names spoken in a low tone, between Shoreham and Boylston. Yours truly has swallowed everything from baked beans to insults, but when it comes to MUD!!!! not for me."

The *Searchlight* offered box scores of contests among Charlie and his chums at such games as Pit, Tiddly-wink, and something called Whyhoo, but it gave bigger play to the opening of the Bruce checker season on New Year's Eve 1919 and its conclusion on March 31, 1920: "The Bruce series of 24 games is finished, and results stand: C. Bruce, 13 wins. W. Bruce, 11 (and about

20 draw games)." In three winter months, by the light of a kerosene flame and the warmth of crackling birch and maple, the fifty-six-year-old father and his thirteen-year-old son had played more than forty checker games. I suspect Will threw a few, but no one will ever know.

Homesickness is not just a feeling among Maritimers—it's a tradition. Its companion is the longing of those who have waved farewell on hundreds of railway platforms and docks and over countless picket fences as buggies and cars vanished into western horizons. Will and Sarah knew, long before it dawned on Charlie, that there'd be a deadline on their sweet years with him, that he would follow his sisters away.

None of "the Bruce girls" had ever been allowed to ride The Place's beloved old horse, Doll, but Charlie rode her. None of them had ever had a crack at four years of university life, but the whole family would soon back Charlie while he earned his B.A. (and the nickname the Bard) at Mount Allison University in Sackville, New Brunswick. At fourteen, like hundreds of thousands of other young Maritimers both before and after him, he was already getting restless. In his last *Searchlight*, he told his Cape Breton subscriber: "With the coming of June comes also sundry *trubbles*, including planting, gardening, brush chopping and burning, and worst of all, nothing doing—that is, in any other line than the above mentioned evils. This old place is dull! dull! deathly dull!!!! Still, it's much nicer than Russia, Poland, or Cape Breton."

He finished his local schooling just after he turned sixteen, but Mount Allison ruled he was too young to enrol there. Rather than kill a year at The Place, he took a job forty-odd miles away, at Kirk's hardware store in Antigonish. "If you do not like the work, and there is too much outside work at delivering in the cold and wet," Will wrote, "if I was you I would throw it up. . . . Look out, and have plenty dry socks and clothing, and be sure not to catch cold. If you do not like the place come home, and we will chop wood and logs, and you can get books and study in the evenings. Your father, W.H. Bruce." On December 3, 1922, Will asked, "How about Christmas? I suppose it will be hard for you to get home and perhaps will be too busy at the store. . . . I wouldn't mind seeing that old truck [the Bruce's Model T] once more if you were at the steering wheel, and it was on the road back of our shop."

Will's salutation was "Dear Charles." Sarah's was "Dear Charlie Boy." She wrote: "I want you to write me all about yourself, what clothes you got, and what you want, and if you are acquainted with any of the church people. . . . You never told me whether you got the money or the box I sent you. Your father sent some in the last letter. Be sure, dear, & let us know if you got it, as I did not register the letter. . . . Ed said he was sure he saw you in town [Guysborough] last Thursday. It must have been some one that looks like you. . . . Sunday evening seems the *lonesomest*. That doesn't sound very elegant. I don't know if it is even correct. . . . If you could only peep in and see how eagerly we *devour* your letters when they arrive. I guess it would make you feel you were of *great* value to us. . . . Lovingly, Mother."

Nine months later, Charlie was living at Mount Allison. He dropped into a well of homesickness so deep his classmates thought he was physically ill. Mooning for The Place, once so deathly dull, he could barely eat or talk. Alone and palely loitering, like John Keats's knight in *La Belle Dame Sans Merci*, he seemed half-paralyzed. He'd never go back now, except for quick trips in summer and autumn and long trips of the mind. He learned to love Mount Allison, too, but in a life that later took him to Halifax, New York, Toronto, back to New York, back to Toronto, London, and back to Toronto again, The Place never stopped haunting him. On the last page of his last novel—a book he did not live long enough to polish or see published —the hero, Christopher Harris, strolls along the muddy road where he'd once awaited delivery of *The Family Herald*. He remembers the different men he had been in far-off places and meets the boy he was:

> They seemed now, some of these Christophers, almost like chance acquaintances, not always likeable, though all were I, alive in this middle-aged man who walked the Devon Road. But closest, the boy.
>
> I let my fancy play a little. What if he should say, "You didn't turn out to *be* much, did you?"
>
> I thought of a reply into which I would put as much good nature as I could: "Maybe not. You were no hell yourself, you young slob."

Christopher Harris was Down Home in space and Down Home in time, and Charles Bruce was not the first novelist to finish a book and then realize he had created the man he wanted to be.

2

MARITIMERS ARE LIKE A MOTORCYCLE GANG

Driving to The Place from Halifax, I stopped to pick up beer in Antigonish because, unlike my forebears, I did not fear my soul would be at risk if I were to crack open an ale while building a fire in the kitchen stove. I didn't want Moosehead, Schooner, Alpine, Ten-Penny, Keith's, or any other Maritime brew. I was feeling disloyal, and extravagant. I wanted Heineken.

"Excuse me," I said to a beefy clerk, "but where's the section for foreign beer?"

His blue gaze was expressionless between his thick sideburns, and he said nothing. He simply pointed—at boxes of Molson, Labatt's, Carling's, and other imports from national breweries in Upper Canada. They were foreign enough for him, and perhaps a shade *too* foreign.

Novelist Hugh MacLennan once swore he heard a Customs inspector in Halifax tell disembarking passengers, "Nova Scotians in Aisle A, aliens and Canadians in Aisle B." MacLennan, incidentally, was a steamship passenger himself, homeward bound from England, when he first met American writer Dorothy Duncan. She couldn't figure out his nationality. "I'm a Nova Scotian," he finally allowed, and in *Bluenose: A Portrait of Nova Scotia*, she wrote: "He hadn't said a 'Canadian,' and he obviously didn't think of himself as a Canadian. What could Nova Scotia be like, that its people gave this name to themselves with such pride in their voices that one felt they were convinced of a superiority palpable to the rest of the world?" MacLennan went ashore at Halifax, leaving Duncan to reflect that the American passengers "had met and come to know a Nova Scotian, and through him we had encountered a people. And we were none of us likely to forget." She certainly didn't. Four years later, she married MacLennan.

Elderly folk artist A.L. Morrison said in his introduction to *My Island Pictures* not that he fought for Canada, or the Allies, or freedom during World War Two, but that "I joined the RCAF and went to do my fighting for Prince Edward Island." Powerful loyalty to one's home turf is scarcely unique to old folks in the

Maritimes. "I never wanted to leave," Halifax prizefighter Chris Clarke said in 1987. "I'm patriotic that way." He was the former middleweight champion of Canada and welterweight champion of the British Commonwealth. He felt he'd have risen even higher in his bloody trade if only he'd accepted more out-of-town fights, but, what the hell, "I'm a Haligonian first, a Nova Scotian second, and a Canadian third."

For saying something similar, a premier of Prince Edward Island enraged the entire venerable panel of the national TV show "Front Page Challenge." He was Angus MacLean, the most gentle, affable, and decent of all Canadian premiers. When he let it drop that he was a Prince Edward Islander first, a Maritimer second, and a Canadian third, the panel reacted as though he'd honked his nose on the Canadian flag.

Like a Doberman aroused at midnight, Pierre Berton barked at MacLean. Like an angry poodle, Betty Kennedy snapped at his heels. Like an elderly bloodhound, Gordon Sinclair wagged his head and fumed as only he could fume. They seemed to regard MacLean's statement as flirtation with treason. But MacLean knew where his friends were—they were Down Home. And sure enough, a blizzard of letters from Maritimers, enraged by the way those Upper Canadian boors had mauled one of God's gentlemen, one of God's *Maritime* gentlemen, blew into the show's Toronto office for weeks on end. Moreover, Down Home newspapers carried rafts of letters that denounced the panel's pillorying of this elder statesman as nasty, unkind, bullying, divisive, disrespectful, disgraceful, distasteful, and, since the Canadian way to treat guests was supposed to be with courtesy, as downright un-Canadian. Nothing unites Maritimers so effectively (if briefly) as an Upper Canadian's sneer at either one of their own or an aspect of their regional character.

*   *   *

Many Canadians see the Maritimes as an amiable family that, despite its dependence on the pogey, remains cheerful and loving. But from province to province, island to island, county to county, town to town, and from bay to cove and river to beach, Maritimers have been fighting and plotting to get the upper hand over one another for a couple of centuries. Down Home communities are often about as co-operative as the Hatfields and the McCoys, as harmonious together as a convention of fishwives. Each town has its own way of doing things, its own self-interest, history, and traditions to protect, and perhaps its own grudges to nurse and grievances to cherish. The old dream of Maritime Union therefore remains an old farce, and in the face of every argument to rationalize higher education, the Maritimes go right on funding no fewer than eighteen universities for a population not much bigger than greater Vancouver's.

Nova Scotia won continent-wide applause for Industrial Estates Limited (IEL), a crown corporation that lured huge industries in the sixties. But no matter what outside praise IEL reaped, no matter how carefully Premier Robert Stanfield chose its directors to represent all parts of the province, and no matter how conscientiously IEL tried to distribute its clients' factories, it was forever being flayed for favouring one district over another. Every corner of Nova Scotia resented whatever another corner got; IEL could never dissolve local paranoia.

Any journalist who honestly describes a Maritime village risks infuriating its people. Reports on poverty, crime, unemployment, or collapsing industries are seen as the work of saboteurs from evil media empires in heartless cities. But if the peddlers of bad news are fiends, the peddlers of good news are simps. If they say the seaside is beautiful, they're perpetuating travel-ad clichés. If they say the folks are friendly, they're patronizing twits. Even the most skilled, knowledgeable, and good-natured writers take wrong steps in the Maritimes' minefields of local resentment. Kennedy Wells is such a writer.

Wells grew up in Alberton, P.E.I., became a journalist overseas, returned to Alberton in 1975, and five years later felt confident enough to write about the nearby village of Tignish. His story appeared in *Atlantic Insight,* and the way the magazine set it up revealed his approach: "Tignish retains its co-op spirit, its superb old Catholic church, its Acadian-Irish flavor, and nicknames so fantastic they amount to a third language. . . . It's the end of the line in western P.E.I. It's the spirited home of Muckapucks, Dadools, Ernie Poopers, and other fine folk with weird names." Wells's entire story struck a note of affection and admiration, and no sane reader could possibly have seen it as anything remotely resembling an attack on Tignish. But when a man from Alberton writes a story about Tignish, he cannot count on all his readers being sane. A Tignish fellow who saw an insult even in Wells's reference to the town's "scrappy coach and able rink manager" sent the magazine this bizarre reaction to the whole piece:

If you have any sense of justice, maybe you will let someone from Tignish write your article about Alberton. I'm sure we can find out about *their* history by looking at all the tombstones. It seems Kennedy Wells got some information and then just enlarged on it from his overactive imagination. Maybe our people are not grand enough for Kennedy Wells but we are "real" people. And scrappy? Who says? Perhaps you are referring to some minor tussles we have at the rink.

And last, but not least, where do you get off talking about an English-Acadian question? We are all very happy and intermarried, so we get along just fine, thank you. If people like yourself kept quiet, we wouldn't even think about differences. After all, we are all ordinary human beings.

*   *   *

When I first attended Mount Allison University, in Sackville, New Brunswick, its enrolment amounted to only about seven hundred ordinary human beings, and all but a handful lived in stone dormitories that huddled against the raw, salt-heavy winds. After flowing for mile after flat mile across the creepy grandeur of the Tantramar marshland, the winds howled into Sackville, lashed the gritty red sandstone walls of our little fortress of higher learning, and made it feel like the cosiest university in North America. The cosiness, however, could not smother the differences. Despite militant promotion of a campus-wide "Mt. A. spirit," university life failed to sap the loyalties that youngsters brought to Sackville along with their luggage. I was a rail-thin teenager from darkest Toronto, and it perplexed me to see the tiny student body at that intimate college gleefully split itself into regional clubs.

New Brunswickers, Nova Scotians, Prince Edward Islanders, and Newfoundlanders each had clubs of their own, each with its own executive officers and exclusive parties. Moreover, the West Indian students had their Club Tropicale, and somewhere below this on the ladder of status came the Upper Canadian Club. Since its members were mostly affluent Anglos from Montreal, I argued that it should properly be called the Lower Canadian Club, leaving me and a Toronto girl I happened to adore as the only members of the Upper Canadian outfit. I was brutally overruled, and thereby learned for the first time that when Maritimers say Upper Canadian, they mean anyone from anywhere in Canada beyond the neighbourhood of Edmundston, New Brunswick. Such persons are suspect.

My second nonscholastic discovery at Mount Allison was that young Maritimers revelled in interprovincial ridicule. Nova Scotians and New Brunswickers liked to remind Prince Edward Islanders how puny P.E.I. was and pointed out that if Yankee Stadium were filled with Islanders there wouldn't be a soul back home to watch the harness races. This was merely one of the milder expressions of birthplace bigotry in "the family" of Maritimers and Newfoundlanders at the men's residence. Cape Breton Islanders, the Prince Edward Islanders insisted, were "just Newfoundlanders with their brains bashed out."

Thirty-two years after I left Mount Allison, Billy Rix reminded me of those harsh, humorous, college-boy judgements. Rix is a sawed-off, fast-talking industrialist from the Island, and his business interests keep him hustling around the region. He curses as naturally as he breathes. He told me, "The people of Cape Breton have got to be the finest people on the face of this goddamn earth—to *party* with! Look, I can't think of any people I'd rather shoot golf with, eat blueberry pie with, or drink black rum with. But holy Jesus, they're a wretched lot to *work* with!"

Back at Mount Allison, I never participated in the nightly ritual of swapping provincial slurs. Since I feared becoming an Upper Canadian with his brains bashed out, I remained an observer in foreign territory. One thing I observed was that men students from everywhere in the Maritimes except Halifax agreed that certain Halifax girls might indeed be beautiful—they dressed more expensively than girls from Montague, P.E.I., or Buctouche, New Brunswick—but they were not worth pursuing because Halifax bred nothing but frigid snobs. Halifax girls probably didn't even like the music of Hank Williams.

Many Maritimers see Halifax through the same eyes that Timmins and North Bay see Toronto: rich, lucky, powerful, greedy, devious, puffed-up, and just not nice. Dartmouth, Halifax's sprawling twin city across the harbour, has long resented not only the muscle and hoggishness of Halifax, but also the idea that its own best feature is simply the splendid view it offers of its historic neighbour's skyline. C.J. Matthews, a former Anglican minister, helps run Gowrie House, a superb inn at Sydney Mines, Cape Breton. He says he's often tempted to turn away all would-be guests from Halifax. He finds Haligonians so smug, superior and generally insufferable that "they're just about as bad as people from upper New York State."

Whenever Cape Breton Islanders curse the day the Island ceased being a separate colony and rejoined Nova Scotia, they are really cursing the fact that for 168 years power that belongs in Sydney has remained in Halifax. Nor is hostility to Halifax confined only to Nova Scotia. The most satisfying moments for Moncton hockey fans occur while their team is whipping any squad from the city Kipling called "the Warden of the Honour of the North." Port boosters in Saint John see Halifax as a ruthless rival that fights dirty.

Town rivalries, like elections, used to find expression not only in platform oratory but also in thudding fists, spurting noses, and cracked skulls. They still do, especially among hard-knuckled, hard-drinking young bucks at backwoods dances, and outside taverns after ball games. The tradition is old. Writing for *Ballou's Monthly Magazine* in 1885, one Addison F. Browne said "a squad of ruffians" from Halifax picked a fight in New Glasgow and "were decidedly worsted":

> Not being satisfied with this lesson the defeated party organized another raid, this time in sufficient force to make cleaning out the place an apparently easy matter. But although the Scottish yeomen were entirely unprepared for this attack, and opposed by ten times their own number, their terrific defense, in which old as well as young took part, was speedily successful, and those of the assailants able to get away fled from the scene, leaving behind a score or so, including the leader, too much bruised and cut to escape. When the doctors got them patched up, these fellows had a taste of Scotch law, which in their cases did not prove over lenient.

*   *   *

The spirit of wrangling and the vigour of parochialism arose centuries ago. For generations before 1763, France and Britain fought for jurisdiction over Acadia, and winds of division ruled the region. Under the French, some parts of Acadia were economic satellites of New England, while others served Quebec, and still others France. After the defeat of France, colonial administrators in London carved up the territory as four colonies. Later, some Maritimers wanted economic integration with the United States, others wanted it with the British Empire, and quite a few thought the region should bet its future on central Canada. Maritimers had economic attachments to Boston, London, and Montreal, but had no dominant city of their own. Smaller Nova Scotian ports fought the rise of Halifax, and Saint John failed to control competing river systems even in New Brunswick. Saint John and Halifax sabotaged each other's plans so often that, among federal politicians from elsewhere, their feuding became a national joke.

Maritimers all had different ideas about what was historically important. To the descendants of the Scots in eastern Nova Scotia, it was the landing of Highlanders at Pictou in 1773, the waves of Scottish immigrants who followed, and their contribution to everything superior in the Nova Scotia character. To the descendants of Loyalists in the lower valley of the Saint John River, it was the arrival in the 1780s of Loyalist heroes who had founded their province and contributed to everything superior in the New Brunswick character. To the descendants of the pre-Loyalists (many of them New Englanders) in Halifax and the Annapolis Valley, it was England's triumph over France, and the founding of Halifax in 1749. To the descendants of the Acadians, it was their own lost Golden Age, the misty time before the expulsion of 1755, before all these other interlopers had usurped their sweet lands. Maritimers, as a whole, had no common history to call their own.

Geography and the sea isolated communities from one another. Your friends were the folks who lived along your own road, helped you haul your nets, and pitched in at haying time. Subsistence farming and fishing were hard ways to fend off starvation, and they nurtured attitudes of fierce independence rather than the promotion of anything so distant and abstract as regional identity. From politicians, the important thing was to get what you could for *your* outport or village.

Moreover, sharp religious differences kept Maritimers at each other's throats. In New Brunswick, for example, the government ruled in 1871 that all public schools had to be nonsectarian; it would no longer fund Roman Catholic schools. For the next four years, religious bigotry tore around the province. Feelings got so hot that an Irish Catholic bishop—the Acadians didn't get bishops of their own till the twentieth century—called the

Protestant lieutenant-governor "a brainless and raving bigot."
Two men died when police fired on rioting Acadians in
Caraquet. Campaigning with such slogans as "Vote for the
Queen against the Pope," the government party in 1874 won a
record majority. Though many Protestants hated Catholics, they
also disliked other Protestants. As Methodists, Baptists, Presbyterian sects, and Low- and High-Church Anglicans all beat the
bushes for converts, rivalries within New Brunswick Protestantism were stubborn and bitter.

Nor was the Catholic Church a happy ship. Irish Catholics
took control of the Church in New Brunswick, and leaders of
the multiplying Acadians found them even more despicable
than Orangemen. By the late 1800s Acadian nationalism was
stirring in all three Maritime provinces, and after conventions
at Memramcook, New Brunswick, and Miscouche, Prince Edward Island, the Acadian *nationalité* boasted its own anthem,
flag, feast day, and patron saint.

Nova Scotia, meanwhile, also had its Anglicans, Methodists,
Baptists, Acadian Catholics, Irish Catholics, Scots Catholics,
and, particularly in Pictou County, its furiously feuding Scots
Protestants. During the first half of the nineteenth century, the
Presbyterians of Pictou County actually got along better with
Catholics than they did with each other. The Kirkmen were
Tories, and the Antiburghers Grit. Elections were not just politi-
cal events: they were religious wars, with crudely armed mobs
marching under banners. It was said that a prudent man made
his will before casting his vote. All of this was part of what the
historian Donald Creighton called "the incurable diversity of
Nova Scotian life."

If history and religious life were wildly varied in the
Maritimes, so was the economy. By the early 1900s mining and
manufacturing depended on freight subsidies and tariff protection to sell their products in Canada, while fishing, farming, and
lumbering still sold goods at prices set by international markets.
But the better the National Policy was for mines and factories,
the worse it was for men who sold fish, apples, potatoes, and

two-by-fours. It jacked their production costs. This fundamental split on economic policy caused vicious political skirmishes. Moreover, myriad fishing villages demanded their own government wharfs, and for lack of a well-placed breakwater, the sea smashed down waterfront buildings and drowned good men. In these circumstances, a politician fought for the survival of his own people, and to hell with the gang down the shore. Thus, Maritime politicians often found themselves at each other's throats. The prickly political climate not only handicapped the region in its competition with the rest of Canada, but according to historian Ernest R. Forbes, it also turned Down Home politics into "the art of obtaining and dispensing local favours."

Nowhere in the Maritimes was loyalty to one's own turf more powerful than in Cape Breton. The first Highland settlers were fishermen who grabbed the best waterfront land. Later arrivals had to move inland, but as Charles W. Dunn explained in *Highland Settler*, "they and their descendants came to love the mountain fastness." Born in 1830, one Donald MacDonald grew up on a mountain in "the rear" of southwest Margaree. When he went down to "the shore" to work, Dunn wrote, "he found life, nature, and the people different from what he had known out back, and in every respect inferior."

In typical Gaelic fashion, he whipped off a song, calling it "Moladh a' Chuil agus Di-moladh a' Chladaich" (Praise of the Rear and Dispraise of the Shore). He had hurled down the gauntlet. Defending the honour of the shore, Duncan MacLellan wrote "Moladh a' Chladaich agus Di-moladh a' Chuil" (Praise of the Shore and Dispraise of the Rear). In short, two men whose homes were within walking distance were busily duelling away in verse, each one boasting about his own community while sneering at the other's. The few dozen people here at Port Shoreham felt for generations that they were socially superior to the even smaller gang down at St. Francis Harbour, which is all of six miles away. At the heart of the Maritime character lie loyalty and defensiveness about exactly where you come from.

This feeling surges in the hearts of city dwellers as well as among rural folk. When men boast about their boyhood not just in Halifax, but in tough old *north-end* Halifax, they sound like an exclusive and hardened tribe with little use for much of the city and none for the sissy south end. In Saint John, folks on the west side of the harbour have known for a century that they have more community spirit and less crime than the rest of the city. They know they are more neighbourly, and although not richer than other Saint John people, they are somehow better.

Working-class Charlottetown people, many of them Irish-Catholic, long lived on downtown streets near the water. The neighbourhood had its east end and its west end, each with its own set of community bonds, street history, and sense of separateness. As people moved to the suburbs, they often settled in groups of former east-enders and former west-enders, but this clustering sometimes failed to conquer homesickness for downtown haunts. One old man and his wife moved to a fine new suburban bungalow, but each evening after supper he returned to the east end to sit with lifelong friends on their doorsteps. At the bungalow one afternoon, a woman visitor, dreaming of Hong Kong, said, "I've never been to the Far East. Wouldn't it be wonderful, just once in your life, to visit the East?" The old man's five-year-old granddaughter piped up, "Me 'n' Grampy's goin' down there after supper. You can come with us."

*　*　*

Politicians saw it as their duty to make sure the railways gave jobs only to local men, and never to intruders from other parts of the Maritimes. In 1904, for instance, political pressure forced the Intercolonial Railway to recall from Cape Breton a bluenose mainlander it had sent there on promotion, and also to remove two Nova Scotians from a survey in Prince Edward Island. As late as World War Two the school board of Saint John refused to hire teachers, no matter how good, if they were not Saint John natives. All other applicants were "foreigners." Nor are such attitudes dead today. Salisbury is an English-speaking village in southern New Brunswick. In the summer of 1987 hundreds of outraged townsfolk violently opposed Canada Post's decision to replace the retiring postmistress with an outsider. The newcomer was Lyn Lévesque, a bilingual Acadian from the north. When a few locals defended her appointment, claiming that an anti-French faction was disgracing Salisbury, they received death threats.

But just as Acadians sometimes forget *ésprit de clocher* (spirit of the parish) long enough to promote their "national" interests in the face of hostile Anglos, Maritimers as a whole sometimes forget local rivalries long enough to broadcast their common plight in the face of national indifference. One of these rare periods occurred during the 1920s when the three provinces promoted Maritime Rights, a reform movement that aimed to halt the decline in the region's influence under Confederation and to promote the protection, restoration, and introduction of federal programmes to bolster the east-coast economy. A result of the fuss was that the feds appointed Sir Andrew Duncan, a British lawyer, to investigate Maritime grievances. Recommendations of the Duncan Commission did lead to increases in certain subsidies and reductions in certain freight rates. During the Dirty Thirties, however, hope turned to cynicism, and nothing as unifying as the Maritime Rights Movement has swept the Maritimes in more than sixty years. Its only legacies, says Ernest R. Forbes, the authority on the movement, are "regional resentment and vestiges of co-operation."

* * *

To be a Maritimer, a student from Ontario wrote, is to be used to rain, and to wake up each morning to radio news of lost ships, oil-rig disasters, and bankrupt industries. It's to be someone who drinks tea, hates fish, drives a pickup truck, bears a mild resentment against central Canada, and sees a trip to Prince Edward Island as other Canadians see a trip to Bermuda.

To be a Maritimer, a student from the Maritimes wrote, is "to be able to breathe fresh air (most of the time); to feel, hear, and see the ocean; to be unhurried; to be able to enjoy solitude; to be happy in the fall when the tourists go home and leave us alone. To be the only one on a sandy beach . . . to live near one's family," and to be self-sufficient.

Both students were at Mount Allison at the same time, a generation after my own Mt. A. immersion in Maritime meanings. They were responding to questions from Professor William B. Hamilton in a Canadian Studies course, and their answers struck me as one more scrap of evidence that Maritimers and non-Maritimers rarely come anywhere near agreeing on what the Maritimes are all about.

The richer provinces tend to see them as the runts of the Canadian litter, the welfare bums of Confederation, a safe harbour for the lazy, a scenic nursing home for poor relations who suffer a congenital defect that makes them incapable of surviving without handouts from their betters. In 1977, while Quebec threatened to declare itself an independent republic, Toronto columnist Joey Slinger cracked, "*Chutzpah* is René Lévesque taking Quebec out of Canada, and insisting we keep the Maritimes." This was a whole lot funnier in Hogtown than Down Home.

For Maritimers see themselves not as shiftless deadbeats, but as the exact opposite: hard-working, hard-headed adventurers. They feel that they're resilient folk who are ever ready to leave a good home to find a good job and to tackle challenges and endure hardships that other Canadians are too timid to try, or too soft-handed to bear. They imagine they're a lot like their ancestors, who were as tough as cold tar. The Down Home skippers who sailed from Rotterdam to Rangoon were gamblers but realists, romantics but businessmen. Before them, the pioneers had been footloose but stubborn. Murdering coasts had forced them to become gritty and adaptable. Either that or die.

The Acadians returned as losers. Once master farmers on juicy meadowland, they now found themselves dumped on salt-lashed tracts of coastal scrub and promptly transformed themselves into master boat-builders and fishermen. The Scots arrived as losers. After the slaughter of Highland warriors at Culloden in 1746 came the crushing of the clan system, crop failures, and the infamous expulsion of unprofitable tenants in favour of profitable sheep. Hordes of Scots sailed away forever, and many of the tens of thousands who came to the Maritimes had to learn a dozen skills they'd never before known: how to handle an axe, build a cabin, pull roots, move stones, make barrels, repair nets, patch sails, control a balky horse. They also had to learn that keeping their families from starving or freezing to death was forever a matter of making do with whatever lay to hand. These immigrants would raise able and venturesome emigrants.

The Loyalists, too, arrived as losers. Choosers of "the wrong side" in the American Revolution, they fled the victors' bullying, dragooning, and pillaging. In the words of a lady from Georgia, "The scum rose to the top," and nearly a hundred thousand losers pulled out. Not all those who escaped to the Maritimes liked what they found. Many moved up the St. Lawrence River and on to the Great Lakes, and more returned to the country that had so recently maltreated them. Some boarded ships for the motherland, but roughly thirty thousand toughed out their first grisly winters in the Maritimes and stayed on to help populate a region that, more than any other corner of Canada, still loves the royal connection.

Here at The Place, lights from the houses of Loyalist descendants twinkle at us each night from the bay's far shore, five miles to the south. The villages over there include Dorts Cove, Halfway Cove, and Peas Brook—punctuation marks on a seaside cliff that runs for twenty-five miles, like a ruled line going due east, from the head of Chedabucto Bay clear out to Canso. On mainland Nova Scotia, Canso is as far east as you can go. The cliff defines a fault, and it was along this fracture that geological pressures shoved all southern Nova Scotia into place some 250 million years ago. From our southern windows, the view of that far, brooding escarpment is dramatic, but most of the soil over there is so poor it could scarcely sustain an annual turnip. The Canada Land Inventory identifies it as the lowest of the low, Class 7: "Soils in this class have no capability for arable culture or permanent pasture. This class also includes rockland, other non-soil areas, and bodies of water too small to show on the maps." It was on this land that, in the summer of 1784, British officialdom encouraged the settlement of a few dozen Loyalist families.

The fathers were men of the 60th Regiment, disbanded vets from a foreign legion the British had recruited among American colonists of German and Swiss birth. Soldiers of the 60th had helped capture Louisbourg in 1758, Quebec in 1759, and Montreal in 1760. They'd fought for the British throughout the American Revolution, and when their battalions were dispersed in 1783, the reward for some was a rock grant, posing as a land grant, on the shores of Chedabucto Bay. It's unlikely the soldiers had ever seen a fish-knife. But the woods grew pine for boats, and the bay that washed the feet of the ancient cliff boiled with mackerel, and the soldiers went down to the sea. Describing them in 1950, local historian A.C. Jost wrote, "Knitting their own nets in the winter evenings, fashioning the rude 'killicks,' which served as boat or net moorings, constructing their own lobster pots, tending their gardens or cultivating the sterile soil, they have passed their self-contained and peaceable existences." And the lights across the bay will twinkle again tonight because, more than two centuries ago, a bunch of battle-weary German foot-sloggers had the moxie to teach themselves how to catch fish.

Nor were they the only adaptable Loyalists who joined our neighbourhood in the 1780s. A dozen miles east of The Place, and even before construction of the ribbon of mud that would one day arouse the ire of boy editor Charles Bruce, forty-eight families from the Carolinas and Georgia arrived at the Strait of Canso. For generations they'd farmed in the lush American South. Now, with winter coming on, they found themselves between the sea and the woods (on Class 7 land), in a climate more vicious than any they'd ever imagined. God only knows how they survived, but survive they did.

The trick was to become a jack-of-all-trades. My grandfather Will wasn't much of a grocer, but he could build a house, a boat, a rocking chair, a barrel, a muskrat trap. In his time Down Home, which lasted till the fourth decade of this century, it was still usual for a man to be a farmer, fisherman, pulpwood-cutter, and a bit of a blacksmith, too. All over the Maritimes, the sons and daughters who went away for good from farms like The Place took with them a matter-of-fact willingness to go anywhere and try their hand at anything. The qualities that gave the Maritimes able pioneers later gave the rest of the country lawyers, judges, and lieutenant-governors, bank presidents and university presidents, scientific wizards and financial wizards, mariners, and missionaries. Maritime men who rattled west on Harvest Excursion trains every summer for forty years were treasured on the prairies, not simply because they were happy to sweat twelve hours a day for a couple of bucks but also because they could handle horses. Teachers' salaries out there were triple what they were Down Home, and doughty schoolmarms from the Maritimes once taught half the youngsters in the Canadian west.

My aunt Bess taught in Edmonton for three decades before returning for good to the bay shore in 1953. My aunt Anna, who's been back Down Home for twenty-two years now, spent much of her life as a beloved teacher in Saskatchewan. In a cupboard in The Parlour at The Place, photo albums with black, crumbling pages, strung together with bootlaces, still hold snapshots of the big grain elevator at Turtleford in 1933; a teachers' outing at "Edmonton Beach, 1932," and another at White Mud Creek; a team of horses pulling a buggy across "Battle River Bridge, Alta."; boxy, black Model A Fords, hunched on the snow-smothered streets of Edmonton; the sleepy main drag of Vermilion, Alberta; four smiling young women on horseback against a grass skyline that's as flat as a calm sea; and chasms, rivers, and glaciers along a railway line into the western mountains. Similar scrapbooks, with similar photos, gather dust in countless thousands of Maritime cupboards.

Considering the virtues of compatriots who travelled far, older Maritimers mention men like prizefighter Jack Munroe. Munroe was one of a dozen Cape Breton Islanders who went to Montana in 1901 to mine copper. On December 19, 1902, the heavy-weight boxing champ of the world, Jim Jeffries, came barnstorm-ing into Butte with an offer of $500 to any man who could survive four rounds with him. No challenger had ever lasted even two rounds. But Munroe's buddies from Down Home shoved him into the ring, and he gave the champ a fearful past-ing. Munroe pocketed the $500, became an instant American celebrity, beat some of the toughest prizefighters of his time, eventually lost a second fight with Jeffries, sacrificed an arm and won the Military Cross with Canadian forces in World War One, made a killing at prospecting in Northern Ontario, wrote a novel, and died in Toronto in 1942. He was tough, brave, smart, famous, and colourful.

When Maritimers discuss compatriots who've chosen to be "goin' down the road," they naturally prefer to dwell on the Munroes rather than on the good-for-nothings. Among hun-dreds of thousands of expatriates—between 1945 and 1965 alone net emigration surpassed 200,000—some were bound to be failures, but Maritimers resent any suggestion that the famous brain drain has also been a deadbeat drain. That's why Calgary mayor Ralph Klein reaped a whirlwind of abuse when, in 1982, he told the Calgary Newcomers Club that some newcomers were "creeps and bums."

Since many newcomers to Calgary were from Down Home, Maritimers furiously assumed he'd smeared the whole region. He hadn't even used the word *Maritimers*. As he tried to explain, his "creeps and bums" applied "to people anywhere who rob banks and snatch purses and mug senior citizens. It just so happens that most of the robberies here last year were committed by recent arrivals. People either didn't get the intent of what I said, or what I said was misrepresented. I never said easterners were creeps and bums." Despite his elaboration, Maritimers were slow to forgive him.

The Social Planning Council of Metropolitan Toronto once proposed machinery to help make Toronto less miserable for migrant workers. It suggested that certain young Maritimers, who lacked skills useful to big cities and who drifted up to Toronto, soon faced worse problems than whatever had inspired them to leave Down Home. The result, among some, was hard drinking, broken families, listless children, petty thievery, desperate prostitution, and sad times all around. Researchers identified an unfortunate "windbreaker group": Maritimers who were conspicuous by their habits of speech and dress, their sheer numbers, and their clustering together to relieve loneliness and homesickness. The council's intention was humane. It wanted to persuade Toronto politicians to use Toronto taxpayers' dollars to improve the lives of Maritimers who'd settled among them.

Yet the reaction in the Down Home press was one of rage bordering on paranoia. The Fredericton *Daily Gleaner* felt these well-meaning Toronto social scientists had tarred "all Maritimers with the brush of hatred." The Halifax *Mail-Star* demanded to know "what Maritime city . . . would put up with the marijuana hippie haven, plagued by infectious hepatitis, that is Toronto's Yorkville?" The Moncton *Daily Times* speculated, "Perhaps the truth of the matter is that the migrants [from Down Home] are a naturally happier kind of people than those who inhabit the 'Big City' and have no time to take a break from the rat race and share a human relationship. This could be the tip-off that all those stories of Toronto being a cold and impersonal city are only too true."

To restore the correct image of the Maritimer abroad, the Moncton paper added, "It is an undeniable fact that great men and women in every walk of life, men and women who have contributed not only to Canada but to Britain, to the United States, to all mankind, have emerged from these easternmost provinces. Their contributions should not be forgotten." Windbreaker group, indeed! The Maritimes, as every true Maritimer knows, sent forth her sons and daughters to make Canada a great nation, and Canada, for a century and more, has returned the favour by extending to everyone Down Home the muddy end of the stick.

* * *

New Glasgow is one of "the four towns" in Pictou County, Nova Scotia. The others are Trenton, Stellarton, and Westville, and they're all cheek-by-jowl. Strangers cannot tell when they've left one and entered another. Even though the combined population amounts to fewer than 24,000, all campaigns to unite the towns in one city have been swallowed up in canyons of village pride as deep as the schisms over Presbyterian doctrine that once divided the pioneer Scots. "That's what goes on inside the county," Lance Hale explained to me. "Once you get outside, it's a whole different ball game." Hale, a Stellarton native who moved to Halifax, continued: "Right now, I know everyone in Halifax of my generation who came from any of the four towns. I know their names, the number of their children, and who they married. Outside the county, we're one big, loyal family, with our own jokes and inside references, and an attitude that says it's us against the world."

"Would you say that, even by Maritime standards, Pictou County people are unusually proud of their roots?"

"Absolutely," Hale replies. "No doubt about that."

"And they're almost fanatically loyal to their county?"

"Most of them, yeah."

"And they have these secret jokes. They fight at home. They unite like brothers away from home, and they feel it's them against the world."

"Sure. So what?"

"Well, listen, Lance. Don't you think your beloved Pictou County sounds sort of like one huge motorcycle gang?"

"Yeah, you could say that," Hale laughed. "But you could also say it about the whole of the Maritimes."

3

CONFEDERATION, CARPETBAGGERS, COME FROM AWAYS

When I moved from Ontario to Nova Scotia in 1971, the relent-
lessness with which the Maritime press carped about the shafting
the region got from greedy Upper Canada made me think I'd
parachuted into the 1890s. Were these people *still* whining about
the deal struck in 1867? Where were the gas lanterns, horse-
drawn streetcars, hoopskirts, and brigantines? In July 1977, the
Halifax *Chronicle-Herald* marked the hundred-and-tenth birthday of Canada with a six-part, page-seven series entitled "The
True Story of Confederation." For any "Come From Away," as
some Maritimers call outsiders who've settled among them, the
series offered a wonderfully educational analysis of one of the
sturdiest grudges in Canadian history. The writer was Alexander
P. Paterson of Saint John, New Brunswick, and to document
Canada's betrayal of the Maritimes, the *Chronicle-Herald* gave
him space for no fewer than nine thousand words.

The gist of Paterson's argument was this:

Before Confederation, the Maritimes were prosperous, self-
sufficient Crown colonies, while Canada "writhed in the travail
of many troubles of dire combination." Equal representation by
Ontario and Quebec had deadlocked their government, and
cancellation of reciprocity with the United States threatened
their economy. War with the Americans loomed, and Canadian
trade through U.S. ports was in danger. The colony was too hard-
up to obey London's order to fortify Montreal. In England, and
even Canada, many favoured letting the whole nuisance drop
into the Americans' lap. Canada had no winter ports, and without safe rail connections to Atlantic seaports, it "could hope for
no real future as a British community." Thus, it was *Canada* that
wanted Confederation. Indeed, Confederation was "imperative
to her very existence." The Maritimes didn't need it and didn't
want it. "The suppliant was in travail, while the supplicated
basked in the sunshine of substantial prosperity."

Canada wanted Confederation so badly "she literally forced it
upon the Maritimes, having actually enlisted the Imperial Government to that end." Maritimers were citizens of the Dominion

of Canada not out of choice, but because Upper Canadians had seduced some of their leaders and Britain had shoe-horned the region into Confederation. (On this point, even so eminent a lover of all things bright and British as Nova Scotia politician Joseph Howe complained: "Even French girls who would have no objections to being married don't like to be ravished.") But, Paterson continued, "misleading propaganda" soon led Central Canadians to believe a monstrous lie: "That, in 1867, Canada *permitted* Nova Scotia and New Brunswick to join her, and that, ever since, she has found these Provinces a very heavy burden. In the hazy distance, beyond the blue hills of Quebec, such people see in the Maritimes a strange folk who, when not fishing or lumbering, are insistently clamouring for financial aid from the Federal Government."

Central Canada soon confirmed the worst fears of the wise herring chokers and bluenoses who'd valiantly fought Confederation. The British North America Act was supposed to have been "an Agreement," but Canada "speedily lost sight of her sacred obligations to the Maritimes" and "shattered sacred pledges." The most important pledge was to build the Intercolonial Railway and to run it not as a commercial line, but as "a National Work" to enable Maritime goods to flow profitably into Upper Canadian markets and to bring the foreign trade of the new nation through Maritime ports. Sir John A. Macdonald himself had promised that Ontario and Quebec "will cheerfully contribute to the utmost extent in order to make that important link without which no political connection can be complete. Build the road and Halifax will soon become one of the great emporiums of the world. All the great resources of the West will soon come over the immense railways of Canada to the bosom of your harbour."

Later generations of Upper Canadians, however, betrayed Macdonald's dream by insisting that "the Maritimes should be compelled to pay freight rates that would render the Intercolonial a commercial success. . . . During [World War One], and under the plea of patriotism and the need for money, these Confederation rights were wholly cancelled. Freight rates that discriminated against the Maritimes were established; and finally, the old I.C.R.—'The People's Road'—ceased to exist as such." There were other injustices, and one was the lie that the Maritimes were in debt to the rest of Canada.

Paterson insisted the exact opposite was true, that the Maritimes had contributed millions more to "the Confederation Scheme" than they'd ever received from it; that the feds had pumped tens of millions of Maritimers' dollars into projects from Quebec to British Columbia, while allowing Down Home industries to die; and that Maritimers had been forced to help finance transportation improvements, such as the St. Lawrence Seaway, that spelled their own economic ruin. "The obvious unfairness of this is pathetic," Paterson wrote, and he rolled on from there to a resounding summary of grievances:

> The people of the Maritimes have been compelled to the conclusion that, for many years, there has been continued, consistent action to sacrifice their industrial and commercial future for the benefit of the Middle Provinces which, by reason of their financial and political dominance, have most certainly achieved that end.
>
> As a result, Maritime industries have languished and died, so that most of the present Maritime consumption of industrial products emanates from the tariff-protected factories of Central Canada. The shattering of Confederation pledges, upon the inviolate fulfilment of which the Maritimes innocently confided, is accomplishing their economic strangulation. The whole tragic circumstance is the direct outcome of a self-centred disregard for the sacred interests of three Provinces by the political dominance of Central Canadian financial and commercial interest. Consequently they have denied the Maritimes the right to participate in the general progress and prosperity of Canada.

Ploughing through "The True Story of Confederation," I gathered that Paterson had not written it to any deadline the *Chronicle-Herald* had imposed. The newspaper acknowledged the series was written by the *late* Alexander P. Paterson, but neglected to say when. Clues lie in the text. It appears that, when the *Chronicle-Herald* published his exposé in 1977, roughly half a century had passed since he'd written it. I found this weird. The job of a newspaper, I thought, was to tell what happened yesterday or this morning, not to trot out long-winded opinions that a dead man had written decades ago. But the longer I live in the Maritimes, the better I understand that, when it comes to the treacherous nature of Upper Canadian power, the news is never old.

* * *

Many Maritimers still blame the betrayals that followed the Confederation deal for the flight of their people and capital, the collapse of their industries, the feebleness of their economy, and the fact that their social services are poorer and their pay cheques smaller than those of other Canadians. They know they live in a dependent colony of the Canadian empire, and that their plight is a direct result of a gigantic double cross.

It is as though X sold a house to Y, granting Y a long-term mortgage. Y moved into the house, then quit making mortgage payments. X was too weak to force payment, or to dislodge Y, and was therefore reduced to endless begging at what was once his own door. After a century of this, big Y saw little X as a whiner it could safely ignore. The Atlantic provinces, Premier Frank Moores of Newfoundland said in 1978, remain "the only region in Canada that hasn't the affluence to do much else but be indignant." And to remind Ottawa, decade after decade, of old and broken promises.

For the first seventy-odd years of Confederation, the forgotten promises were not part of a master plan to torpedo the Maritimes. The federal government promoted immigration to settle the west, but it did not deliberately arrange Canada's population growth so it would sap the Maritimes' influence in Parliament. Central Canadian greed and competitiveness undermined the Down Home economy, but no one specifically orchestrated them for the destruction of east-coast industry. With the arrival of World War Two, however, came the arrival of a federal government policy not just to let the Maritimes slide backward, but to shove them backward. The villain in this scheme, from a Maritimes view, was the American-born minister of munitions and supply, C.D. Howe.

Howe is often celebrated as the strong man who put Canadian industry on a war footing and reconstructed the country's postwar economy. But recent research reveals that he was so determined to fatten central Canadian industry with government money, while starving Maritime industry, that he did so even at the cost of bungling the war effort. The historian Ernest R. Forbes has described part of the dismal story.

The Dominion Steel and Coal Company (DOSCO) was the largest industrial employer in the Maritimes and one of Canada's "big three" steel producers. The other two were the Steel Company of Canada, in Hamilton, and Algoma Steel Company, in Sault Ste. Marie. While granting the two Ontario firms huge subsidies to modernize and build new mills, the feds were so tight-fisted with DOSCO that its president, Arthur Cross, complained to Howe in 1941 that his was "the only primary steel producer in this country which is receiving no government assistance." Cross suspected that Howe's team had "deliberately formulated a policy which is bound to discriminate against the postwar future of this corporation and in favour of its central Canadian competitors."

As Howe's gang concentrated steel-making, shipbuilding, and even the repair of fighting vessels in central Canada, skilled workers flowed inland from the Maritimes. Having caused a labour shortage in the Maritimes, the feds now used it as an excuse not to bolster Maritime war industries. Another bureaucrat's excuse was "distance." But it wasn't the Maritimes that were distant from The Battle of the North Atlantic. It was central Canada. Howe's anti-Maritimes bias, along with the political clout of Montreal, forced warships to go for repairs not to convoy headquarters in Halifax, but all the way up the St. Lawrence. "The navy," Forbes wrote, "was reduced to the desperate expedients of leaving some vessels frozen in St. Lawrence ports for the winter, routing others to British Columbia, and sending still others on the dubious gamble of breaking into refit schedules at American ports."

Some argue that Canada's failure to set up an efficient, year-round, strategically located repair centre turned the Canadian navy into bystanders, while British escorts beat the Nazis on the North Atlantic. As early as 1940, British naval authorities objected to Canada's policy of building vessels at inland yards. Ice barred the new ships from the ocean for almost half the year, and winter damaged them even before they could be launched. Moreover, the British specifically asked Ottawa to build a decent repair centre at Halifax, with graving docks for their biggest vessels. "The Americans, too, were surprised by the Canadian nonchalance at the state of their repair facilities," Forbes wrote. U.S. investigators surveyed the port of Halifax and told their government to "send tugboats to Halifax to rescue 'vessels of all nationalities . . . detained for an unreasonable length of time in Canadian waters awaiting repairs.'" The U.S. survey irritated Howe, but it did not get Halifax the repair centre the Allies needed.

If Maritime industry did not draw its share of government investment during arrangements for war, neither did it draw it during arrangements for peace. In 1944 Howe took charge of the new Department of Reconstruction, which used a formula to make sure government assistance went only to profitable companies that showed promise of making a successful transition to peacetime production. By July 1, 1945, all of 5 per cent of the funds had gone to the six Maritime and Prairie provinces; Ontario had received 48 per cent, Quebec 32, and British Columbia 15. It wasn't the Maritimes who'd hogged the blessings of the plump federal teat. It was central Canada.

Maritime industries such as DOSCO survived the war, but thanks to the government-fuelled expansion and modernization of Ontario, competitors found themselves badly weakened in the marketplace. Over the next quarter-century, DOSCO would be taken over by British interests, milked of its capital, and dismantled. Forbes concluded that, in the long run, the impact on the Maritimes of the government's wartime policies was bad. They accentuated and consolidated all the old trends toward regional disparity.

Howe was so antagonistic to DOSCO that in 1944 he told his steel controllers to use it "to the minimum extent possible, even if we have to buy the steel from the United States." He had close ties with Sir James Dunn, head of Algoma Steel, and Dunn's empire collected more than 80 per cent of the government's direct wartime grants to the steel industry. Dunn buttressed the powerful lobby on behalf of Great Lakes ports with his own anti-DOSCO lobby, and touted the concentration of Canadian manufacturing on the shores of the Great Lakes. Howe was the MP for Port Arthur, and he had earned much of his private pile by building grain elevators on the lakes. He shared the vision of "a centralized manufacturing complex closely integrated with the United States," but the vision, Forbes continued, "apparently did not include the Maritimes in any significant role."

Howe has been celebrated as a man who succeeded brilliantly at running Canada's war-production programme. But thanks to Maritime scholars such as Forbes, it is now clear that Howe screwed up Canada's war effort at sea, and at the same time screwed up the Maritimes.

While richer provinces feel the money that flows from them through the federal government to the Maritimes proves their generosity, Maritimers have never regarded federal aid as charity. They see federal grants not as handouts or dole, but as *rights* and as inadequate payment on the tremendous debt Canada owes them for having sacrificed Down Home interests to Toronto and Montreal. "I find something quite unreal about the Bay Street friends of mine who say the Atlantic provinces are a bottomless pit of federal funding," Donald Jamieson said in 1986. An eloquent Newfoundland politician who served as Canada's minister for external affairs, Jamieson spoke for four provinces when he added: "The next time, I say, don't bail out the banks, bail out Atlantic Canada. There is no necessity for any underdeveloped or disadvantaged part of this country to feel like some kind of mendicant when it starts looking for benefits from the government in Ottawa."

          *   *   *

Nothing annoys Maritimers more than the hoary notion that they are the alms-seekers of Canada. "Too often, we are stereo-typed as recipients, as needers rather than givers," Nova Scotia premier John Buchanan told the Canadian Club in Toronto in 1979, "as part of the baggage of Confederation." The idea is particularly repulsive in light of the billions the feds have poured into central Canadian benefits such as the St. Lawrence Seaway, the Mirabel Airport boondoggle, fast trains on the Windsor–Montreal corridor, and assorted subsidies and tax breaks for auto plants, aircraft factories, paper mills, and other industries sprinkled about southern Ontario and Quebec.

For the image of the Maritimes as the leeches of Confederation, their people have blamed Upper Canadian propagandists, including Toronto historians. "Unfortunately," Alexander Paterson wrote, "Central Canadian publications have teemed with just such singularly unfair mis-statements." Thus, Upper Canada was guilty not only of betraying the Maritimes but of slandering them as well, and the slander eased the betrayal. Like more evil forces in the world, Upper Canada distorted history to promote its own imperialism.

Writing five decades after Paterson, William Y. Smith told readers of a Maritime journal that Toronto professor Abraham Rotstein was wrong to write, "There are few tasks in Canada that have ranked as high on our list of priorities as regional development." The truth was, Smith said, that "the only time in Canadian economic history when regional development has had a recognizably high priority in Ottawa was, perhaps, 1969–72."

Moreover, "the federal program of industrial incentives for regional development has never been much more ambitious than it was in . . . the fiscal year 1975–1976, when the entire DREE [Department of Regional Economic Expansion] budget for industrial incentives for designated areas across Canada was only $92 million, almost exactly equal to the research budget of the federal Department of Agriculture." Since the days of Oliver Mowat, premier of Ontario from 1872 to 1896, "Ontario has been big and powerful enough to impose its concept of federalism on the whole country, a form of federalism geared, of course, to the interests of Ontario rather than to balanced growth across the country."

Rebuttals such as Smith's are becoming more frequent. If all Maritimers feel in their bones that Central Canadians have a distorted view of them, experts in Maritime history have begun to document the distortions. They've taken to exposing the way Canada's best-known historians twist the Maritime story while jamming it into the national story. J.M. Bumsted, for instance, has analysed the picture of Prince Edward Island at Confederation as it appeared in works by W.L. Morton, D.G. Creighton, and P.B. Waite. Lumping together descriptions by these national historians, one learns that Islanders were complacent, yet somehow bitter, feuding, and violent. They were isolated, parochial, narrow-minded, self-obsessed, smugly self-sufficient, and so immersed in a weird kind of local patriotism that they were incapable of larger loyalties. In the grand national perspective, Islanders were simply too stupid to recognize their glorious chance to join Confederation.

But Island ships were sailing around the world, Island farm products had good markets in the United States, and Island manufacturing was mushrooming. It was not till 1873 that the economy became so shaky that the colony joined Canada. A decade earlier, as Bumsted wrote, "the self-sufficient attitude of the Island's politicians in the Confederation debates . . . had a sound basis in reality." Moreover, feelings of local patriotism "were not, as the national historians would suggest, curious, but legitimate responses to circumstances." Historians trained in central Canada couldn't see this. They didn't know enough.

Maritime scholars repeatedly complain that general histories and textbooks about Canada betray disgraceful ignorance about the region. Before writing about the Maritimes, Canadian historians often neglect to read even the easily available research by Maritime scholars. When historian John G. Reid assessed nine recent books about Canadian history, he found that most gave short shrift to the Maritimes and some made stupendous mistakes about the most elementary facts in the region's history. To Reid, *Twentieth Century Canada* was especially annoying. It was the work of five of the biggest guns among Canadian historians: J.L. Granatstein, Irving M. Abella, David Bercuson, R. Craig Brown, and H. Blair Neatby. Yet it offered the amazing news that, *before Confederation*, Nova Scotians were struggling "to break free of the superior power and economic strength of the Canadas." This was codswallop, and Reid skewered it: "To be sure, 'Empire Canada' was in full operation by the turn of the twentieth century, but to date its emergence before 1867 seems fanciful at best."

From *Twentieth Century Canada*, Reid reported, "we learn that 'in the Maritime Provinces the Depression made less of an impact . . . only because these provinces had experienced an almost continuous depression since Confederation.' After that revelation, the region mercifully disappears from the text for a hundred or so pages." From start to finish, Reid said, *Twentieth Century Canada* portrayed the Maritimes as a laggard and poor cousin, and "to see this tired and misleading nonsense trotted out again in 1986—and by five historians of national reputation at that—is not so much infuriating as saddening."

* * *

Like the attitude of a child toward a capricious parent, the attitude of the Maritimes toward the federal government swarms with contradictions. No matter how hostile the Maritimes' opposition to granting Quebec special status within Confederation, they saw only good in the idea that they themselves should enjoy such special privileges as free trade with New England and exclusive rights to funds from the Department of Regional Economic Expansion. No matter what wrongs Confederation

imposed on them, Maritimers regard their own separatists as
kooks and cranks. No matter how callously Ottawa treats the
Maritimes, and no matter how vigorous the lip-service their
politicians and newspapers pay to the virtues of provincial
autonomy and self-reliance, the region remains Canada's
staunchest supporter of strong central government.

The federal government may never have shared the wealth
fairly, but at least it knows that sharing the wealth is part of its
duty. One recent survey indicated that 80 to 90 per cent of
Maritimers and Newfoundlanders felt Confederation had been
good for Atlantic Canada. "Only Ottawa Can Turn the Tide,"
declared the headline of an editorial in the Moncton *Times* in
1970. "Despite all their well-worn grievances," Maritimer Carman Miller wrote in 1982, "the Atlantic provinces editorial
writers remain firmly wedded to the Canadian option, if only
because existing economic exigencies seem to make it the best
bargain available."

That's why the Halifax *Chronicle-Herald* was suspicious of the
Meech Lake Accord: "For Nova Scotia, the most serious aspect
is its general concession to the rising power of the provinces . . .
Nova Scotia and its sister Atlantic provinces, so dependent on
transfer payments from Ottawa, must be concerned about the
erosion of federal power. As frustrated as we sometimes are by
the federal government's insensitivity to the region, most
Atlantic Canadians would rather appeal to Ottawa in times of
need than to premiers in Victoria or Toronto."

No one understood this unpalatable line of reasoning better
than Alex Campbell when he was premier of Prince Edward Island. If Quebec pulled out of Canada, Campbell told me in
1978, "we'd be alone on the Atlantic Coast, and we're *not* self-
sufficient. Ever since Confederation, there's been a decline in
our self-sufficiency. We've allowed the region to become a market of central Canada. You know, 40 per cent of all the personal
income in Prince Edward Island comes directly from the federal
government. We'd be without that. The population of the At-

lantic provinces would drop by at least half, and you know who'd leave first. The work force and the entrepreneurs. We'd be left with the very young and the very old. We'd face half a century of doubt and uncertainty. Even united as an Atlantic nation, it would take us fifty years to turn things around and get back just to where we are right now."

* * *

Resentment against central Canada and its selfish manipulation of the federal government is as natural to Maritimers as fog at Ship Harbour, Nova Scotia, muddy roads near Montague, P.E.I., or a storm-stayed basketball team at Campbellton, New Brunswick. Indeed, it's part of the regional identity, just as bitching about the CBC is part of the national identity. It expresses itself not only when a federal shipbuilding job goes to Sorel, Quebec, rather than Saint John, not only when a federal contract for the maintenance of fighter planes goes to Montreal rather than Halifax, not only when tens of millions of federal dollars go into jazzing up the Toronto waterfront while wharfs rot throughout the Maritimes, but also in every field from transportation to sports:
• When a blizzard imprisons ferryboats at Cape Tormentine, New Brunswick, any Prince Edward Islander with an ounce of constitutional knowledge can tell you that, for at least the three thousandth time, Canada has reneged on her ancient pledge to the Garden of the Gulf. The Island sourly joined Confederation in 1873, and to sweeten the deal, hadn't Canada promised "efficient steam service" to the "Mainland of the Dominion, winter and summer, thus placing the Island in continuous communication with . . . the railway systems of the Dominion"?
• When the Canada Council refuses grants to a Maritime dance company, the troupe complains that this is not because its performances are less than excellent, but because a narrow-minded clique in Upper Canada controls the Council's funding and funnels the money to friends up there.
• When the Canadian Intercollegiate Athletic Union chooses

a fullback from western Ontario as the most valuable college player in Canada, rather than a star tailback at Acadia University, a Halifax sportswriter says the CIAU has "once again snubbed its nose" at Maritime football. Moreover, "this latest snub by the CIAU" may not be as old as Confederation, but it is certainly "nothing new." The superior player from Acadia is too classy to complain, "but deep down, it has to hurt. Just as the latest slap in the face must hurt all the players, coaches and fans in the Atlantic provinces."

• When the CIAU then overlooks two hot basketball teams from Nova Scotia for wildcard spots in the national championships, local coaches, sportswriters, and even the leader of the opposition in the provincial legislature send up a chorus of wailing.

• When opening ceremonies for the Canada Winter Games in Sydney are so impressive that Cape Breton columnist Bill Dunphy says, "One couldn't help feeling proud as a peacock," he feels obliged to add, "And it didn't need an uppity film director from somewhere in Ontario to show us how to do it."

• When the federal cabinet orders the death of the most successful long-haul passenger train in the Maritimes, a ticket agent in Saint John says the decision is typical of the feds' attitude: "Forget the Maritimes. They only started Confederation. To hell with them."

Such items are not exceptional. They're typical of a strain of anger and resignation about the Maritimes' status in Canada that's as routine in the regional press as weather reports and the funnies. But even worse than snubs and injustices is the feeling that Canada has forgotten the Maritimes and acts as though they've disappeared under the ocean. When Albertans flaunted bumper stickers saying, "Let the eastern bastards freeze in the dark," it didn't comfort Maritimers that the target was Ontario, because that meant westerners didn't even know where the *real* east was. The real east was Down Home, and its people would rather be bastards than nobodies. Nothing arouses apoplectic editorials in Maritime newspapers more surely than a description of a "coast-to-coast" trip that starts in Montreal and ends in Victoria, or federal government travel bumf that gives short, inaccurate shrift to the east coast.

Maritimers dislike the Upper Canadian notion that because they're far from Toronto they are, by definition, isolated. Halifax was an international port when Toronto was a Mississauga encampment. Many Maritimers believe it's not they who are parochial but Torontonians. Born in Cape Breton, raised in Halifax, and celebrated everywhere as a pioneer of Canadian literature, Hugh MacLennan once told me he endorsed fellow novelist Robertson Davies' opinion of Toronto: "Rob says a Toronto audience won't laugh at a joke unless they've got a written guarantee that it's already been laughed at in New York. They're a terribly narrow, provincial people. Nova Scotians aren't like that." MacLennan, it's true, had never forgiven Toronto critics for crucifying his novel *Return of the Sphinx*, but even so, those who describe the city as provincial have a point. Toronto wraps her own people in a careering ball of energy, ambition, desire, and images of their own excellence. A cloud of self-interest insulates the ball and prevents Torontonians from grasping that, all across Canada, there are other spheres in which millions of Canadians are very much in touch with everything that's important to them.

"Oh yeah, I forgot," a Toronto newspaper editor told me by phone. "You're so out of touch down there, aren't you?" While watching the seagulls glide over Chedabucto Bay, I had confessed to him that I knew nothing about an impending strike on his paper. His response griped me a bit. What did he know about the oil rigs abandoning offshore exploration, or pollution in Halifax harbour, or the renovation of the Saint John waterfront? What did anyone in that self-satisfied, self-absorbed, self-mesmerized city know about the latest blow to the steel plant in Sydney? Who, really, was out of touch? And with what? Who in hell was Toronto to define for Port Shoreham the things with which it was important to be in touch? One convivial night I poured another rum for a fierce and native son of the Nova Scotian soil, and I told him about all this, and he said, "My God, Harry, you're becoming a Maritimer."

＊　＊　＊

Beneath the celebrated friendliness of the Maritimes, there lurks a bowel-deep suspicion of outsiders, and nowhere is this more true than along the strip of Nova Scotia's south shore that includes Barrington Passage, Doctors Cove, Shag Harbour, Woods Harbour, and Charlesville. The coast is often foggy. It's low, bleak, rocky, and speckled with alder bushes, stunted spruce, and stringy tamaracks. The industry here is fishing, not farming, and you wouldn't want to fall on your face while chasing a fly ball at the local ballpark. The field is dusty, gravelly, and, with scarcely a blade of grass, as hard as a supermarket parking lot. The bleachers are rickety, and behind centre field two crumby outhouses endure the corrosive weather. The ballpark looks no more inviting than the vats and pipes beyond the sign that says, "Acadian Seaplants Ltd. *Les Algues Acadiennes*. Cultivation Site. NO TRESPASSING."

Strung out along the snaking highway, within sight of acres of eel grass and the gray sheet of ocean, the houses wear clapboard and shingle. None will ever win an award from a house-and-garden magazine. Drowned fishermen lie in the graveyard by the small, steepled churches, and at Shag Harbour gaudy green wreaths and red, white, and blue anchors—made of plastic flowers, bright and gross in the pearl mist—lie beside a little cairn that commemorates "They that go down to the sea in ships, 1785–1985." There's a real anchor here, too, glossily painted in the usual colour: black. Farther up the road, a sign promises "For Whosoever Shall Call Upon The Name of the Lord Shall Be Saved," and it's easy to believe that the people who live on this melancholy and spooky coastline are God-fearing, superstitious, and wary of strangers.

"You've got the old Anglo-Saxon prejudice around here," Kirby Nickerson told John F. Burns of *The New York Times*.

Nickerson's forebears had been local seafarers for 150 years. He was twenty-nine, and Burns said he "belongs to a caste that sees little merit in outsiders." Nickerson told the reporter, "The attitude toward folks we don't know is, 'We don't know who they are, and they aren't from around here, so they can't be any good.'"

But Burns had come to the neighbourhood because it had just endured the biggest invasion of outsiders in its history, and the story had gone around the world. On Sunday morning, July 12, 1987, in a bay that strangers rarely dare to enter without a pilot, a rusty freighter somehow picked its way through dense fog and dumped 174 Sikhs on a deserted beach at Charlesville. A family of Malones awoke to a sight they'd never forget: bearded men, in turbans and flowing robes, milling around on their front lawn. The Malones gave them water from a garden hose, and pretty soon buses took the illegal immigrants to the firehall at Woods Harbour for grub.

From her kitchen window, a local woman saw one bus go by, noted it was full of hairy men with headgear, and decided that some strange sort of baseball team was on its way to town. But if the Sikhs astounded the shore, surely the shore astounded the Sikhs. For the people here have responded to the bleakness of sea and stone by turning their community into the lawn-ornament capital of the Maritimes. The buses carried the Sikhs through a corridor of daffy figurines: Garfield the comic-strip cat, Sylvester the Pussycat, Bugs Bunny, the Seven Dwarfs, umpteen Smurfs, wooden ducks "4 sale," wooden butterflies, lions lying down with lambs, geese, eagles, swans, flamingos, clattering wind toys, model ships under full sail, a Sambo holding the Nova Scotia flag, and at one house a flaming pink mooring buoy dangling from a tree like a gargantuan Christmas bauble.

Some religions have house gods; the people of Woods Harbour have lawn spirits. They also have tents, tent-trailers, trikes, bikes, pickup trucks, picnic benches, swinging lawn benches, power mowers, barbecue rigs, TV dishes, all-terrain vehicles with balloon tires, lobster boats, lobster buoys, and whole fields of stacked lobster traps. All these were on display for the wet, dazed, and sea-weakened Sikhs. They had no idea where they were. One asked if he could hire a taxi to take him to Toronto, some twelve hundred miles inland.

By the time the buses rolled up to the firehall, townsfolk had gathered there with food. Some Sikhs doubtless pondered a written command near the immaculate red trucks: "Don't smoke in bed. Make love instead." But they were mostly in the part of the firehall where dances ("I.D. required, couples only") and bingo occur. It's directly across the road from L & B Takeout, with its big cut-out picture of a strawberry ice-cream cone, and not far from Flossie's Bed and Breakfast, Kathy's Kustom Hair Care, and Karla's Hair Affair.

When I drifted along the coast a few days later, the firehall was locked. I parked and began to snoop around, but then a tall guy in his thirties came out of the building. He locked the door behind him. He had a rusty moustache and a baseball cap, and for a man from these parts who'd just found a no-account stranger rattling doorknobs and peeking in windows, he seemed amiable enough. "Yeah," he said, "we tried them on hot dogs and hamburgers, but they were vegetarians. We got out the peanut butter. We told them it was made of nuts. We just kept pointing at it and shouting 'Nuts! Nuts!'" So the Sikhs' first breakfast on Canadian soil consisted of peanut-butter-and-jelly sandwiches, pop, and Kool-Aid—all provided by the supposedly suspicious denizens of this gloomy shore. But the people here know about the sea, and they also know, as Maritimers have always known, that you must do what you can for wet, cold, hungry strangers who have come in from the ocean.

As the summer progressed, village parades throughout the province featured derisive floats bearing men dressed up as Sikhs, some of them waving placards that demanded Premier John Buchanan give them cab fare to Toronto. New characters joined the lawn population in Woods Harbour: small, dusky, bearded men wearing bright turbans and billowy blouses and

pants, each with a Canadian flag jutting from his lap. Outside
naval buildings in Halifax, where the government held the real
Sikhs before they moved west, a man in a yellow shirt waved a
sign that said, "Go home, trash." He said many Nova Scotians
shared his opinion but lacked his courage, a courage that did not
extend to his telling the press his name. For lack of other
dramatic footage, local television news showed him again, and
again, and again. All over the province, men and women in
drinking joints cracked nasty jokes about "the ragheads," and
angry bluenosers wrote furious letters to newspapers about the
vile "queue-jumpers." If the behaviour of the people of Charlesville and Woods Harbour on the gray morning of July 12 showed
one way Maritimers treat outsiders, the bitter, province-wide
reaction to the illicit human cargo from the mysterious freighter
showed another.

* * *

Most of the Sikhs were bound for Toronto and Vancouver.
They'd never intended to stay Down Home, and perhaps that
was wise. Many Maritimers mistrust all people from away who
choose to settle among them for more than two weeks in summer. Though the doubts might be strong about possible settlers
from India, they are also strong about real settlers from Toronto.
One can never tell about such people, can one? One doesn't
know their parents from Adam. Suppose they are of the same ilk
as those snake-oil salesmen, con artists, and disarming champagne guzzlers who suckered the Maritimes into Confederation?
These modern carpetbaggers wouldn't have come here unless
they sought something they couldn't get in Ontario, would they?
And yet Ontario already *has* everything. What do they want
with us?

"Who's that hairy-headed creep?" a Halifax viewer demanded
of the CBC switchboard when I first appeared as host of the
suppertime talk-show, "Gazette." "What rock did he crawl out
from under?" The man's anger was understandable. I was the successor to a line of smooth, garrulous, confident, and lovable

hosts, Down Homers tried and true, who for eighteen years had been making "Gazette" adorable in the eyes of the bluenose bingo crowd. But I was a stammerer, a blusher, a squeaky-voiced chump whose hands shook, a complete fumblebum among television interviewers. As for my hairy head, it was indeed in the style of what a woman friend in Toronto liked to call "WASP Afro." But it wasn't my hairiness or incompetence that most enraged the caller. It was that the new host "sounds like he's from Toronto."

So many viewers soon lodged that same complaint that I wanted to say on camera, "Yes, yes, I'm guilty, I'll sing, the jig's up. I forced my mother to give birth to me in, ugh, Hog Town. I've lived with the hideous shame of my birthplace for four decades, but listen, I beg of you, my father was born in Guysborough County, and his father farmed and fished herring and wore real rubber boots. Doesn't that count for anything?" But I was never brave on television.

My TV career was short. Returning to print, I attacked a building-supplies store in Halifax because its clerks were doltish and as lazy as toads at the bottom of a well. I suggested that no self-respecting Toronto store would retain such sluggards, but judging by the furious response of my readers, you'd have thought I'd said Joseph Howe molested children, Robert Stanfield sold secrets to the KGB, and Angus MacAskill, the legendary Cape Breton giant, wore elevator shoes. My assailants did not say I was as wet as dung about the clerks in the store (which, incidentally, soon went belly-up). They didn't bother to defend this local industry, because, to them, my point was not *the* point—which was that I, as a Hog Town immigrant who'd lived here only three years, had the gall to crap on any Halifax institution. I had bad-mouthed something Nova Scotian without having served my apprenticeship as a Nova Scotian. (I'm not sure how long the apprenticeship is supposed to last, but an old man, born in Lunenburg, once told me the townsfolk had never regarded him as a true Lunenburger because his father had come from P.E.I.)

Shortly after settling in Nova Scotia, I mocked Premier Gerald A. Regan in *Saturday Night* for his posturing as the Father of Fundy Tidal Power. The consequences were ugly. The piece enraged Regan. To get revenge, he phoned the president of Nova Scotia Light and Power, the private utility where I worked as editor of a house organ, and demanded he fire me. The president refused but issued me a gag order: while employed by his company I was never to write anything about any Nova Scotia politician for any publication. "If only you'd been living here a little longer," one of Regan's aides told me, "the preem wouldn't have been so pissed off."

In moving Down Home, I wondered, had I fumbled my future? I was a writer. I was from a city that expected to read raucous criticism of politicians and institutions and tolerated millions of newcomers. The newcomers endured labels, to be sure, but native Torontonians never called them Come From Aways. Could I be happy in a society where simply writing nasty comments about local situations drew midnight telephone calls demanding, "If you don't like it here, why don't you go back where you came from?" It turned out that, with a little help from my friends, I could.

*   *   *

"If you're from away," Libby Oughton told me over lunch at a Lebanese restaurant in Charlottetown, "you're from away, for ever and ever." She had come to the Island after a publishing career in Toronto and lived in Charlottetown for five years before being invited into the house of any Charlottetown native. Fully 90 per cent of the people at the parties she gives and attends are still Come From Aways.

As a challenger of the Island's fortress mentality, Oughton is conspicuous, like her flashy bangles and leopard-spotted pants and shirt. She's a trim, wiry woman with short mahogany hair, strong forehead, intense blue eyes, and a fast, wide mouth. Oughton is stubborn, energetic, and smart as a bee. She's a feminist. When she talks about what she does on the Island, which is run her own book publishing company, her manner seems to say, "I'm a fighter, and you'll never deck me." Some might want to cold-shoulder Libby Oughton even in the relatively tolerant corridors of Toronto publishing, but she chose to settle down and build a business in an island society so intimate it not only distrusts boat-rockers from away but also can't help being fascinated, and sometimes repelled, by whatever it is that sets even one of their own apart.

What sets Premier Joe Ghiz apart, in some minds, is his swarthiness and the fact that his father came from Lebanon. During the 1986 provincial election, his ancestry was a "hidden issue" of such power that, in one of his most moving speeches, he brought it out into the open himself. His Liberals won the election, but during a steamy debate in the new legislature, a furious Tory lost his head long enough to call him a "black boy." (The Tory later apologized, saying he meant no racial slur.) Historically, blacks have not been popular in Charlottetown. In the 1920s, British traveller George Nestler Tricoche visited the city, and in *Rambles Through the Maritime Provinces of Canada*, he claimed: "Persons who are still in their prime will tell you how amazed they were when they first saw a coloured man, for it is only a few years ago that the first specimen of that race put in an appearance at Charlottetown. It is related that people ran after him in the streets, as if the poor fellow were escaped from a menagerie."

But perhaps some of those Charlottetown persons in their prime were stringing Tricoche along. At least half a century earlier, blacks had been living in a neighbourhood known as the Bog. During the trial of two white men for the shooting death of a teenaged mulatto in 1878, defence lawyers viciously exploited local bigotry against the people of the Bog, where the murder occurred, and Crown witnesses swore they heard the killer boast, "I killed one black son of a bitch, and I'll kill another before I leave." The defence sneered at evidence from "the colored brigade," and the white jury found the accused not guilty. No one was ever convicted.

Tricoche was on firmer ground when he described how it felt to be a stranger in town, though he made himself sound like adventurer Richard Halliburton being gawked at by aboriginal Asians. A newcomer to Charlottetown was "often stared at in public places, such as banks, railway stations, or in a shop; but there is no effrontery in it, for it is the puzzled, half-amused stare of the child—or of the primitive being." Tricoche found the natives friendly, but he wasn't staying for long, and he was no threat to "the Island Way of Life."

Future visitors would not always appear so harmless, and P.E.I. would try to discourage them with vicious, hasty laws. After a strike vote at Canada Packers in 1947, the government of Premier Walter Jones, who rejoiced in the nickname Farmer Jones, declared the strike illegal, took over the meat-packing plant, ran it with scabs, and outlawed all unions with off-Island affiliations. Cabinet member Horace Wright defended these extreme measures on the grounds that "a communist agent from Toronto" had set foot on the Island, and it was essential "to keep communism out of this province." Premier Jones believed a tame labour force was essential to Island prosperity, and workers who didn't agree could "go somewhere else." The legislation was so ugly, however, that in 1949 the government succumbed to pressure—much of it "from away"—and scrapped it.

The potential enemy in 1971 was not commies and labour agitators from Toronto, but tens of thousands of rock music fans from across North America. Faced with plans for the Island's first big outdoor rock festival—this was two years after the famous inundation at Woodstock—older Islanders feared an invasion by raucous, hairy, dope-zonked, and sexually abandoned freaks. This would never do in the land of Anne of Green Gables, and the government of Premier Alex Campbell panicked. With help from the Opposition, and probably the approval of most Islanders, it whipped up a legislative package that amounted to a gross violation of human rights and rushed it through the legislature. You'd have thought war had been declared. The attorney general now had authority to cancel any public gathering "which in his opinion may contribute to the disruption of public order." Fortunately, national publicity once again embarrassed the Island. The government repealed the legislation almost as fast as it had been passed.

Comparing the anti-labour laws of 1947 and the anti-festival laws of 1971, political scientist David A. Milne wrote: "Each pointed to the use of extraordinarily heavy-handed measures to defend the Island from what were regarded as threats to the community. In each case, the principal danger was seen to come from external agents—people 'from away.' Each incident betrayed a state of siege mentality which directly accounted for the careless drafting of repressive legislation. . . . For such knee-jerk insularity, the province earned from *Time* the unlovely epithet of 'uptight little Island.'" Milne's remarks appeared in *The Garden Transformed*, a book of essays distributed by Ragweed Press, the publishing house of that unmistakable Come From Away, Libby Oughton.

The Come From Aways who most annoyed the uptight Island in the 1970s were the hordes of highly paid professional planners that the provincial government imported to help shape the Island's future. Many Islanders saw them as an insensitive gang who suddenly had the power to tinker with the Island's hallowed character and yet had no sense of its history or values. Also writing in *The Garden Transformed*, Donald Nemetz said: "Without question, the principal mistake made in the management of development on Prince Edward Island has been the manner in which outside experts were introduced and utilized. Isolating them organizationally was the worst possible arrangement. . . . The experts talked only to each other and were forced to make too many assumptions."

Though a businesswoman rather than a bureaucrat, Libby Oughton arrived in Charlottetown as an outside expert—in publishing—"and my first two years here were the loneliest of my life." She hurled herself into such community services as the local arts council, and feels she's gradually earned a grudging respect. Still, she remembers small slights. While running a bookstore, she responded to a woman who asked for a local newspaper by saying, "Yes, we have the *Pay*triot." The woman snapped, "It's the *Pah*triot." Some slights were not so small. No one could fathom a woman trying to run her own business, and when she applied for a loan on behalf of her Ragweed Press, a bank manager said, "No, no, dearie, you don't want a business loan. You want a personal loan."

If Islanders have begun to respect Oughton, it's because she's beaten the odds imposed by their wariness and served them well. For the Department of Education, this crusty outsider has produced the first major textbook to be written and published on the Island. *Abegweit, Land of the Red Soil* is by local history professor Douglas Baldwin, and it's introducing thousands of schoolchildren to the story of their home and native island. Ragweed has also produced fine children's books, regional cookbooks, and much poetry and fiction by Maritime writers.

Its radical feminist literature and lesbian erotica, however, are not high on the reading lists of most Islanders. In July of 1987, shortly after the *Globe and Mail* mentioned the lesbian verse in a feature about Oughton, someone torched the historic wooden building that housed Ragweed Press. Was some anti-lesbian madman out to punish her? She didn't think so. There'd recently been a whole rash of arson cases in Charlottetown. "But you know, Harry," she confided, "arsonists are *never* women."

She was soon back in business, running her one-woman publishing empire from second-floor quarters in the heart of the city. After the fire, she had not once toyed with leaving the Island. "I'm here to stay," she said. "I've nowhere else to go." She had spent seven years chiselling out what the *Globe and Mail* called "an extraordinary niche for Ragweed Press," and I've a feeling her isolation is just about over. Islanders eventually come to cherish the very outsiders they once reviled as crackpots and nuisances, particularly if the intruders prove they can give something useful to Island society. What they give might be books, paintings, theatre, or simply intelligent participation in the endless debate about the character of tomorrow's Island; but in the end, even these Come From Aways find acceptance and sometimes admiration. The process just takes longer than it does elsewhere. Nova Scotians and New Brunswickers also take years to size up a stranger. One morning, however, the stranger wakes up and realizes that a whole decade has passed since anyone has asked, "Why are you *here?*"

Long after Leon Major left Nova Scotia, he remembered that baffling question. He arrived in Halifax in 1963 as the first artistic director of the Neptune Theatre. *Maclean's* had called him "a bushy-browed hustler from the hardest-bitten Jewish district of Toronto." A brash, ebullient, cigar-chewing work addict, Major surfed into Halifax on a wave of publicity about his role as the boy genius of Canadian theatre, and again and again, at cocktail parties of the affluent south-end burghers who supported his theatre, he found himself trying to frame an acceptable answer to that odd query: "If you're so good, Mr. Major, why are you *here?*"

Major was normally as quick with an answer as Groucho Marx, but he could never figure out the motive behind this question. Surely these people didn't really believe he was too good for Nova Scotia? Did Maritimers feel *that* inferior? Or was the question just an expression of suspicion? If so, why had they chosen him to run their theatre?

Now that I've lived in Nova Scotia for seventeen years, I know what the question was all about. Wearing their monkey suits, with their bare-shouldered wives all dolled-up beside them, those Halifax businessmen who'd backed the Neptune with a few of their bucks were squinting at Major over their crystal highball glasses, and what they were really saying was something like this: "You've never lived here, Mr. Major. You've never played poker at the Halifax Club. You've never sailed out of the Royal Nova Scotia Yacht Squadron, and when you were a young buck you never got laid under the pines at Point Pleasant Park. *We* know why this is the best damned city in the best damned province in Canada, but *you* can't possibly know. So, Mr. Major, why are you *here?*"

Without actually uttering it, a fisherman put the same question to me in a limpid channel among the stone blobs in the sea off Prospect, Nova Scotia. I was messing about with my wife and three kids in *Moonshadow*, our little green yawl. The wind was light, the ocean placid and glittering, and the sun gorgeous at high noon. Since we were looking for an easy spot to clamber onto an island with our sandwiches, pop, and Moosehead Ale, we'd furled the sails and started to nudge the boat ahead with oars. The roar of an unmuffled engine shattered the bliss. An open powerboat, thirty feet long if an inch, tore out from behind an island. It looked old enough and fast enough to have done duty as a rum-runner half a century before, and it came at us as though it were going to cut us in half. Then, like a hockey player making slivers fly as he puts on the brakes, it veered sideways and stopped, bobbing there beside us. We were beam to beam, so close that the skipper could clap his hands on our starboard gunwale.

His eyes swept our boat from stem to gudgeon. His face was lean and coppery and about as friendly as a coastal cliff at midnight. A bearded man in his twenties sat in the bow of their vessel and eyed us meanly. The older fellow grunted a question. His accent was so thick and strange I couldn't make out his words, but it was obvious both men wanted an answer to "Why are you here?" Once they knew we were neither setting out lobster pots in their territory nor poaching from their own traps, their manner miraculously changed. They were all sunshine, and all of us together were just a bunch of wonderful Down Home folks sharing a fabulous day on the dancing ocean.

The skipper produced a mickey of straight rum, took a swig, and shoved the bottle at me. I downed a slug and then, forgetting that earlier I'd spread white medicinal grease all over my mouth to prevent the sun from blistering my lips, I passed the bottle over to the younger bruiser. For a second or two, he looked at the white smears my lips had left on its neck. He'd been ready to believe I was a lobster poacher, a type of human that fellows like him regard as lower than necrophiliacs, but now he seemed to be wondering if his wiping off that bottleneck with his shirttail might not hurt my feelings. He decided it would. He put his own lips over the guck that had covered mine and drank deep. "Ahhh!" he said, pulling the bottle from his mouth and grinning at the squawking gulls. "That's some good." White stuff clung to the black curls of his beard. It may take Maritimers a while to trust a stranger, but once they accept you, they *accept* you.

*   *   *

In the late 1700s, Scottish settlers in Pictou County, Nova Scotia, knew that whenever they were a few miles from home they could stop at any house and eat and sleep there as naturally as they would in their own places. Strangers from far away enjoyed the same generous treatment. Much later, in the 1850s, Isabella Lucy Bird, one of those redoubtable Englishwomen who liked to tour the colonies, stopped near Pictou town for afternoon tea at a house run by "Nancy Stuart of the Mountain." Along with her tea, Miss Bird received not cucumber sandwiches but thick oatcake, fresh butter, and gobs of raspberry and cranberry jams. A log fire crackled, and under the deer and cow horns pinned to the blackened rafters, Miss Bird happily filled her stomach in the company of "some handsome, gloomy-looking, bonneted Highlanders" and "large ugly dogs." When Nancy Stuart discovered that the English lady spoke Gaelic, she refused to accept any payment for the tea. Halifax had not impressed Miss Bird, but now she was beginning to like Nova Scotia.

More than one hundred and twenty years later I, too, repeatedly wallowed in Pictou County hospitality. I was writing a book about a local boy who'd stayed home to make good. He was Frank Sobey, a blunt, bald business whiz who'd parlayed his father's butcher shop into an empire of supermarkets, real estate, and stock-market investments worth hundreds of millions of dollars. The biography was his son Donald's idea, not his. Frank was wary, reticent, even grumpy. Prying anything interesting out of him was like trying to shuck oysters with a swizzle stick. But at the end of each boring morning at his pretentious mansion— Crombie—outside New Glasgow, he'd say, "You'd better stay for lunch. Want a Scotch first?"

He'd pour the two drinks himself and chunk in the ice, and after a while we'd go into his dining room, a small banquet hall really, and an elderly woman servant would bring us breaded haddock, never overcooked, and crisp fish cakes, vegetables, and white wine. After apple pie, cheese, and coffee, he'd climb into his blue Mercedes with his black lab and drive a few miles to the Sobey business headquarters where, at seventy-nine, he was still kicking ass. Frank Sobey and I never got to be friends, but on the other hand, I never left his house without a meal. He was a Pictou County man.

Friendly acts still startle me in the Maritimes. One June afternoon in 1987, I was wandering about old Saint John with a map and a guidebook. Three different men asked, "Pardon me, but may I help you in any way?" Two delivered little history lectures before ambling off on whatever their business was. A fourth man stopped his shaky green Ford beside me at the foot of Prince William Street because I was taking notes at a plaque under the Three Sisters. These are navigation lights on a trident, dedicated to local harbour pilots, and the plaque commemorates the seven-man crew of a pilot boat that a steamship sliced in half in January 1957. The man rolled down his window and asked, "You want to know anything more about the monument?" His offer was so unexpected my answer was abrupt: "No, no. I'm just writing down these names here."

"Well, one of them was J.W. Cunningham," he said. He was blocking traffic, but no one honked. "If you want to know more, his son works just up at the U.N.B. campus. His name is Jack, Jack Cunningham." The man drove off, leaving me to wonder what people from New York City think when they visit Saint

John and run into this unpaid, unsolicited, unbaited helpfulness. Do they think it's part of some city-wide con game?

In industrial Cape Breton, I rarely got away with simply asking someone for directions, receiving them, saying thank you, and departing. At Victoria Mines, for instance, I saw a lanky, knobby-jointed bloke pushing a power mower through the ditch in front of his house. I wanted to know where Waterford Lake was because it was there, on June 11, 1925, in one of the worst incidents in Cape Breton's grisly labour history, that a coal-company goon panicked during a union demonstration and shot miner William Davis through the heart. I thought I should see the scene of the outrage. As I approached the man with the mower, he switched it off and faced me. Yes, he knew where the lake was, but there was nothing up there worth seeing, and why would I want to go up there? So I was a writer, was I? Well, that must be an interesting line of work, and where did I say I hailed from? Guysborough County across the Strait, you say? And do you happen to know a MacIntosh family over there?

This man combined classic Maritime characteristics: nosiness and courtesy. He had to *place* me, and we stood out there together, while the breakers on Spanish Bay roared behind my back, and I told him I was born in Toronto but moved to Halifax with my family in 1971, and now my wife and I were living on the farm where my father was born, and our children were in Upper Canada, but some day they'd return, and. . . .

His face was all bumps and crags. He was a retired miner, a man who'd survived decades of lung-sooting labour, and maybe the odd bone-crushing tavern brawl as well. But he had grace, and in his manner, great gentleness. I have buttonholed strangers for information in dozens of towns throughout the Maritimes, and over and over again, I have encountered that same gentle dignity. It lights up Down Home faces from the inside.

*   *   *

For dirt, toughness, hard luck, and hopelessness, no spot Down Home beats Whitney Pier, Sydney, Cape Breton Island. A sooty cluster of hillside houses, The Pier has been a catchbasin of misery for much of this century. In the near west—above a vast, bleak, fenced zone of railway tracks, rusting boxcars, and black mountains of stockpiled coal—looms a skyline of grim chimneys, tubes, cannisters, cranes, and scaffolding. The steelworks. In the near east, on a slope beyond Victoria Road, lies a Catholic cemetery that's full of MacNeils and Zagorskis, MacDonalds and Gnieweks, Gillises and Kolankos, Murphys, Reillys, and Butlers, and Etiennes, Josephs, and Candeloras. At the turn of the century, when industry speechifiers gloated that the great German steel syndicates "trembled with misgivings" at the potential rivalry of Sydney, European workers flooded into town so fast that in eighteen months the population shot from three thousand to ten thousand. From the farms of Cape Breton came descendants of Scottish pioneers, and Sydney quickly boasted the most polyglot crowd in the Maritimes.

Controlled by ruthless investors from away, the steelworks dominated and tormented Whitney Pier for generations. As the plant's fortunes rose and fell, so did the steelworkers' hopes for a decent living for their families. The Pier was a workers' ghetto for men who, as often as not, had no work. Along with injustices in the nearby coal mines, the cruelty and niggardliness of the plant's management helped arouse some of the most bitter and bloody labour strife in Canadian history. Meanwhile, decade after decade, the plant sent its harsh, ceaseless din rattling through the little streets of Whitney Pier, and the towering stacks spewed smog over the wooden houses, trim lawns, flowering bushes, picket fences, clotheslines, churches, shops, traffic, street children, and, indeed, over everything and everybody. From a distance, the smoke looks like orange plumes over the blue harbour; it's Sydney's most distinctive feature. But when you're *in* the stuff and there's a breeze, it's a spinning, hellish fog of pink, vermilion, fuchsia, red, and rust. With the sun setting behind it, the smog looks black, like a coal-miner's lung.

Whitney Pier people opposed plans of the Cape Breton Development Corporation (DEVCO) to stockpile coal near their homes in 1987, and DEVCO president Derek Rance infuriated them by suggesting that since the neighbourhood was already "the worst-polluted environment in the province," a few more heaps of coal wouldn't make much difference. (It had been a while since a company president in Sydney had said anything quite that insensitive, and the federal government fired Rance.)

The main drag of Whitney Pier is Victoria Road, and it was here, on a summer Sunday in 1923, that a squad of "special police," riding horses and swinging three-foot clubs, galloped into a crowd of worshippers who were strolling home from church. The steelworkers were on strike, the strike had already turned violent, and the purpose of the cavalry charge was to teach them a lesson they'd not forget. Recruited from the Montreal and Halifax waterfronts, the special police included thugs and boozers, and though employed by the province, they served as company goons. On that black Sabbath in 1923, they not only knocked down fences, smashed windows, shot a dog, and split open the heads of young and old in the street, they also charged into houses in search of more victims. Bloody Sunday remains one of the most infamous days in the history of labour strife in Nova Scotia.

On another Sunday, sixty-four years later, I took a melancholy stroll of my own along Victoria Road. It was a cold afternoon in mid-May, and nothing much was doing. Sundays in strange cities are depressing, and I wished I had someone to talk with. "I'll have a Caramilk bar," I told the girl at Pier Confectionery. Her skin was snowy, and her dark hair and red lips curly. I liked her not only because she was beautiful but also because she did not tell me to have a nice day. Instead she said, "Bye now." I ambled past Neville Memorial Park ("Home of the Cape Breton Pepsis"), but there'd be no ballgame there this evening. Polish Village, run by St. Michael's Polish Benefit Society, was locked up, and so was the Royal Canadian Legion, Whitney Pier, Branch 128.

The grass was already deep green. A fine lace of budding leaves, a paler green, shrouded the trees and looked delicate in the rolling, orange smoke. Many houses were small and, to defy the gloom in the air, brightly painted. I passed a black Chrysler Cordoba with flat tires, a green Dodge Duster, and other wrecks in driveways and backyards. After a while, I asked a middle-aged guy in a windbreaker where the horrors of Bloody Sunday had occurred. He pointed out Holy Redeemer Church, a solid, red-brick building where five loud boys were playing ball hockey. A fat kid on the sidelines urged a player who was enamoured with his own stickhandling to pass the ball. "Don't be a hero," he chirped. "Up and over, up and over." Tonight, I remembered, the Stanley Cup finals would begin. At least I'd have something to watch on television.

I walked west toward the steelworks—only one of six stacks spewed smoke—and then came back up Dominion Street to Victoria Road. From a distance, the intersection looked choked with cars. Beyond the traffic I could see dozens more cars, and people standing beside them, looking at some activity in a field. Good, I thought, a softball game. Just the ticket for the late-Sunday blues. When I reached Victoria Road, however, I found not a softball game but the most wacko sport I've ever seen. The field of competition was a grassy swamp, roughly two hundred feet wide, and the contestants were deliberately, recklessly, and gleefully driving their cars and trucks into the muck till their wheels sank and they could go no farther.

All the vehicles had four-wheel drive, and the idea was simply to see who could make it across the bog to the dry slope on the far side. Dozens of spectators hung around over there, and here on Victoria Road I stood among a hundred or so connoisseurs of this zaniest of auto sports. I watched a Lada, Toyota, Datsun, GMC, and Chevrolet charge headlong into the swamp, roar and bounce and slither three-quarters of the way across, and then wallow to a halt and sink to their fenders. All-terrain vehicles with balloon tires buzzed around them like flies around stricken water buffalo. Each time a car or pick-up truck bogged down— and none that I saw reached the far side under its own power—a grinning guy waded out with cable and chain from a tow truck on firm ground, and pretty soon the filthy vehicles were back on our side for another try.

From fender to fender, from roof to exhaust pipe, they were lathered with black, glutinous muck. Windshield wipers created the sole clean patches, and by nosily peering through the glass, I discovered that wives or girlfriends sat beside some of the happy drivers. Spotting me as a stranger, a Pier character called Frenchy told me the contest occurred every Sunday night. Another guy said the swamp restored its own shape naturally, taking exactly one week to smooth out the gouges that tires opened, and to make conditions flat, ripe, and tempting for a new round of assaults. One driver was a tall fellow with a rusty beard, white forehead and rosy cheeks, and he volunteered that this wasn't the only spot where he and his buddies drove their trucks and cars into thick muck. Good bogs often sprouted behind shopping malls and parking lots on the outskirts of town. It was 6:30 P.M. now, and all afternoon he'd been plunging his pickup truck into the best slime pits Sydney could offer. "Yeah," he said, with a touch of weary pride, "I been goin' hard since two o'clock."

The evening confirmed a cliché for me. The cliché says that generations of deprivation in the Maritimes have bred a people who know how to make their own fun and how to share it. Here was I, alone on a Sunday night in one of the hard-luck capitals of the region, and here were all these crazy guys slogging around in a cold, useless swamp. Every driver had mud up to his thighs. Some were bearded, some clean-shaven. Most had peaked caps and wore either windbreakers or what I call the Down Home Shirt, the one with red and black checks. All of them, and all of the Pier people who'd come out to see them, seemed to be either laughing or on the verge of laughing, and even though I was a stranger and taking notes like a cop, people welcomed me into their conversations as easily as if I were their brother. On my way back to my motel room, where no one waited, I felt like singing.

4

WE'RE ALL IN
THE FAMILY

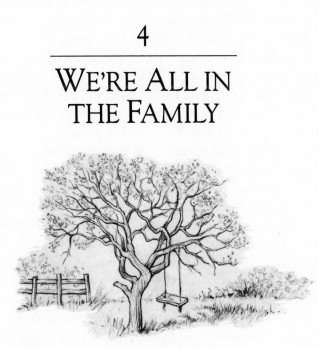

Robert Stanfield phoned me one night in 1979. He was sixty-five. A dozen years had passed since he'd been premier of Nova Scotia and three since he'd been leader of the opposition in the House of Commons. Now, he was Canada's most respected ex-politician, but I barely knew the man. I'd once told *Star Weekly* readers why Pierre Trudeau would make a better prime minister than he, and in 1972 *Maclean's* had published a piece by me about what Truro had been like while Stanfield was growing up there. The story included a flattering description of his mother as a political asset to his father. Months after it appeared, Stanfield and I found ourselves awkwardly standing together at a Neptune Theatre party. Neither of us were masters of small talk. "Uh, Mr. Bruce," he said, "I, aah, I just want to thank you for the nice things you said about my, aah, my *mother*." Seven years passed before I picked up the phone at my Halifax house to hear him talking to me again.

For ten minutes, I had no idea what he wanted. He told me that Lord Elgin, chief of the House of Bruce, was coming to Halifax for a few days, but I had never taken the slightest interest in my Scottish roots, and my unspoken reaction to this news was, "So what?" Stanfield told me he'd once stayed at Broomhall, Lord Elgin's estate in Scotland, and it was certainly a lovely place. Elgin was not at all lordly in his manner. He was a pretty regular guy, and he had "a nice wife, yes, very nice." Elgin's name, Stanfield continued, was Andrew Bruce. There were lots of Bruces in Scotland, of course, but did I know that there weren't really all that many Bruces here in New Scotland? There was Allan Bruce who ran the Palliser Motel outside Truro, and there was a Bruce fellow who had a car dealership in the Annapolis Valley, and a few Bruces down around Shelburne on the South Shore, but when you came right down to it, Nova Scotia wasn't really a hotbed of Bruces. Weren't my people from Guysborough County? There were plenty of Grants in Nova Scotia, that was for sure, and many of them had Bruce connections, but . . .

As this inexplicable flow of bluenose-Bruce lore continued, I

thought of my drinking acquaintance Doug Harkness, a dangerous man when moved to make mischief. He had often used his
uncanny ability to imitate Stanfield's voice to play fiendish telephone jokes. I was about to issue an obscene order to "Stanfield"
when he told me that, although Lord Elgin had a tight schedule
in Halifax, his lordship wanted to meet Bruces. Would I be so
kind as to join him for a quick breakfast at the Lord Nelson
Hotel the following Monday? This just wasn't Harkness's style,
and, sure enough, when I went to the hotel the chief of the
House of Bruce awaited me. He and his wife, Victoria, were
exactly as Stanfield had described them. Lord Elgin gave me a
biography of Robert the Bruce, we began to correspond, and a
couple of years later my wife and I followed Stanfield's tracks to
Broomhall for a four-day visit at Hogmanay.

Stanfield's telephone performance no longer strikes me as
mysterious. For all he had done was call me on a family matter,
and in the Maritimes, family counts for more than it does anywhere else in Canada. To know you, Maritimers must place your
family. If they do, they are confident, even before they've met
you, that they have a line on your character. Older businessmen
still talk about having hired a man because he came from "good
stock." For generations, a factor in the loan decisions of bank
managers was the reputation of an applicant's family. Though
the power of such considerations is fading, they remain stronger
Down Home than anywhere farther west.

Nowhere in Canada have I heard more talk about nice, fine,
talented, hard-working, honest, and lovely families, and also
families "with a few bad apples," and those that are "a bad lot."
I've listened to these assessments at garden parties and afternoon
teas, in boardrooms and bars, over beer on a beach and whiskey
at a wake. Obsession with family may be natural to any society
that's both old and intimate. It binds people together, but it
has its dark side. Through lost opportunities, many Down Home
sons and daughters have had to pay for the sins of their fathers
and mothers. It's hard to shake the taint of having sprung from a
bad family.

The Maritimes may be the last Canadian stronghold of the traditional family business. A Central Canadian who's made his fortune in one business may proudly encourage his children to excel in entirely different fields, and the son who joins his father's firm sometimes arouses the suspicion that he lacks moxie. Maritimers, however, admire father-and-son business teams and think it's right for families to stick together to run anything from a fishing boat or potato-chip truck to an industrial, investment, and real-estate empire worth hundreds of millions of dollars, or in the case of the Irvings of New Brunswick, untold billions.

Outside the Maritimes, it's common to see business ambition and attachment to family as a war in the heart of every successful man. Business is one compartment of his life, family another, and those who lock themselves inside the first sacrifice the second to neglect. The man who fails to know his anguished and disintegrating family while hurling himself along the treadmill of business success is a cliché of the times. But whatever the cliché's accuracy with regard to the big-city businessmen of North America, it's been pretty well irrelevant to the Maritimes for most of the twentieth century. Down Home, a man's wife and children were not isolated benefactors of his business triumphs, but contributors to his business survival. Sons of fishermen hauled nets. Daughters cleaned fish, taught school, and brought their pay home. The children of few Annapolis Valley farmers grew up without knowing the pain of blue fingers while picking apples on an icy November morning, and not one of grocery magnate Frank Sobey's three sons escaped regular exile to the family's basement to sprout and bag spuds. While a boy in Toronto, I disgusted my father by asking for twenty-five cents after shovelling snow off our front walk. Where he'd come from, no kid ever dreamed of asking his father for cash for milking a cow, cutting hay, or splitting firewood.

The usual questions about the split between a tycoon's work and his family often don't apply in the Maritimes. As children who've been drawn into a family business grow older, they're liable to complain not that they see too little of the patriarch, but that they see too much. (Frank Sobey, in his last years, suspected that his three sons tried to keep him out of his office, and their hair, by secretly arranging golf invitations for him.) In the heads of men like Sobey, and the even richer financier Roy Jodrey of Hantsport, Nova Scotia, one's family, business, travel, and life itself were all mixed together in a rolling ball that could only keep getting bigger. Long before the deaths of Jodrey and Sobey, they hired the craftiest lawyers they could find, not only to freeze their estates to beat taxation but also to set up companies to guarantee that their empires would remain indefinitely in the hands of their descendants.

When a wilful man struggles all his life to erect a successful business in central Canada, his sons may either blow the chance to keep it growing, or, wanting no part of the old man's creation, let it pass into outsiders' hands. "What you often find," Halifax bond-dealer J. William Ritchie told me, "is that one son's a drunk, another's in jail, and the third guy's off in Tanzania or somewhere." Noting that Frank Sobey's father had started the Sobey business, and that Frank's grandsons were now rising in its supermarket and real-estate branches, an elderly Toronto banker marvelled to me in 1982, "How many family companies survive four generations in Canada? Damn few."

Some economists speculate that business nepotism has drained the Maritimes of entrepreneurial vigour, that the smartest and most ambitious executives in family-owned companies see their way to the top blocked by the dull offspring of the founder, get fed up, and head west. The theory has holes. Harrison and Wallace McCain of Florenceville, New Brunswick, both worked for the mighty Irving-family empire, but they did not get fed up and head west. They got fed up and founded the mighty McCain-family empire, a worldwide food-packaging business with headquarters in their hometown.

Moreover, if business nepotism drives out the brightest and best, how does one account for the success of the Olands, brewers since the nineteenth century; the Sumners of Moncton, merchants for five generations; the Jodreys, whose multifarious interests are chiefly run by Roy's son, John, and grandson, David Hennigar; the Sobeys, whose business affairs are in the hands of Frank's three sons, and increasingly a nephew and some grandsons; the Stanfields, who've been manufacturing underwear in Truro, Nova Scotia, since before the Klondike gold rush; and above all, the Irvings, whose stupendous international holdings and Down Home industries are ruled by K.C. himself, now eighty-eight, and his three sons? Far from driving out executives with entrepreneurial hustle, many of these family businesses have helped reverse the notorious brain drain by importing senior management from Upper Canada.

It 's easy for even a huge enterprise to play its cards close to its chest when the players who hold all the best cards are brothers. If the biggest businesses in the Maritimes are excessively secretive—and business journalists have been insisting for decades that they are—it's because the families that own them regard their business affairs and family affairs as indivisible. For them, secrecy in business is not only a smart way to operate, it's also a matter of family privacy and good taste. Poorer families don't tell their neighbours how much money they make, the size of their mortgages, or the details of embarrassing interviews with bank managers. Just about all families have financial secrets. The difference is that the business decisions of families such as the Irvings, McCains, Sobeys, and Jodreys are so huge they may affect the lives of tens of thousands of smaller families. These dynasties, however, do not believe their power imposes on them some special responsibility to blab to the media about an important business decision. It's all in the family, and smart families know how to keep their mouths shut.

*　*　*

Families are significant Down Home not only in business but also in everyday conversation. Like gossip or sports trivia, talking family is fun. It confirms that the talker knows a territory. It is as though the Maritimes were an endless novel and the readers were forever sorting out the characters. If someone in a Halifax bar mentions a certain Murray, someone else may wonder aloud if this particular Murray isn't one of the Murrays from Pictou town. Yes, he'd be a brother of Jock Murray, dean of the Dalhousie medical school, and didn't he have eight brothers and sisters? No, nine. Quite a family, that. The father ran the weekly paper in Pictou, and just about all ten kids went to St. F.X.— St. Francis Xavier University, Antigonish. Someone at the bar remembers playing hockey with one of the Murray boys. Someone else knows a fellow who, a quarter-century ago, dated one of the Murray girls. Different Murray names are introduced and then rejected as having no connection to the Pictou Murrays. I've heard such family talk ramble on for half an hour before the boozers change the subject to the latest political scandal.

When Maritimers discuss family, they inevitably discuss history. I have never met Joseph Salter, for instance, but when I phoned him in June 1987, we ended up yakking about generations of Bruces and Salters. I had called him on a hunch. I'd noticed a dull wooden building with a hip roof on Commercial Street in North Sydney, Cape Breton Island. Two six-foot anchors sat outside, and a small cannon faced the harbour. What intrigued me, though, was a sign advertising Salter's Agencies, an insurance outfit. Another sign identified the law office of Joseph L. Salter, and across the street a waterfront building housed Joseph Salter's Sons, Ltd., coal brokers, ships' agents, and ships' chandlers.

The odd thing was, I had only recently learned that no fewer than sixty-nine years before, my old Aunt Zoe, then a farm-fresh girl of twenty, had graduated from a secretarial course and gone straight to work for some Salters in North Sydney. Moreover, they'd run a ships' chandlery, and Zoe's job there was her first big step away from The Place at Port Shoreham. For the rest of her life, she'd return only for short visits. Meanwhile, her kid brother Charlie missed her and sent her his secret hand-written weekly newspapers. He also mailed her an eight-line poem. Zoe showed it to her boss, one Joseph Salter. Salter showed it to the editor of the *Cape Breton Post*, who printed it. "Master Charles Bruce," future winner of the Governor General's Award, was now a published poet.

Zoe told me all this in a letter from San Bernardino, California. She remembered a day in North Sydney "when the captain of a huge Dutch ship, in for coal, sent word to Mr. Salter that he would like to invite me for lunch on board the ship. Consent was given, and the absolutely huge first mate, in uniform, came for me. We were rowed out to the ship by several sailors. They were stripped to the waist, which I am sure shocked me. At that time men were not allowed on the beach without tops to their bathing suits. (Shades of bikinis!) I climbed up the rope ladder, and I remember being entranced by the beautiful wood in the captain's cabin. All I remember about lunch was soup, though I'm sure we had more. The captain presented me with a teak-wood napkin ring, which has been lost in my moving around."

Zoe's sister Carrie also worked for Salter, and at ninety-two, she wrote to me jocularly about the smoke in the office, "from vile tobacco"; the crunching sound when one of the Salter men bit an apple while "all the rest were appleless"; and the morning ritual of spreading Dustbane, "and the broom's clean sweep along the middle, scorning all the corners." The working day, Carrie recalled, did not end till six at night, and then the building was left to the mercy of four raucous Newfoundlanders who rented rooms on the second floor.

Within a few weeks of receiving my aunts' letters, I happened to be in North Sydney. They and their ancient adventures were the last thing on my mind. Then, however, I saw the name of Joseph L. Salter, barrister and solicitor, in a front window of that unexceptional building, and I called him on a pay phone. He did not think it at all odd that a stranger should interrupt his morning's work, calling out of the blue to ask if, back around the tail-end of the Age of Sail, one of his forebears might have employed two sisters from a Guysborough County community whose name he'd never heard. In fact, as fast as I told him about the Bruces, he told me about the Salters. Even faster.

His great-grandfather, also Joseph Salter, had been a quintessential Maritime adventurer. Born in Hants County, Nova Scotia, he joined a Halifax trading firm as a teenager, and by the time he was twenty-three he had made so many voyages to Africa that his friends called him Africana. In 1839 he suffered seven attacks of malaria before he could leave Sierra Leone. "He helped quell a mutiny, or something," his great-grandson told me, "and was awarded half the cargo. That gave him enough money to stay ashore and start a business." By the 1850s, while still in his thirties, Salter was the mayor of Moncton. He was one of the biggest shipbuilders in the Maritimes and a man who'd crossed the Atlantic thirty-six times. After both Moncton and his shipbuilding business went bust, he founded a gold mine near Halifax and plunged into the coal business in Cape Breton. He managed a colliery at Victoria Mines and opened a ship brokerage in North Sydney. It also dealt in coal and lumber, and its name was Joseph Salter's Sons, Ltd.

One son was Joseph Salter, Jr., grandfather of the man telling me all this. At the end of World War One, in this same building with the cannon out front, Joseph Salter, Jr., was indeed my aunts' boss. They were Methodists, and so was he. "He supported missions in Africa," his grandson said, "and he went around preaching, playing music—he could play anything—and saving souls from the demon rum." From Sarah Tory Bruce's point of view, Joseph Salter, Jr., must have seemed the perfect employer for her daughters.

Even as I write this, my phone rings to remind me how hard it is to escape family talk Down Home. The conversation goes like this:

"Is that you, Dave?"

"No, it's Harry Bruce. You've got the wrong number. The phone's acting funny today."

"Harry Bruce, eh? Well, this is Neil Torrey. I think we're related." (My grandmother's branch of the family had changed the spelling to Tory.)

"If you're a Tory, that must be true. My grandmother Bruce was a Tory."

"I know, and my grandmother Torrey was a Bruce."

"Is that right? I guess we're related twice, then."

"Yeah. We should get together some time."

We probably will.

* * *

Family lies at the heart of the whole Acadian drama. Like the immigrant Scots, another punished people, the Acadians relied on a clan system for comfort, survival, moral example, and cultural tenacity. During the Expulsion of the 1750s, the British broke up families, hoping to disperse them so thoroughly that they'd lose their customs, loyalties, language, and common sense of history. With luck and time, maybe they'd even forget where they'd come from. But the British misunderstood their victims. No sooner had they dumped the Acadians in various parts of the thirteen colonies than many of the exiles began to ramble around in search of lost relatives. If the British had kept families intact, and given them land to farm in one spot, the legend of the heroic wanderings of the Acadians might never have flowered.

As the wanderings continued, and as the Acadians rounded up strays, many dreamed of returning to their homeland. By the late eighteenth century, hundreds of families had made their way back to the Maritimes from England, France, Massachusetts, Georgia, and the Carolinas. Their return was stealthy. The Acadians, Antonine Maillet wrote in *Pélagie*, "came home by the back door, and on tiptoe. And when the world got round to noticing, it was too late; Acadie already had springs in its shanks and its nose in the wind."

Back home, though rarely on the choice land of their fore-bears, the Acadians repeated their old settlement pattern: a family would form a clan-village around the holdings of its first settler. As more exiles of the same name returned to the family mecca, as villagers married among themselves and children were born, communities grew faster than surnames. In many Acadian towns, more than two centuries after the earliest return of exiles, a single family name is still overwhelmingly predominant. Along "the French Shore" in western Nova Scotia, for instance, it's Comeau in Comeauville, Saulnier in Saulnierville, d'Entremont in West Pubnico, and Deveau in Salmon River.

Like Acadians who'd been booted out of one homeland, Loy-alists who'd been booted out of another came to Saint Mary's Bay with their families in the 1780s. Like the Acadians again, they weren't much interested in either conquest or riches. They wanted to be free of warfare, left alone to crank out of a sea-blasted coast enough food and fuel to keep their families healthy. Not only in western Nova Scotia, but in farm towns and coastal communities throughout the Maritimes, family networks were often so extensive that visiting, receiving and chatting up relatives consumed the time that later generations would blow on movies, television, taverns, and bingo. In the Acadian vil-lages in particular, family gossip not only guaranteed that everyone knew what everyone else was thinking and doing but also enforced a standard of behaviour. Crime was rare.

If certain Acadian families were exceptional for their local power, Down Home families from other historical backgrounds also served as co-ops for production, sources of entertainment, judges of behaviour and thought, and funnels for political patronage. Both the Acadians and the others had a phenomenal grip on family history. In Lunenburg County, Nova Scotia, fam-ilies can still rhyme off their lineage right back to the first Ger-man settlers of the 1750s. "It is not uncommon in Cape Breton to find those who can name their father, grandfather, great-grandfather, all of whom were perhaps born on this side of the Atlantic, and their great-great- and great-great-great- and great-great-great-great-grandfathers, who were born in Scotland," Charles W. Dunn wrote in *Highland Settler*. One Cape Breton Islander, Alexander the Ridge MacDonald, could "trace his own paternal line back seven generations to a Highland chief and from him back into the misty past of Gaeldom until his total list included twenty-three names."

Kinship binds Acadians everywhere. A Poirier from Meteghan Centre, Nova Scotia, may feel as at home in France as a MacNeil from Cape Breton feels on the island of Barra. In *My Acadian Heritage*, Léonie Comeau Poirier wrote of Acadians, "We're like a large family. I have been called 'cousin' by people living in France whose ancestors were deported from Grand Pré in 1755. Their homes are open to me whenever I visit France. Visiting Acadians are treated to their sumptuous cuisine and wines . . . because we are family."

The Acadians and Scots had something else in common. Their families were so big they kept running out of names to give their chidlren, and both cultures used patronymics. "If Angus MacIsaac called his son Donald, like dozens of others, neighbours would style him Donald (of) Angus, with his surname seldom mentioned," David (Big Christopher) MacDonald explained in *Reader's Digest*. "His kids might then become Little Angus Donald Angus or, for that matter, Big Annie, etc. Thus the third user of one name became Tommy Tom-Tom." Acadian neighbours of the Scots used the identical technique. Among the people of Chéticamp, Cape Breton Island, Father Anselme Chiasson said in *Chéticamp: History and Acadian Traditions*, "it is not necessary to say Placide Poirier of Joseph Chiasson, but simply Placide à Lazare and Joseph à Henri. As it often happens that a boy is given the same name as his father, to distinguish him from his father he is called 'le petit' (the younger or junior), as in 'Petit' Placide à Placide, a name he will keep all his life, even if he grows bigger and taller than his father."

If a patronymic didn't do the job, a nickname did. In Chéti-camp, to take the example of just one Acadian village, local characters have been known by the French terms for ox, poodle, spaniel, dog, cat, field mouse, rook, raven, rooster, otter, had-dock, beetle, yellow lamb, little monkey, and wolf fart. One fellow was the Plough, and another the Little Pint. One woman was the Funk, another the Fury, and still another the Little Kettle. The town boasted the Beak, the Mouth, the Great Nose, the Plum, the Paw, the Blockhead, the Hammer, the Sledge, and both Molasses-Eater and Ashes-Eater. In Father Chiasson's history of Chéticamp, he lists more than two hundred old nick-names as proof of "the teasing spirit of the Chéticantins, their easy repartee, and their gracious witticisms."

Nor were the Down Home Scots any slouches when it came to nailing neighbours with tags that stuck for life. Their nicknames often linked the owner to an incident, place, or habit. "Among all the John Chisholms," David (Big Christopher) MacDonald reported, "it then becomes possible to distinguish John the Schoolhouse, who lived near one, from John Jesus, who was much given to profanity. Similarly, the manifold MacDonalds could sort out Allan the Ridge, Alex Big Painter, and Maggie in the Sky, who roomed on the top floor of the tallest building in Antigonish, three stories up." A Cape Breton coal-miner with arms of different lengths was Alex the Clock; physical char-acteristics inspired such other nicknames as: Curly Dan, Johnny Hot, Six Foot Angus, Hector the Itch, and the unfortunate Jim Smelly.

Little Rory Donald Dhu (Gaelic for "black") of Washabuck, Cape Breton, found himself with a new and unwelcome name after his daughter, who'd come home from Boston for a visit, persuaded him to build a privy. The neighbours, who still used the nearby forest as a latrine, thought the outhouse pretentious. They mocked its owner as "proud Rory what does it in a box," and, succumbing to peer pressure, he tore the box down. This sacrifice, however, failed to wipe out his new nickname. For the rest of his life, he was Little Rory the Backhouse. He had made the mistake of trying to look better than his neighbours. Maritimers dislike show-offs and ostentatious spenders.

*   *   *

On August 19, 1954, the *Bridgewater Bulletin* on the South Shore of Nova Scotia printed a complaint from Emmerson Weagle of Danesville, Queen's County, and it struck a Halifax newspaperman as so funny he clipped it and mailed it to my father in Toronto. My father died in 1971, and I found Weagle's letter in his files. I've kept it because, thirty-three years after it was written, it remains a blunt but superb expression of an abiding characteristic of the people Down Home: the fear that others may think that *you* think you are better than they are. Some of the richest Maritimers work hard at never giving anyone an excuse to call them snobs.

"Would you please make a correction in your paper this week?" Emmerson Weagle asked. "In last week's paper you announced that I was arrested in Danesville at a Garden Party on Thursday. I would like to inform you I was not arrested at a Garden Party, nor was I arrested in Danesville. I would like to have it corrected, and whoever put this in the paper, I would like them to make a correction in the Halifax paper also. I was arrested at a dance held at Harry Whynott's at Italy Cross, and at no Garden Party. I am, Yours Truly, Emmerson Weagle."

Weagle didn't care if all of Nova Scotia knew he'd been arrested, but it horrified him to think that even one newspaper reader might get the idea that he'd abandoned his earthy ways and rowdy dancehall habits in order to sip tea with the genteel at garden parties. Let no one think he was a sissy or, worse, a social climber. Let no one call him Emmerson Garden Party Weagle. He set the record straight for somewhat the same reason that Frank Sobey, as he got richer and richer, took each new car he bought and drove it through puddles. An immaculate Mercedes-Benz sets its owner apart from his neighbours more surely than a muddy one does. Sobey, like Garden Party Weagle, wanted to remain one of the good old boys.

So do most Maritime millionaires. Pressure on the rich to behave like just plain folks is stronger Down Home than anywhere else in Canada. A man who can easily afford six Rolls-Royce limousines wonders if his buying even one might not attract the same sort of derision as Little Rory endured in pioneer Washabuck. In Europe and Asia, Frank Sobey slept and dined in hotels favoured by oil sheiks, rock stars, and royalty; but while leaving Halifax to begin these travel orgies, he flew economy. He didn't want Nova Scotians, particularly ones from Pictou County, to see him pampering himself in the first-class compartment. His friend Roy Jodrey of Hantsport, Nova Scotia, once said, "I don't drink liquor and I don't give a damn about drinking my coffee out of a china cup. Why in the hell should I pay for first-class?" Once, in a miracle of persuasiveness, bluenose friends did succeed in getting Jodrey to buy a first-class ticket so he could sit with them. He planted his fatness in his roomy seat, glowered at the cabin's luxury, squirmed guiltily, and grumbled to no one, "The people of Hantsport will know about this before I even get home."

Jodrey was the staunchest of all champions of the Down Home virtue of not showing off one's wealth. He believed in the old saying, "The man with money to burn never lacks for a match," and he owned neither an executive aircraft, a yacht, a swimming pool, nor palatial estates for seasonal pleasures. He did not throw lavish parties with exotic food, imported flowers, society orchestras, oceans of liquor, and squads of servants. Nor did he collect horses, dogs, old books, exquisite china, antique firearms, figurines, or women. His only impressive collections were a stunning array of common stocks and timber lands, and he said he needed no expensive hobbies to help him relax because nothing could possibly have been more relaxing than the sound of his own paper-plate factory next to his own house.

There was nothing in what Jodrey, his wife, Belle, and their offspring ever said publicly, told the neighbours, or showed in their style of living to draw attention to the family fortune. Indeed, they were so reluctant to appear rich that one of Jodrey's own grandchildren was on the verge of manhood before he had even an inkling that he might one day be an heir to an empire. He learned it while at college. Another student showed him a *Maclean's* calculation that his grandfather had fifty-six director-ships, more than anyone else in Canada.

"They should never have printed that," Jodrey complained. The story made him appear mightier than he was, and being in the spotlight embarrassed him. What would the neighbours think? Would the people who'd helped build his investment and industrial empire blame him for hogging the glory? All his life he'd disliked publicity. When the Bank of Nova Scotia named him a director in 1950, it had a tough time getting him to supply for its files even a head-and-shoulders photo of himself. The Modest Giant, as a Halifax paper called Jodrey, was past seventy before he let himself be listed in *Who's Who in Canada*.

Frank Sobey was never as tight-fisted as Jodrey—perhaps no one was—but he shared the desire to be seen as a fellow whose character was so solidly grounded in Down Home virtues that no amount of wealth could ever turn him snooty. Near New Glasgow on the Abercrombie Road, he built a waterfront mansion. Though made of red brick, it had a vaguely Dixieland look, as though it were the Tara of Pictou County. He called it Crombie and explained that, of course, he'd never really wanted such a large dwelling, but he was now president of Industrial Estates, a provincial Crown corporation, and therefore it was vital to the economic health of Nova Scotia that his home be suitable for entertaining government officials and industrial giants from foreign lands.

Crombie fascinated the county. It seemed to Frank's wife, Irene, that rubberneckers would never quit coming up their driveway. Still, he refused to erect a No Trespassing sign. He did not want anyone to think he was inaccessible or, as the saying goes, full of himself. His name was on his letterbox, his number was in the phone book, and his life had always been among the people of these towns and hills.

One summer Saturday, at his cottage in my own Guysborough County, he served me a no-frills New England boiled dinner. The cabin sat on the west bank of the dark, gurgling, ocean-bound St. Mary's River and was lined inside with heavily varnished knotty pine. It was full of stuff that suggested not wealth but schmaltz: ceramic ducks on the walls; china statues of turkeys over the fireplace; framed photos of Dennis Morgan and Ginger Rogers; seven rocking chairs, most of them leatherette; an ashtray that declared the golden anniversary of Kraft Foods in 1963; a four-foot-long cribbage board; a sign that showed a cartoon skunk and asked, "Why be disagreeable when, with a little effort, you could be a real stinker?"; and a cornball painting of a young blonde with long hair, huge eyes, Bardot lips, and a blue, breast-revealing shirt. Frank was pleased to explain that in 1945 he'd hired friends to build this place for him and his family with war-surplus lumber, on what was then Crown land. It hadn't cost him much. In addition to Crombie, the Sobeys owned a house in Bermuda and an apartment in Florida, but this riverside cottage—the cheapest of all his real-estate holdings, and scarcely better than the summer cabins of a thousand coal-miners, truck-drivers, and tradesmen—was his favourite spot in the world.

He wore a checked flannel shirt and khaki workpants and, even at eighty years of age, looked ready for a brisk hike to a trout stream. His real passion, however, was fly-fishing for salmon. Once, when his sons had been boys, the river that still ripped southward just below these windows had been jumpy with salmon, but those days were long gone. Three black cormorants boldly rode the current. They looked messy and devilish, and their necks were snaky. "I'd like to shoot those bastards," Frank said. "All they do is eat fish and shit, eat fish and shit."

A local character dropped in, uninvited. He was in his seventies, a sometime guide for anglers, and Frank grilled him about who'd been catching how much of which fish and where. The fellow declined dinner. He sat in the living room, drinking

Frank's gin, puffing on his own Player's, barking out his bits of gossip, while Frank heaped my plate, his own, and Irene Sobey's with steaming foothills of carrots, potatoes, parsnips, onions, turnips, cabbage, and the finest corned beef that money could buy at a Sobeys' supermarket. Blankets of fat swathed the stringy, red meat, and the whole meal, the biggest that anyone has ever shoved my way at midday, would have horrified devotees of *nouvelle cuisine*.

But Frank Sobey was proud of that boiled dinner. He'd boiled it himself. He'd been looking in on the simmering meat all morning. Sure, he was a multimillionaire. He was the guy who'd built up a retail empire that would soon gross a billion dollars a year, and he was a colossus of the bluenose business establishment. But no one would ever be able to say of him that he was too self-important to whomp up a New England boiled dinner with his own hands.

"You like fat?" he asked as we sat down.

"Well, yes, but just a bit."

"Yeah, so do I," he said. He found a blob of hot, white flab, the size of a baseball, and slapped it down beside my brick of beef.

While we ate, Frank conversed with the local character by shouting over his shoulder, and I marvelled at the speed with which Irene Sobey dispatched her dinner. She was small, frail, uncertain. She had Alzheimer's disease and would be dead within a year, yet her appetite might have put a lumberjack to shame. Within fifteen minutes her plate looked as though a panther had been licking it, and she smiled gratefully as Frank dumped still more meat and vegetables in front of her.

"Want some more?" he asked me.

"Well, ah, no, I don't think so," I said. "That was really delicious, but it's a bit more than I usually have for lunch."

"Don't eat much, do you?"

He served bowls of canned peaches for dessert, and tea. He rinsed out the pickle jar we'd just emptied, filled it with milk, and brought it to the table. Irene looked sorrowfully at the jar.

Her illness was so serious she rarely spoke, but perhaps she was remembering the banquets at Crombie and the way she'd been able to seat her guests at linen tablecloths that glistened with crystal goblets, sterling cutlery, glossy china, and silver candlesticks. She considered the milk in the pickle jar, smiled gently, and sighed, "Oh, Frank." He said, "Look, Rene, I'm not going to wash out a jug if I don't have to, and I'm sure as hell not going to let you do it." This was his family cabin, dammit, a place where for forty years no one had put on airs or dared to be pretentious.

* * *

The typical Acadian, Father Anselme Chiasson claimed in *Chéticamp: History and Acadian Traditions*, "rarely acts highbrow or superior. In him, there is nothing of that proud or arrogant self-conceit which believes itself above others, and shows itself unconsciously." In *My Acadian Heritage*, Léonie Comeau Poirier recalled that among the lessons she learned at Sacred Heart Academy, Meteghan, Nova Scotia, was, "A person should not draw undue attention to oneself by spectacular dress." Catholics, however, were not alone in their distaste for the vain and their suspicion of flashy clothes. Pre-Loyalist New Englanders brought to the region a Puritan leeriness of all foppishness and sartorial finery. Margaret Marshall Saunders, author of the dog epic *Beautiful Joe* (the first Canadian book ever to sell a million copies), was the daughter of a Baptist clergyman. While growing up in Halifax during the 1870s, she learned from her parents, "First you must clothe your mind in the finest raiment. Your body can wait for handsome habilments."

Scottish Protestants saw extravagant clothing and efforts to dress attractively as the work of the Devil himself. In 1840 Reverend Norman McLeod complained by mail, "O! Pictou, Pictou! Thy sins are fearful." One of Pictou's sins was the "maddened itch for immoderate dressing . . . more notoriously in reference to females." In Cape Breton "extravagance in dress is . . . one of the crying sins of our times. . . . Her Majesty Victoria is not half so proud of her royal robes, her diadem and diamonds, as our mushroom maids are of their own belts and beads, busks and bonnets, combs and crisping-pins, rings and ringlets, lace and lockram, locks and linings."

By the early twentieth century, Down Home periodicals were filling up their columns with such pithy advice as, "The wise man spends money right, the spendthrift right and left," and, "The guy with the loud clothes usually has a weak voice." On September 17, 1920, the *Pictou Advocate*, in an editorial entitled "What's the Matter With Canada?" offered a superb summary of Maritime attitudes toward foolish spending, soft habits, and personal ornamentation. Among the things wrong with Canada were these:

Too many diamonds, not enough alarm clocks.
Too many silk shirts, not enough flannel ones.
Too many pointed-toed boots, not enough square-toed shoes.
Too much decollette and not enough aprons.
Too many satin-upholstered limousines and not enough cows.
Too much oil stocks and not enough savings accounts.

Almost seventy years later, similar ideas still rule the behaviour of even the richest Maritime businessmen. The Sobeys, for instance, dress in a way that would keep them inconspicuous at any Rotary luncheon in any small town in Canada. David Hennigar, the bear-shaped luminary of the Jodrey empire, dresses as though he shares his grandfather Roy Jodrey's scorn for men's fashions. It amuses some that the style of his shoes, with toe caps, suggests he inherited them from Roy. The way the Sobeys live is a balance between affluence and not putting on the dog. "The boys"—Frank's three middle-aged sons—are like any small-town businessmen whose idea of luxury is a second car for the wife and a second home for the family in summer.

The sons of K.C. Irving are cut from the same Down Home cloth. "For the three richest young men in New Brunswick," *Maclean's* reported in 1964, "they lead surprisingly unpretentious lives; they don't collect art, they drive Fords and Mercuries, their homes are nothing special, and their visits to the Irving fishing lodge on the Miramichi River are brief and infrequent." Twenty-two years later, business journalist Diane Francis made almost the identical point: "Despite their billions, the Irvings are still imbued with the Protestant work ethic. The sons live in modest homes, draw small salaries, and are listed in the Saint John telephone book. They travel mostly by commercial airline and lead low-key lives. It's a family that does not have—and would not tolerate—high-livers, playboys, or layabouts."

Down Home tycoons, in short, are totally unlike the faddish, gonzo, quick-buck artists of western Canada described by Peter C. Newman: "[Men who] seem to be perpetually just shy of forty years old, the most outrageous of them sporting dyed beards and tousled curls. If they decide to wear diamond pinky-rings, order new Cadillac Eldorados every April or, like Vancouver's Nelson Skalbania, paper a bedroom ceiling with $100,000 worth of gold leaf, who in the hell is going to tell them it's not *bon ton?*" In the Maritimes, such tastes would mark a man as pretentious, risible, and stupid enough to lose his money.

Another way in which Maritime magnates strike some in-landers as quaint is that, although some have extra-marital affairs, very few trade in their wives for newer models. Moreover, the wives of the Maritime business establishment also work hard at being just plain folks. In *Debrett's Illustrated Guide to the Canadian Establishment*, Peter C. Newman devoted a page to the McCains, who run a billion-dollar frozen-food business from Florenceville, New Brunswick. While discussing their lack of pretentiousness, he quoted a local woman who said, "When you go to a church dinner, the McCain women will be there, cook-ing and serving just like everyone else." Eleanor McCain, sister to the brothers who founded the worldwide food business, mar-ried Patrick Johnson, a Britisher who became headmaster of what was once Canada's snootiest boys' school, Upper Canada College in Toronto. Despite Mrs. Johnson's rubbing shoulders routinely with Hog Town's more snobbish families, *Maclean's* reported: "She remains a girl from the potato-and-lumber country, ever ready for a good bash at the old Legion hall, the nutty vitality of a backwoods election scrap, or a sleigh ride on the hills of home."

One reason why rich Maritimers dress, talk, and spend in ways that don't let their wealth distance them from others is that they fear losing the respect of people they've known all their lives, of people whose forebears their own forebears often knew. Their style is not calculated. It's the result of their having absorbed a relentless principle of small-town life: if you can't get along with neighbours and customers, you are deficient in character and deserve to fail.

It's not just the business community that shrinks from anything that smacks of the phony, flashy, or sniffish in the Maritimes; it's just about everyone outside an ancient clique or two in south-end Halifax. Before coming Down Home from Toronto, I'd naturally heard of vain, proud, haughty, boastful, snotty, snobbish, conceited, self-centred, self-important, swelled-headed, puffed-up, and even hubristic people. I knew the meaning of "She's stuck on herself" and "He's hung up on himself," and somewhere I'd heard that memorable comparison, "as proud as tom-tit on a turd." But never once, until I came down east, had I heard anyone denounced as "big-feeling."

The term struck me then—thirty-five years ago at Mount Allison—as a pungent expression of the scorn Maritimers feel for all those who dare to put on airs. When a student from Campbellton said a student from Yarmouth was "too big-feeling for me," I could taste the contempt in his voice. It was as recognizable as salt on the tongue; and, for me, instructive. For I had come from Toronto, a city already under suspicion as a bastion of the big-feeling, and I instantly sensed that here on this small campus in this small town at the geographic heart of these small provinces, I should avoid arousing any suspicion that I was a big-feeling Upper Canadian. Big-feeling Upper Canadians were a repulsive people, and when you live for three years at a place as intimate as Mount A. you want the respect of your neighbours. I hid my natural Toronto conceit and passed myself off as the small-feeling son of a Nova Scotian writer and as a fellow with no side.

Maritimers prove in myriad ways that they are not big-feeling. When they go to a party, for instance, they invade the kitchen, leaving the showier parts of the house empty. That was one of the first things that Englishman Peter Luckett noticed when he moved to the Maritimes. Luckett runs Pete's Frootique, a fruit-peddling operation at the Saint John City Market. In only half a dozen years his jokes, stunts, sales banter, and zany cheerfulness have helped make him not only a successful merchant but also a town character. In *Atlantic Lifestyle*, Luckett wrote: "No matter how many rooms you have prepared for dancing, eating or drinking, most of your guests will gather in the kitchen, shoulder to shoulder, using empty beer bottles as ashtrays, and sitting on the counters, asking in apologetic tones, 'Am I in your way?' As if you usually work in your kitchen with fifty tipsy assistants. Believe me, the only way to move them is to run out of beer."

Titles never impress the Maritimer who is truly without big feelings about himself. After my father got a D.Litt. from Mount Allison in 1952, our local druggist in Toronto addressed him as "Dr. Bruce." My father said, "Don't you ever call me that again, George. It's Charlie, just plain Charlie." I thought of him when I chanced upon an article by historian P.B. Waite. Discussing a volume of Sir Robert Borden's letters, Waite wrote: "Borden's marvellous impatience with pretence comes through again and again. One reason he disliked Mackenzie King was King's eternal preoccupation with precedence, role and appearance. That stuff was not for Borden. When he was dying, in June 1937, he said to his nephew: 'Remember, Henry, none of this Sir stuff at the cemetery, just plain Robert Laird Borden, born Grand Pré, Nova Scotia—1854; died Ottawa, Ontario—1937." If a man comes from Down Home, he knows that merely being a knight of the realm and a former prime minister is no excuse for becoming big-feeling.

* * *

Coming from Toronto, I was astonished to find at Mount Allison students who had the same love of hillbilly music as gum-chewing waitresses and ignorant truck-drivers. These youngsters, who would become doctors, lawyers, accountants, and engineers, liked what I considered contemptible ditties for hicks by Hank Williams—"Cold, Cold, Heart," "Your Cheatin' Heart," "Lovesick Blues," and so on—and it mystified me that the death of Williams in 1953 plunged a college boy from Truro into such sorrow that he skipped classes to mourn by himself. I saw such people as backward, but as trends in popular music would eventually prove, the campus fans of Jimmie Rodgers and the Carter family were more in tune with the future than I was. Country and western music barged into the mainstream of popular culture, and its stars became as famous as Frank Sinatra and Muhammad Ali. In *The Story of English*, Robert McCrum, William Cran, and Robert MacNeil state, "The ballads of the Scots-Irish that travelled here during the eighteenth century are imitated and reproduced from Arkansas to Alberta, by singers like Dolly Parton and Kenny Rogers who have internationalized a style that was once confined to the hills."

The early popularity of country music Down Home was partly a matter of roots. The music comes directly from folk songs, popular songs, and ballads that English, Scottish, and Irish settlers carried to the southeastern seaboard of the United States. Like so many Maritimers, some of my contemporaries at Mount Allison came from families that had not only descended from English, Scottish, and Irish settlers but also had stayed put on the same land since their first forebears had taken axe to tree. If their love of country music was a throwback to old times in the old country, so perhaps was their love of tales.

Within the memory of these students' grandparents, every culture in the Maritimes had boasted legendary spinners of yarns. Before electronic entertainment and easy escape by cars to bars and shows, storytellers who were revered for their narrative magic terrified and captivated family gatherings with hearthside fables of triumph and horror, heroic ancestors and evil spirits, mystery ships, sorcerers, apparitions, devils, and the inexplicable. Most Mount Allison students of the early fifties were too young to have heard the semiprofessional storytellers weave spells with ancient tales, and they knew both radio and movies. But television was still a rumour to them, and in the younger years of their own parents no amusement had been more dominant than simply paying visits, exchanging gossip, and telling stories, old and new.

Far more than teenagers I'd known in Toronto, the young Maritimers at Mount Allison told stories. On my way to Sackville, I'd wondered how I'd hold my own in bull sessions on existentialism, whether God was dead, whether a falling tree made a noise if no one heard it fall, and if it was right to murder an innocent stranger if, by doing so, you'd save a million lives. But the nightly gatherings that I attended in the men's residence weren't like that at all. They were story-telling sessions. The stories were neither the legends of a race nor jokes that began with "Did you hear the one about?" Instead they were embellished versions of real events: some guy's disastrous failure at seducing a girl; a fight at a backwoods dancehall; a politician's masterful squelching of a heckler; the time the umpire pissed at the crowd during a riotous baseball game at Springhill; the time the roof fell in during a collegiate hockey game in Antigonish; and the time a classmate got drunk in Amherst, fell asleep during the train ride back to Sackville, looked out the window at the Sackville station, thought he was still in Amherst, went back to sleep, and at three in the morning, with no money, was kicked off the train and into a blizzard at Dorchester, New Brunswick. That kind of story.

Stories still dominate the conversation of the guzzlers in Maritime taverns. A specially good story—perhaps an epic about how some locally notorious drunk outsmarted the forces of law and reason—may get told again and again. If three men know a story and a fourth doesn't, the three will agree that one of them should tell it to him. The narrator will not be able to tell it, however, without enduring interruptions, corrections, improvements. The solitary yarn-spinners of past centuries have been succeeded by garrulous committees. Watching them from a distance is a little like watching a television commercial for Moosehead, Keith's, or Schooner beer. One of a dozen men who met for lunch at the Seahorse Tavern in Halifax in the mid-seventies was a Nova Scotian newspaperman who built his career in Ottawa, came home for several years to run a weekly, and eventually went back to Ottawa. I found him nursing a beer one night in the National Press Club. "Ottawa's okay," he said. "But the trouble is, nobody ever tells any *stories* around here. How's the gang at the old Seahorse?"

Maritimers not only tell stories more than other Canadians do but they use distinctive words, accents, and rhythms to tell them. Most native-born English-speaking Canadians talk in a way that's so standardized it never reveals a speaker's birthplace. Someone from Kingston, for instance, can't hear the talk of someone from Red Deer and conclude, "Aha, he's from Alberta." With a few notable exceptions—the Ottawa Valley is one—this is true from Quebec all the way west to the Pacific Ocean. But is it *not* true from Quebec all the way east to the Atlantic Ocean. In any tavern, anywhere in Canada, I could detect the Maritimer in the crowd just by listening to the talk. I might not be sharp enough to tell what county, cove, or valley he'd come from but, *by the holy old twist*, I'd surely know he was from somewhere Down Home. I'd have to be *deaf as a haddock* not to figure that out.

In my freshman year at Mount Allison, the thing that amazed and bewildered me was the rhythm, imagination, and humour of the blasphemy that shot from the lips of certain male students who were not studying theology. There's nothing remarkable about eighteen-year-old boys trying to sound like men by using curse words, but these were curse-word combinations I'd never heard before: *by the lord liftin' Jesus, by the holy old dynamiting Jesus, holy old snappin' arseholes,* and the milder *holy chain lightning, holy old mackinaw,* and *holy whistlin' frig.* (It was only the politer guys who used the euphemism *frig.*) Mount Allison youngsters also introduced me to such useful expressions as *skindog* and *whoremonger,* which struck my citified ears as positively Shakespearian. Ah, the joys of higher education.

The pronunciation of Down Home students was new to me, too. It had always struck me as strange, and a trifle embarrassing, that my father pronounced *calm* as *kam,* and *wash* as *warsh.* But now I lived among swarms of teenagers who said *noice* for *nice,* and *crick* for *creek.* Many made *aunt,* which I rhymed with *ant,* sound like *haunt,* and *route,* which I rhymed with *root,* sound like *spout.* To me, all of this was some strange. In *The Garden Transformed, Prince Edward Island, 1945–1980,* English professor T.K. Pratt said, "We would certainly not conclude an overview of Island or Maritime English without some attention to . . . *some* as an intensifier: *some good, some hot, some terrible.*" Other intensifiers were *desperate,* as in *It's desperate cold out* and *I'm desperate glad to see you,* and *right,* as in *right nice.* Another word scholar, Lewis J. Poteet, has compiled two dictionaries of old words and phrases from the South Shore of Nova Scotia, and he describes a scale of goodness: *good, some good, right some good,* and *right some Jesus good.*

Down Home speech offers bolts of vividness that are more startling and energetic than anything you normally hear in any big city. Shortly after I emerged from Mount Allison, clutching my B.A. and an honours certificate in English Literature, my father told readers of *Mayfair* magazine about "a look, an attitude, a crispness and imagery of speech you don't find elsewhere. . . . I mean a kind of speech that tells you what happened. Down Home the small boy never throws a stone. He lets drive with a rock. He does not chase an enemy. He takes after him. And when he's overhauled him he does not punch him in the nose. He knocks him into the middle of next week."

Bluenose schooner-builder David Stevens told me that when

his right eye deteriorated, a doctor prescribed potassium pills "that nearly killed me. Giving me those pills was as stupid as going up to the top of your mast to find a leak in your boat." He warned me about buying land from a local hustler who "always has the dollar sign right out in front of him." For the schooner Stevens was now building, he'd gone to a local saw mill and personally selected hundreds upon hundreds of feet of pine planking, and in all that wood "there wasn't enough knots to cover the palm of my hand." For planking, Prince Edward Island boat-builder Johnny Williams had discovered in Newfoundland that balsam fir was better than spruce. He softly pronounced it *var*, and his recital of its virtue was as tight as fine poetry: "It's just like styrofoam—pure white, and light as a cork." Williams lives near Murray Harbour in the southeast corner of the Island, and when I phoned from Charlottetown to ask if I could drive down to see *Lily*, his forty-six-foot ketch-rigged motor-sailer, he replied, "Well, now, isn't that great altogether?" I learned later that pleasing situations were also "fine altogether."

The drift to cities, and television's relentless homogenizing of speech, may kill everything that makes Down Home lingo distinctive and fascinating. But meanwhile, throughout the region, a rural spice still flavours the way people talk. On the matter of meanness, for instance, one of my neighbours recently told me tales about long-gone characters who were such notorious skin-flints they survive in local folk history. Without a hint of affectation, self-consciousness, or reaching for the right comparison, he dropped three new images of meanness on me in ten minutes. As easily as if he were offering another shot of rum, he said one fellow was *as mean as black cat shit*, another was *so mean he wouldn't pay a dime to see the Statue of Liberty piss*, and a third—my nomination as the heavyweight champion of meanness—was *so mean he wouldn't shit away from home*.

Lewis J. Poteet reveals that on the South Shore a raincoat *fits just like a smack on the lips*; the wind is so sharp *it cuts the whiskers right off your face*; and someone is *not worth two cents to jingle on a*

tombstone. A man moves so fast he's *goin' like greased lightnin' thru'
a gooseberry bush,* and a boy looks so sad he *has a face like a dyin'
calf.* Poteet lists *making love to* something as a euphemism for
stealing it and gives an example from Upper Port La Tour,
Shelburne County, Nova Scotia: "Don't leave that battery char-
ger in the bait shed. Somebody might come along and make love
to it." A woman who grew up near Pugwash, some three hundred miles away, tells me people there used *making love* in
precisely the same way.

This woman was a descendant of Scots and Irish on her father's side and Yorkshire settlers and Loyalists on her mother's, and
she wrote to me about *tire.* In a column for *Atlantic Insight,* I had
mentioned Poteet's discovery that people in the remote outport
of Blanche still used *tire* to describe the apron a young girl wears
to keep her dress clean. Shakespeare often used the word, and
according to the *Oxford English Dictionary,* a tire was "a pinafore
or apron worn to protect a dress" as far back as 1425. The
woman from near Pugwash simply wanted me to know that, half
a millennium after that, "When I was a small child, my little
apron, worn to protect my dress from spills, was always called a
tire." My aunt Anna, at ninety-five, remains as smart as a bee,
and I asked her if she'd ever heard the word in Guysborough
County. "Oh, yes," she said. "I had tires. All the little girls
around here wore tires. Adults had aprons." With four
daughters, my grandmother Bruce must have washed a heap of
tires in her time.

Another *tire* letter arrived from an eighty-year-old woman in
Edmonton. She'd been born in Five Islands, Nova Scotia, where
the fabulous tides of the Bay of Fundy shoot past Cape Blomidon
and into Minas Basin, swirl around the five spooky islands, and
roll right up to the hayfields. From 1918 to 1926, when her family moved out west, her father and his brother-in-law ran the village store, Harrison and Chisholm. "Those were the days when
men congregated in the store in the evenings to swap yarns and
discuss politics." My correspondent had come back Down Home

on visits many times, "and only my arthritis keeps me from making one last journey." Her letter was a tribute to the power of a single word to bring the past alive. The word was *tire*:

> With that one word came a flood of memories: my little dog, Buster, my constant companion . . . my swing under the old apple tree . . . the lovely little brook, flowing gently through our farm. Just behind the barn, my little brook tarried. As if to rest awhile before dashing off to the river and then losing itself in the sea, it formed a delightful pool, shaded by ferns, alders, and a lovely old pine tree. Here, I sailed my imaginary boats, made mud pies, and picked little red berries I called pigeon berries. Further along the gently sloping banks, I watched for the first violets of spring and the first strawberries. Nearby grew a clump of stately purple iris, and a gnarled old apple tree whose fruit tasted like bananas. Oh, those lovely, hazy days of summer!
>
> For more than sixty years, my home has been Alberta, where brooks are called creeks, and where I miss the Fundy tides, and the sound of the sea—and Nova Scotia is always and forever Down Home.

THE LAND'S LOUSY—
AND UNFORGETTABLE

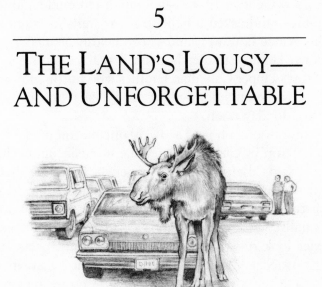

American tourists who carted skis to Ontario resorts in August were an annual joke when I was a boy in Toronto, but the tourist joke in Halifax starred an American who looked out his hotel window, saw Georges Island—a lump of red mud amid the harbour traffic—and asked a bellhop, "Say, fellah, would that be this here Prince Edward Island I been hearin' about?" A sturdier joke Down Home, sturdier because it really occurs every summer, features Upper Canadian families who hurtle into northern New Brunswick on Friday night with plans "to do the Maritimes" by Monday noon.

A Toronto friend phoned at 10:30 one morning. He was leaving Fredericton by car and wanted me to meet him for lunch in Halifax. I said, "Better make it supper, Jack. You're three hundred miles from Halifax." He later confided he'd thought touring the Maritimes would take no longer than rattling around a couple of small counties in England. On the map of Canada, the Maritimes look tiny, cosy, crowded with roads, ports, and villages. Knowledge that down-east settlement began in Shakespeare's time reinforces the idea that the entire region is like one of its own Historic Villages: a place to find much history in a few hours.

Statistics support the illusion. The Maritimes cover only 1.4 per cent of Canada's land surface, and Ontario alone is nine times bigger than they are. But other numbers tell another story: 1.7 million people are hardly a dense crowd when the perch they share on the Atlantic Ocean amounts to 52,000 square miles. The six states of New England boast only 66,000 square miles, but they're home to twelve million people. Belgium, the Netherlands, and Denmark add up to a mere 44,000 square miles, but their combined population, about twenty-eight million, is sixteen times that of the Maritimes. Afghanistan is one of the more sparsely populated nations of Asia, but it has more than twice as many people per square mile (seventy-two) as the Maritimes have (thirty-three).

The drive from Edmundston, New Brunswick, to Sydney, Nova Scotia, is more than six hundred miles. That's also the distance from Saint John, New Brunswick, to Ottawa, or from Amsterdam to Milan. Nova Scotia may look no bigger than a hefty lobster on the map of North America, but you can't drive from Yarmouth to Meat Cove without covering five hundred miles, the distance between Toronto and Quebec City. Moreover, a drive Down Home is never as straight as a line fence on the prairies. In the Maritimes, drivers can't zoom along parallel rules from skyline to skyline. Instead, you snake from valley to forest to dykeland to sawed-off mountain. If your route follows a coast, you'd be smart to change all meetings over lunch into meetings over supper. Not counting the more than eleven hundred minor islands that lie off the Maritimes, the coastline of these provinces—which is even more intricate than the crocheted tablecloth I found in the box in the cupboard in The Parlour at The Place—stretches for 5240-odd miles, almost a thousand more than any surface route from St. John's, Newfoundland, to Victoria, British Columbia.

*   *   *

You cannot drive these Down Home roads without sensing that no matter how doggedly Maritimers recite the indignities they've suffered under Confederation, the political legacy of the past hundred years has been gentle compared to the geological legacy of the past billion years.

Near Saint John, Precambrian stone sits on a basement of granitic rock that's 1.2 billion years old, which suggests southern New Brunswick was once connected to the tough old Canadian Shield. Though scientists are uncertain about the geology of the Maritimes during Precambrian times, ending 575 million years ago, they're sure that inland North America was already stable. It responded to forces of uplift and depression, but major faulting occurred only on the seaboard margins. When the Cambrian period began, when the atmosphere was accumulating oxygen and jellyfish were born, an ocean started to open in land that now includes the Maritimes. Oceans do not widen with the speed with which God parted the Red Sea for Moses. The Atlantic is widening even now—at a rate of about an inch per year—and the ancestral sea of the Cambrian period continued to expand for tens of millions of years. Most of the time, Nova Scotia was under water, and there was no Prince Edward Island.

Then, as though a pendulum had swung one way long enough, whole continents began to edge back toward one another, and the ocean shrank. When northern Europe mashed up against Greenland–North America, the sea between them vanished. The last stage of this gigantic disturbance occurred 450 million years ago. It crushed sediments on the shelf against the margin of the continent and raised them, like a plough pushing earth, till they formed a ridge that curved more than fifteen hundred miles from western Newfoundland through eastern Quebec, Vermont, and eastern New York State. This folding was the beginning of the Appalachian mountains, and by then the remaining seas held enough oxygen to support crinoids, with their cup-shaped bodies and feathery arms, the ancestors of squids, octopuses, and crabs.

Though volcanoes spewed from time to time, the margin of North America was fairly quiet for another seventy-five million years. But certain continental plates were again marching in to meet one another, squeezing other oceans. Nova Scotia, once nearly four hundred miles south of the equator, moved north to lie against North Africa, and then the mysterious drift of continents carried it west. Four of the biggest land masses in the world—Europe, Africa, and North and South America—collided to form one gigantic megacontinent. Nova Scotia now lay far inland, and its climate was dry and continental for a hundred million years.

The great collision caused the Acadian Orogeny. An orogeny is a process of mountain-building, especially by the folding of the earth's crust, and this one occurred at the end of the Devonian period, 360 million years ago. It was the most fabulous disruption in the geological history of the Maritimes. "Our Atlantic area and a block on the opposite side of the closing ocean came in contact and all the orogenic structures were compressed between them," wrote Albert E. Roland in *Geological Background and Physiography of Nova Scotia*. "Ancient sections from the Avalon Peninsula of Newfoundland through Cape Breton to southern New Brunswick, were jammed into their present position; and the deposits which make up the greywackes and slates of southwestern Nova Scotia today, along with the developing granitic plutons, were thrust into position or crumpled against the stable northern continent."

Tossed skyward by the Acadian Orogeny, the Acadian Mountains ran from southeastern Newfoundland down the whole length of Nova Scotia and its now-submerged coastal shelf. All of eastern North America ascended from the sea during Devonian times, and the Appalachians likely rose as high as today's Alps. Eons of erosion have humbled the Appalachians and flattened the Acadian range.

From great depths, rivers of molten rock thrust their way to the surface in the Devonian age, and in parts of Nova Scotia and New Brunswick you can still see traces of this ancient granite. The continental uplift followed the mighty intrusion, and erosion has been at work ever since.

But if Devonian times transformed geological structures, they also ushered in creatures and plants. Shellfish swarmed along the coasts, vertebrate fish began to evolve, the shark arrived, amphibians clambered ashore, and flora took root. The first plants were small, but shrubs and trees followed them. In the Carboniferous period, ferns covered the shadowed floors of huge, wet, tropical forests. Again and again seas drowned the woodlands and buried them under blanket upon blanket of sediment, and in the submerged and compressed wood lay the future coal beds of the Maritimes. The source of all the profit, agony, and heartbreak in the coal mines of the Maritimes lurks in the swampy forests of more than 300 million years ago.

The forests thrived in a hot, southerly megacontinent. The terrain was a jumble of valleys, peaks, and basins. Deep in the earth's mantle, temperature changes influenced both the shape and height of the surface. Wind, rain, rivers, and seas sculpted the land. As mountains arose, erosion brought them low. But as a ship unloads cargo, she rises at her dock, and even as wind and water turned mountains into plateaus, the land bobbed up and brought with it rock that had been underground. The surface of the Maritimes was once thousands of feet lower than it is today, but as erosion stripped immense thicknesses of slate and sandstone from the peaks, the land as a whole kept on rising. That's why drivers on Down Home highways can still see blobs and slabs of granite that once lay in the depths of long-gone mountains.

In places, basins sank under the weight of sediment that erosion stripped from mountains. Between sinking lowlands and rising highlands, fractures cracked open in the earth's crust. Mountains continued to rise and vanish. The height of the land above the sea never stopped changing, and, indeed, the countryside between Truro, Nova Scotia, and Moncton, New Brunswick, is subsiding even today. Arms of the sea crept into some basins, and then, as the floods subsided, they laid down enormous thicknesses of sediment. Torrential rains continued to drench vast tropical forests.

The erosion and layering of sediments, the levelling forces of the Carboniferous period, continued throughout the fifty-five million years of Permian times, which ended 250 million years ago. By then, the continental blocks had been glued together for a hundred million years. The land was low, undulating, and covered with sand and gravel. It stretched from the Canadian Shield to what's now the continental shelf, and on to Africa. There was no Bay of Fundy, no Cabot Strait between Nova Scotia and Newfoundland, no wide Gulf of St. Lawrence. The climate was hot and dry. The North American plate inexorably drifted northward, but Nova Scotia, pinioned at the heart of the megacontinent, still lay near the equator.

Then currents in the earth's mantle changed. The continents quit pushing against one another, and their parting released pressure. Up and down the Bay of Fundy, and at Chedabucto Bay, a band of the crust sagged downward in the wake of the retreating shore. Into the new depressions flowed sand from the uplands. Around the Bay of Fundy, for instance, red silt, sandstone, and gravel piled up in a subsiding basin. The break-up of the megacontinent also caused fresh faults in the crust, and lava welled up through the rifts to the surface. Basalt remnants of the 200-million-year-old lava flow still embellish cliffs along the Bay of Fundy and on New Brunswick's Grand Manan Island.

As the continents sailed apart, land that had once been on the far side of an earlier ocean clung to North America. That's how the Maritimes got parts of southern New Brunswick, the foundation of the Cobequid Mountains in northern Nova Scotia, and the Cape Breton Highlands. Moreover, sediments from either African or South American uplands had been crushed between continental blocks during the orogeny; now, 150 million years later, these also stuck to the American side. Altered by later forces, they became the Southern Upland of today's southwestern Nova Scotia.

The time of the dinosaurs had come, and the new ocean was warm and narrow. During the early Jurassic period, a mere 180 million years ago, the land was probably mountainous and the heat intense, as they are now near the Red Sea. Later, the ocean became more like our Mediterranean Sea, and conditions may have been similar to those of today's American Southwest: a hot, continental climate; vegetation so meagre the wind tore away the surface, allowing flash floods to slice the land with channels; and a planed countryside with deep river valleys cutting right down to underlying strata.

Early in Cretaceous times, 130 million years ago, the ocean was half as wide as it is now, and still spreading. Erosion had bevelled off the upraised margin of North America, and the edge was sinking into the rising sea to form a continental shelf. One hundred million years of erosion had probably turned the whole of the future Maritimes into a flatland. When the Tertiary period began, some sixty-five million years ago, the Atlantic had widened to perhaps 90 per cent of its present size. The eastern seaboard became more unstable, rising, settling downward, rising again. For a time, the sea may once more have covered much of the region. By then, the continent had drifted well north of the equator, and the climate was temperate, perhaps like that of the modern Carolinas. Flowering plants arrived, and dense vegetation was possible, and though erosion was gentle, it nevertheless cut into the ancient planed-off surface to carve out the ancestral routes of today's rivers and the chains of lakes that from an airplane look like strung-out necklaces. Though Precambrian events, more than half a billion years earlier, had set the pattern of Maritime uplands and lowlands, it was the Tertiary period, ending only two million years ago, that shaped the topography that Maritimers endure today.

Then came the ice. Invasion after invasion of glaciers ground their way south. In places, the ice may have been more than half a mile thick, three times as high as the highest ridges in northern Nova Scotia. It squashed the Maritimes as a brick might squash a wet sponge, and when it retreated for the last time—only twelve thousand years ago—it left the countryside so low that the sea flooded river valleys, estuaries, and coastal lowlands.

More than any other geological force, it created Prince Edward Island. Some 300 million years ago, when a floodplain covered much of eastern Canada, rivers deposited the red rocks of the Island. But it owes most of its geological character to glacial droppings that ceased to arrive only fifteen thousand years ago. The weight of the ice lowered the land and ocean beds, and for a while a low plain linked the Island to the mainland. But as the glaciers melted, the land rebounded, the sea rose, Northumberland Strait was born, and a mere five thousand years ago—the time of early Trojan culture and the founding of Egypt's Third Dynasty—the crescent shape of the Island emerged as what its people are now proud to call the Garden of the Gulf.

The glaciers scoured the land like colossal road-grading machines, scraping their way far beyond Maritime shores to the continental shelf and all the way south to Kansas. Advancing, the ice plucked rocks, ground them to powder, or dropped them farther south; retreating, it left in its ponderous wake a stony till of sands, gravels, and boulder clay. The eiderdown of alluvium covered nearly all the Maritimes. The glaciers also disrupted drainage patterns, blocking streams, drowning coasts, creating lakes, ponds, and dismal bogs. The ice dotted the countryside with eskers, which look like abandoned railway embankments; the elongated mounds of glacial debris that geologists call drumlins, such as Citadel Hill in Halifax; and other spooky-looking humps, bumps, and lumps. In the Maritimes, the effects of the glaciers were universal. Not an acre escaped their influence. By the time they were gone, they'd shovelled much of the soil into the depths of the sea.

*　*　*

Sailing off-wind in a stiff breeze, a little sloop moves no faster than a jogger, but to the crewman who hikes out to windward with his head soaked in the swoosh of her bow waves, the craft flies over the ocean like a stone skipping on a pond. That's the joy of sailing small boats, and it's a matter of perspective. Perspective also counts when you look at the Maritimes. From an airplane, they are a flat, dull, gray-green mass of vegetation. They look like boring moss on a stone plane that barely emerges from the shimmering ocean. Even from the higher mountains— and the highest, Mount Carleton in northern New Brunswick, rises only half a mile above the sea—the views inland are long but far from spectacular. No snow-capped peaks here, and no mighty rivers that nurtured ancient civilizations. Just the clean, chill wind and a low, undulating skyline in the haze of far counties. You might almost be on a plateau that grows nothing but trees and little to eat. The geological legacy of New Brunswick and Nova Scotia is a farmer's hell.

As you move down, your perspective changes, but the agricultural possibilities don't improve much. Nothing illustrates both points better than the Cape Breton Highlands. Rising only seventeen hundred feet above the ocean, they are puny by the standards of the Rockies, and yet their gloomy, lethal, sea-bashed cliffs are so plainly magnificent that they make you think of a symphony by Sibelius. That's the aspect of the Cape Breton Highlands that awes visitors from around the world. But another aspect of these barrens is that, for farming, they are as useless as tits on a boar hog. Most of the whole region is little better. Gulches cut through uplands. Rivers, bays, straits, and tongues of ocean chop up the terrain, and even in such apparently lush country as the valley of the Saint John River, gullies and ridges keep fields too small for large-scale farming. The Maritimes boast no endless prairies of rippling wheat and no fertile blankets of dark, warm, rich, stone-free loam such as southern Ontario enjoys.

Thick in valleys, thin on uplands, a boulder-strewn glacial till covers the region. In places, flat bedrock lies exposed, useless to all but adventurous picnickers and the gulls that crack open sea urchins by dropping them from the sky. Only the soft finger of the Annapolis Valley prevents the Atlantic upland from covering all of western and southern Nova Scotia. Beyond the valley's South Mountain lies a desolate territory of thousands of low hummocks, smooth ridges, boulders, muskeg, fire-blackened stumps, mist-wreathed ponds, and streams so aimless no lost canoeist could ever count on them for a downstream route out of the wilderness. This country is as eerie as any British moor, and in bad weather, far more dangerous.

When you do find real soil in the Maritimes, the odds are it'll be shallow, stony, mucky, acid, coarse, heavily leached, poorly drained, excessively drained, low in plant nutrients, or lying on hills too steep for easy cultivation. The House at The Place sits on a southward-sloping field, bounded by the highway on the north, scaly apple trees to the west, and aggressive spruce and balsam fir in the south and east. Trees invade our field by spreading up from gullies that hold rattling southbound streams. Much of the higher Bruce land, north of the highway, was once a hayfield. It offered a view of Chedabucto Bay so sweeping that my first son never went up there without promising himself that this was the spot where, one day, he'd build *his* house. But now, a dozen years later, he can see only a corner of the bay. Spruce and fir have taken over the land, and all along the bay shore the forest has recaptured the fields of forgotten farms. The population around here has shrunk drastically since the time of Will and Sarah, and even now the retreat from the hard land of small farms continues across the Maritimes, and the trees rush back to reclaim tens of thousands of acres that it took our forebears generations to clear.

Here and there in my own damp forest, I find neat piles of rocks. God only knows the exact age of these mounds. They're the work of earlier Bruces, men who tore the stones from the ground while creating farmland. Those fellows had no gas-driven machines, and knowing what I do about the one small field that stretches south from the house, I regard their secret heaps of rocks with the same sort of reverence that overcomes visitors to Mayan ruins. How did the local pioneers ever remove enough stones so they could plough the land? The rocks of Port Shoreham don't just sit in the ground in finite numbers. They rise, in relentless hordes, to replace the ones you've plucked. The rock piles in the woods are monuments to bygone sweat.

The earth here is heavy, dense, defiant against shovels. While digging a grave-sized pit for the new outhouse we installed near the traditional Bruce location, I could not remove a spadeful of soil till I'd hacked it loose with a pickaxe. I wanted a hole ten feet deep. I dug down three feet and quit. I've no doubt that now, two years later, stones are rising through the stinking cargo of that shallow pit.

The old well stands as a rebuke to my modern fecklessness. The Place has boasted a drilled well and tap water ever since Sarah and Bess, mother and oldest daughter, returned from Edmonton in 1953 to spend their last years here; but when I came down from Toronto in the summer of 1946, as an eleven-year-old getting his first indoctrination in the superiority of life at Port Shoreham, the only water came from a hand-dug well of uncertain age. "The Bruce well" was no ordinary well in these parts. It had the usual rope, bucket, and windlass, but the hole dropped from a spot within the enclosed porch at the back of the house. Along this shore, the luxury of an indoor well was as rare as Jacuzzis are today. I didn't like it. It was dark and deep, the stuff of bad dreams, and perhaps a voice of doom. It exhaled air that, even in July, was as cold as the north side of a January gravestone by moonlight. The family kept butter part way down, and when I went to fetch it, I found a snake curled around the yellow brick. Years before, I'd heard, a terrier named Patches had fallen into the well.

Four decades after my boyhood summer at The Place, neighbours dropped in for rum and chicken curry. Carl MacIntosh, who'd known our house since his own boyhood, asked, "What ever happened to the Bruce well? Was it filled in, do you think?" I'd owned The Place for three years, but perhaps because ghosts of my childhood dread still rustled in the attic of my mind, I'd never opened the hinged trap door in the floor of the porch. Now, bolstered by rum, I said, "Well, let's have a look." We moved some garden tools, rubber boots, and a chest of drawers, opened the hatch, smelled a puff of air that seemed to come from a tomb, and shot a flashlight beam down the black hole of The Place.

No snakes. Just a round sheet of water glinting at us from ten feet down, green and shiny in the thin light driven by Duracell batteries, and captured in a tube of exquisitely fitted fieldstones. The water was five feet deep. We lowered a bottle by rope, and the sample we raised looked as pure and sparkling as it must have been when some Bruce—probably Richard, with the help of his son, Charles Joseph, and the neighbours—dug that skinny hole, lined it with stones he'd ripped from his own gummy clay, and then, for the first time since laying the last, uppermost ring of rock, put the water to the lips in his bearded face. That would be about one hundred and forty years ago, and by the beam of the flashlight, I marvel now not only at the workmanship but also at the *work* it must have taken to insert that hollow column in this hard soil. What we have under our back porch is an immovable working family antique.

Farther south, our cottage squats on a bluff, just back from high water. The carpenter who built it for us in 1972 (one of his grandmothers was one of my great-grandmothers) says it's just as well we didn't want to pay for a basement because the ground under the topsoil is already as tough as cement. The cottage is close to a hundred feet above the bay, but even up there we find small stones, smoothed and rounded by primeval seas.

Hemmed in by hills and water, even the "good soil" in the Maritimes has flaws that might intimidate farmers from more favoured lands. Poor drainage curses the clay in the Annapolis Valley. While Prince Edward Island is mostly well-drained, some of it is swampy, and its famous red soil is so acidic and so low in plant nutrients that cultivating it requires expensive doses of lime and fertilizer. Though the province touts its image as a garden, only 40 per cent of it comes under the official designation of "improved agricultural land." Still, a mere 4 per cent of New Brunswick is improved farmland, and Nova Scotia is even worse off.

On the mainland, topography imprisoned the patches of soil where mixed farming sometimes thrived. The uplands barred the way between lowland peoples. Roads avoided the uplands. Some headed into them but then returned to lowland corridors. To the dispersed farmers of the Maritimes, the grimness of the uplands made their own small valleys seem all the more precious. Especially in winter, travel was often as agonizing by land as it was by sea, and Maritime villages had time by themselves to learn their own priorities, build their own traditions, and establish their own ways of survival, talk, religion, amusement, and prejudice.

*   *   *

But if the countryside Down Home is short on fertility, it's long on scenic variety. The Bay of Fundy alone offers more in the way of miraculous seascapes than I'll ever live to see. Its shape creates an effect of resonance, and this amplifies the oscillation of the tides as a violin resounds to the vibrations of a plucked string. As the tides race two hundred miles up the bay, they swell magnificently. They average only about three feet down at Cape Cod, but a spring tide reaches a range of thirty feet at Saint John, forty-six feet up toward Shepody Bay and Cumberland Basin, and even fifty-three feet at Cobequid Bay. These bodies of water are extensions of Fundy that plunge inland. Indeed, Cumberland Basin stabs so far into Nova Scotia and New Brunswick that it comes close to cutting right through to the Northumberland Strait. If it did that, Nova Scotia would be an island. The tides are not only the world's highest; they're also stupendously heavy. The St. Lawrence River flows past Cornwall, Ontario, for five days before the volume of water in the flow is equal to one six-hour tidal movement in Cobequid Bay alone.

On the Bay of Fundy, you don't have to go anywhere to see a dramatic change in scenery; you need only sit and wait. A mountain freshet becomes a surging tidal river. Fresh water becomes salt water, and salt water fresh. Oceans of grass and fields of ocean merge in tidal meadows at the heads of bays. In the wink of a day, massive plains of mud disappear under ten thousand whitecaps, reappear, and disappear again.

At Alma, New Brunswick, my wife and I walked out on the ocean floor to meet an incoming tide. The sun was hot, the air clean, and the mud and gravel flats dotted with clam holes and littered with the peerless shells of scallops. We walked straight out for more than half a mile before the bay washed our toes and then our ankles. If we'd stayed there half an hour, we'd have been crotch-deep in shrivelling-cold water. If we'd stayed a full hour, the waters would have closed over our heads. A full spring tide at Alma is enough to submerge a four-storey building.

We dined after dark in a restaurant that overlooked exactly the spot where we'd gathered shells. The red, green, and white lights of a fishing boat swung into view. She came toward us bow-on, chugging along several fathoms above the route we'd walked only five hours before. Thunder crackled and roared, subsided to a grumble, and roared again. A swift wind buffeted the boat, and she slid sideways in the current. She came closer and closer, deftly nipped inside the breakwater, and then—just as the sky dropped curtains of rain on her and the three men on board whooped and hollered and laughed—she nudged the town pier so gently the impact would not have cracked an egg. The men came ashore, and the headlights from a waiting pickup truck lit them up. Since the bay floods the river mouth only in the last hour of a tide's rise and there are only two high tides a day, those fellows had been on the water for the usual, inescapable shift of ten to twelve hours. If they'd stayed much longer, they'd have been stuck out there for another ten or twelve hours. On every Fundy coast, the tidal cycle rules the lives of fishermen.

The rusty-red cliffs that form Point Wolfe Gorge in nearby Fundy National Park loom as a rebuke to all those who think of Maritime scenery as pretty but puny. These cliffs are British Columbian in their grandeur and make you think of bad old movies in which nasty Indians push boulders off bluffs onto the wagon trains and cavalry below. Just *up* the shore from the gorge, tides and ice ceaselessly sculpt a soft brick conglomerate, formed 330 million years ago, and create caves, arches, pillars, giant "urns," and mighty "flowerpots." Just *down* the shore, near St. Martins, New Brunswick, I wandered among smooth, shadowy, dripping caverns that the sea had punched a hundred feet into the land. The argle-bargle of gulls and ravens came from far away, and I wished I were a boy again so I could believe in myself as a pirate.

The caverns, gorge, and teapots are all on the New Brunswick side of the Bay of Fundy. Over on the Nova Scotia side—from Brier Island at the tip of skinny Digby Neck, up to Cape Blomidon and Cape Split, and around to Five Islands and Advocate Harbour—the geological legacy is also spectacular, sometimes brooding, and always surprising. Where the provinces meet, the long rush of Fundy tides expires in caramel-coloured rivers that snake through the Tantramar marshes. The marshes are as flat as the sea, and their grass ripples in the ocean winds all the way out to empty horizons. In winter gloom they are as eerie as any land in Canada, but in spring and fall they're heaven to migrating geese and ducks.

Except in the forests that clothe the uplands of northwestern

New Brunswick, a startling variety of scenery characterizes the whole region. Prince Edward Island is supposed to be neat, pretty, intensely cultivated, and all in all about as wild as a lapdog. But here in the tame land of *Anne of Green Gables* you can walk off a manicured golf course to seaside sand dunes that are the essence of wildness. They look as though they belong in mid-Sahara. The shaping of the Island's whole north coast—the beaches, bluffs, shifting dunes, and symmetrical spits—is the work not of farmers, gardeners, or landscape artists, but of an ancient conspiracy of winds, tides, ice, ocean currents, river currents, and tough grass and shrubs. The red sandstone of the cliffs may be 250 million years old, but the arrangement of beach and dune is always newer than this morning's sunrise.

In the Cape Breton Highlands, cliffs slope gently seaward for a while, then plunge a thousand feet to exploding surf. The highlands boast echoing coves, brooding headlands, desolate capes, bluffs of white gypsum, outcroppings of pink and gray granite, and blankets of fleecy mist. This is the most barren land Down Home, but only a little way south and southwest farms along the Margaree and Mabou rivers look warm, safe, nourishing, civilized. An afternoon's drive away, the South Shore dishes up familiar ingredients of Down Home scenery—lighthouses, storm-lashed fishing villages, combers rolling in off the North Atlantic to thump rock—but only thirty-odd miles inland from there, Kejimkujik National Park offers a different world. It's the mysterious home of plants, birds, and reptiles that normally live much farther south, a paradise for canoeists, a lush jungle of black rivers and gigantic shadowy trees. Some hemlocks are centuries old and so big that two men embracing a trunk from opposite sides can't join hands.

For more than four hundred miles, the mood of the Saint John River keeps on changing. The Maliseet Indians called it Oo-lahs-took, or "godly river," and on its upper reaches it is narrow and calm. But at Grand Falls, as Hugh MacLennan wrote in *Rivers of Canada*, "the flume of the falls, utterly savage, hurls itself, twisted by the contour of the rock, into a huge slide of water before it plunges roaring into a gorge with walls more than a hundred and fifty feet high." Farther downstream the river is wide, deep, and smooth. It slides southward through pastoral bliss, around dreamy islands, past sleepy cattle, and between curvaceous hills. Then, at the Reversing Falls in the heart of Saint John, it wrestles with ocean tides and vanishes in salt water.

Generations ago, some misguided booster called the river the Rhine of America. In the nineteenth century, Down Home cities were forever boasting that they'd soon be the Sheffield, Birmingham, Manchester, Liverpool, or the Ruhr of America. They failed, and in one sense their failure is our good luck: innocent wilderness still nudges Down Home towns and cities. The land here was white man's first accessible wilderness in the New World; south of the Arctic, it may be his last.

More than anywhere else in North America, the Maritimes offer human history and wildlife on the same plate. Not ten miles from The Place, in the district where my people have lived for a couple of centuries, the French had a fort when New York City was only a Dutch village. But bald eagles still soar over our house; white-tailed deer still bound over our field; blue stick-legged herons still fish the abandoned harbour; and porcupines and racoons slump around in our forest. Just out on Chedabucto Bay, a seal escorted our sailboat till we turned off the music from a portable radio. The creature's head was as big as a horse's. The next summer we kept the boat in Halifax. Within a half-hour's sail of the office towers, a gang of porpoises cavorted around us, looped their shiny backs through the air, and zoomed away to astound other sailors.

Near Black Brook, Cape Breton Island, in the winter of 1987, a moose ambled onto a highway and for forty minutes blocked traffic bound for the Canada Winter Games in Sydney. Not long after that, near my own corner of Nova Scotia, so many gray seal pups clambered ashore from floating ice that they, too, became a highway hazard. Seal pups sometimes follow brooks and gullies to find sunny spots and have occasionally reached Lincolnville, ten miles inland on the Guysborough County uplands. Black bears are no strangers to the streets of some New Brunswick cities, and a pilot whale recently beached itself within earshot of factory whistles in the industrial neighbourhood of Pictou County, Nova Scotia. It had come to town on the East River. Half a dozen New Glasgow men managed to shove it into deep water so it could make its way back to the Northumberland Strait. Meanwhile, townsfolk in Mulgrave, Nova Scotia, wanted their council to revoke a law forbidding the firing of guns within the town because coyotes—sheep-killers normally so elusive they seemed invisible—were now boldly trotting among their houses.

One reason why the animals remain is that so many men and women did not. Down Home is still a sparsely settled place. The pull of adventure inspired some to leave, but others had no choice but to get out of the nest. Down Home was too poor to nourish them and yet too beautiful to forget.

*　*　*

The weather is as choppy as the countryside. Maritime weather is volant, an old military term meaning organized for rapid movement, and it owes its speed to complex forces. Tropical ocean air from the southwest, polar air off the northwest Atlantic, and air from the heart of the continent all conspire to keep the weather shifty. The cold Labrador Current, which carries tens of thousands of seals south on floating ice every spring, washes the eastern fringes of Atlantic Canada, while the warm Gulf Stream slides by in the south. Both influence air masses, and so do changes in the volume of offshore ice. The Icelandic Low, a low-pressure system between Greenland and Iceland with anti-clockwise winds, dominates the winters; and the Bermuda-Azores High, with its powerful clockwise winds, brings fine westerlies as it spreads northward in summer. Sometimes, however, terrifying interruptions violate the smooth circulation pattern of the Bermuda-Azores High. Hurricanes roar up the North Atlantic seaboard from the south.

The Gulf of St. Lawrence laps and smashes the shores of five provinces. In *Searchers at the Gulf,* Franklin Russell wrote: "The Gulf was shaped like an eye and set on earth between arctic and equator. . . . Every life within its broad salt waters was charged with this tension of extremes and so the Gulf was a place of compromise. It resisted equally the fanatic ice and the permeating heat. Its lack of allegiance to north or south or hot or cold made it the most diverse place on earth." Barely three hundred miles separate the northern and southern limits of the Gulf. Yet an Arctic blizzard may paralyse the north while a muggy fog, broken by pale sunlight, warmly enshrouds the south. Temperatures in northern New Brunswick plunge to $-40°F$ in winter, soar to $100°F$ in summer.

Storms are not just storms in the Maritimes; they are historic events. Generations after they've struck, newspapers mark their anniversaries. Historical journals give them the scholarly attention they also devote to wars and treaties. The Saxby Gale of October 4, 1869, named after a naval officer who predicted it a year in advance, stuck in the memories of all who survived its terrors. They passed the story on to their children and their children's children, and it became a sturdy legend. The August Gale struck on August 24, 1873, and decades later my grandfather Bruce told my father it had lifted schooners out of the water and tossed them like toys into the upper branches of our trees. Long after many who'd witnessed the August Gale had died, it remained a standard by which lesser storms were measured. Ninety-eight years after the gale devastated Maritime coasts, my father documented it for millions of Canadians in the last magazine article he ever wrote, in *Weekend* magazine.

Words preserve not only ancient gales in the Maritimes but modern ones as well. On February 2, 1976, the Ground Hog Storm lashed western Nova Scotia with winds of more than 120 knots. They roared against the coast for twenty hours, and at their peak, high tides joined them to drive battering-ram waves ashore. The storm flattened fishermen's shanties, house trailers, barns, and timber stands. It turned wharfs into explosions of splinters, tossed boulders onto highways, and wrecked the harbourfronts of entire villages. It flooded roads, shops, and dykelands, and drove boats into bushes. The miracle was that it neither killed nor maimed anyone. The people of this ravaged coast had barely emerged from their dens to look for their own shadows when the amateur historians set to work. Before the year was out, two students at Collège Sainte-Anne, Church Point, had written term papers on the Ground Hog Storm; staff of *The Vanguard* newspaper in Yarmouth had produced *Ground-Hog '76*, "a pictorial account" of the devastation, and J.F. Amirault and A.D. Gates had written *The Storm of 2nd February 1976 in the Maritime Provinces.*

The Ground Hog Storm was a pussy compared to the hurricane that struck the neighbourhood of The Place in 1811. Judge John George Marshall witnessed its horror in Guysborough, ten miles away. Marshall was one of the early luminaries of the town. He had various jobs in Cape Breton, but on the afternoon the hurricane rocketed up from the south he happened to be back home in a house above Guysborough Harbour. He was studying legal briefs at a desk when the house began to shake. Fifty-four years later, the moment was still with him: "I raised my eyes to the window in front of my seat, and perceived that the Parish Church was totally prostrate, and its lighter materials were flying about like so many feathers."

Marshall stuffed his papers in his pockets, went outside, and to keep his footing in the maelstrom, clung to a willow sapling, "which was constantly bending near the ground." He watched an anchored vessel capsize and disappear. "The flocks of geese were blown from the land into water as their own feathers would have been by an ordinary wind. A large part of the roof of a dwelling house, near to the one in which I was lodging, was carried into a field several hundred yards off and driven like a plough share into the soil." Marshall compared the normally benevolent waters of Guysborough Harbour "to the drifting of the snow in the most severe winter storm, so violently was it raised by the wind and driven along in one sheet of white and sparkling foam and spray."

The hurricane vanished as suddenly as it had appeared, and Marshall immediately set out for his Cape Breton headquarters, a hundred miles away. No horse could negotiate the storm-maimed forest, so the judge, with a young man who'd also been visiting Guysborough, went on foot, first heading north toward the Acadian village of Tracadie. They trudged up the Guysborough River for nine miles, passing farmhouses whose roofs had been smashed to kindling, and camped for the night. At dawn they ate "some cakes and other little eatable comforts" that their Guysborough friends had given them, and then they tackled a fifteen-mile stretch of uninhabited forest. Here in the Guysborough Highlands, dense trees and glacial till hid an underbody of shale, sandstone, and volcanic rock, a cement-like conglomerate whose origins lay in late Devonian times, 370 million years before.

Marshall and his companion found the path the locals had recommended, but "immediately on entering it we found the heavy trees blown down from the roots and entangled in every direction so that we could scarcely get on more than a dozen paces without being obliged either to creep under fallen trees or clamber over and under their fallen branches. . . . Hour after hour passed in the same laborious struggle onward." Their clambering sometimes took them high on the fallen branches of uprooted trees, and they inched forward like boys playing tightrope-walking on a rail fence. Then "there seemed, as far as the eye could reach, but little else than one entire mass of fallen and entangled wood, in some places scarcely a standing tree within the compass of an acre."

To keep on course, Marshall had to climb back down to earth and scrabble around on his hands and knees till he found the gravel-covered path. Sometimes "I practised the expedient of passing alternately for suitable distances east and west like a vessel beating in windward, and thus after some time found a spot, which I knew to be part of the road." Thirty hours after Marshall and his young friend started their weird trek through the slaughtered forest, they staggered into a house in Tracadie, and there they got a sweet taste of Acadian hospitality.

"The lower garment of my companion, now called pants (in 1865) but then trousers (in 1811)," Marshall wrote, "had become so tattered and torn that they seemed irreparable." But the companion had an extra pair in his packsack. Marshall was not as well-equipped. He went to bed, and while he slept the sleep of the just, an Acadian girl repaired his pants. Then the Acadians fed the travellers, "and I can well remember that the large pie composed of water fowl and other good things, which was the chief dish, was amply partaken with the keenest relish." Marshall reached his home in Cape Breton four days later.

Much of his path to Tracadie is now a paved road, linking the Trans-Canada Highway to the district of The Place. It takes us all of twenty minutes to zoom over that same route in our little gray Toyota. As we pass the trees that press the road's shoulders, I sometimes wonder if my great-great-grandfather, Richard Samuel Bruce, shuddered at the force of the storm that, in recognition of Judge Marshall's memoir, *The Nova Scotia Historical Review* labelled John George's Hurricane. Richard was the first of my Bruce forebears to be born this side of the Atlantic. He was a boy of only eight when John George's Hurricane hit eastern Nova Scotia.

If Maritime weather is occasionally a murderer, it is always a trickster. Some summers are a string of such warm, sunny, perfumed days that Maritimers gloat, "Only a fool would ever leave here in summer." Others are so cold, rainy, and foggy that the papers dredge up stories about the year in the early 1800s in which a miserable spring drifted straight into a miserable fall and there was no summer at all. Haligonians expect fog in June, which is not invariably busting out all over in Nova Scotia. But when fifty-odd Tall Ships from three continents arrived in port in early June of 1984, the sun roasted the city for days on end, and the dominant smells during the waterfront carnival that blossomed under the freakish blue skies were those of French fries, hotdogs, Moosehead and Schooner ale, and tanning lotions on the bare flesh of bluenose girls seeking foreign sailors and foreign sailors seeking bluenose girls.

When the ships finally paraded out to sea, tens of thousands of Maritimers crowded the piers and downtown rooftops to applaud each vessel as she passed with all her sails raised and to yelp their approval like country-music fans at the Grand Ole Opry. The sun was still beaming as those bonny ships disappeared over the horizon, and though their going was sad, especially for the girls, Haligonians knew that nearly four thousand young sailors from a dozen nations had left town with the beautiful misconception that Nova Scotia in June was like Bermuda in April. If the sailors had returned on the same dates one year later, they might well have thought they'd dropped anchor at Murmansk.

Always, the weather has helped define the character of Maritimers. Among rural and seaside folk, it matters so much that for centuries they've had their own ways of trying to outguess it. They've seen its future in the sounds of foghorns, train whistles, loons; in the way the leaves bend in the wind, potatoes cook in the pot, soot burns in the stove, smoke rises in the hills; in the look of the sun, moon, and stars, in clouds, rainbows, and the northern lights; in the order of arrival of wind, rain, and tide; in the behaviour of gulls, cranes, roosters, hens, earthworms, wasps, cattle, sheep, dogs, cats, spiders, and locusts; in the feel of the corns on their own feet, and in a snowflake's weight. Often, their forecasts have been right. Often the forecasts of the government weather offices have been right. But there has always come a time in which the weather has tragically or gloriously fooled just about everyone.

Moving ice choked all of Chedabucto Bay in April 1986. From our kitchen windows it looked as though we could walk right across to Queensport. But one morning the ice was gone, and the bay smartly marched before a summer breeze from the southwest. Had the Micmac hero Glooscap melted the ice with one hot puff from his divine lungs? Or had he simply blown it down the coast to Halifax? For the first time in more than a quarter-century, ice now jammed navigation at Halifax. Proud to be known as an ice-free port, Halifax found that not even the Dartmouth ferries could venture into her harbour. Ice also postponed the opening of the seasonal ferry between Pictou County and Prince Edward Island, and kept Northumberland Strait lobster fishermen ashore, twiddling their thumbs and counting up losses. In mid-May I reported to Arsenault Monuments Works, near Antigonish, to pay for my aunt Bess's gravestone, and the woman who took my cheque, a frustrated lover of lobster, sighed, "We've been drooling for two weeks."

Crossing by ferry to Prince Edward Island on a blissful July morning, tourists can barely imagine what ice does to the seemingly benign Northumberland Strait, or how it could be that a kind of province-wide cabin fever has struck the natives every winter for generations.

The sea once gave Maritimers a sense of community. It was their best highway. Now, however, they're dependent on roads, trains, and planes, and the same seas that once brought Maritimers together are seen as the prime enemy of efficient transportation. But drifting snow closes roads, blizzards halt trains, fog shuts down airports, and in the end all that's certain about Down Home weather is that winter will be too long, spring too late, summer too short, and fall too early. In the countryside of The Place, we're lucky to get 150 frost-free days a year near the coast, and only half as many a little way inland. Around here, the growing season is as short as a donkey's gallop, and nobody attempts winter wheat.

*　　*　　*

No part of Nova Scotia is more than thirty miles from the sea, and three-quarters of all bluenosers live within six miles of salt water. Bras d'Or Lake, an injection of the Atlantic Ocean, fills the whole centre of Cape Breton Island and splits it in two. All that keeps western Prince Edward Island from being an island on its own is three miles of flatland between Malpeque Bay and the upper part of Summerside Harbour. Driving on the Island, you have to try hard to roll along for thirty minutes without seeing salt water. Even in New Brunswick, where inland forests stretch across millions upon millions of acres, you can't get much more than a hundred miles from the sea. Most New Brunswickers live on salt-water bays, or tidal rivers, and even those herring-chokers in the uppermost forestlands are generally on rivers that they know run down to the ocean. The sea is therefore part of the lifelong consciousness not only of fishermen, yachtsmen, the Coast Guard, and the crew of international ferries but of all Down Homers. Whether or not they *like* fish, fog, buoys, or boats, they cannot grow up and move around the Maritimes without knowing the smells of clam flats and tidal marshes, the sounds of waves on granite and gulls over sumptuous sand, the sights of moon over lighthouse and sun over fishing fleet. I lived in Halifax for thirteen years, and on a thousand wet nights I drifted off to sleep to the long moan of a fog signal down in the harbour.

Some Maritimers love the sea even when she curls her lips and bares her teeth. I realized this one winter morning in 1973, shortly after I moved into Halifax from Prospect, Nova Scotia. A brutal easterly had mugged the province the night before, and though the wind had passed, I suspected gigantic waves were still rolling ashore at Crystal Crescent Beach. Since it's a twenty-mile drive from Halifax and the route ends in an axle-threatening stretch of rocks, I thought I'd be the sole connoisseur of the sea during her spectacular hangover from her fierce midnight indulgence. When I got there, however, dozens of men and women stood with their hands in their pockets and their collars up, facing the terrible ocean, watching from the sidelines as she put on one of the greatest shows on earth. The breakers rushed out of the fog like charging foam. Some were thirty feet high, and as each crashed to its fabulous death, the rock shook under our feet. Every so often a giant among giants thundered toward us, as though it would pluck us off the shore and grind us to powder. Then the ocean-watchers turned in the mist, and with their faces soaked in sea froth, they grinned at one another, and their eyes said, "Boys, she's in some foul mood this morning, ain't she?"

Though the ocean can give pleasure in her most deadly

moods, she can also give death in her most pleasant moods. On a June afternoon in 1987, my wife and I had club sandwiches and rhubarb pie right out of the oven at Fundy Breeze Lodge —"Specializing in Comfort, Pleasant Surroundings, Home-cooked Meals and an Attractive Beach on the Bay of Fundy"— at St. Martins, New Brunswick. The bay was quiet, and the air balmy, and we saw a scarlet helicopter moving along in the summer sunshine. People named Rizzi ran the lodge. They were friendly enough, but our waitress, a woman of about thirty, came and went without saying much. She seemed solemn. When I told her she'd failed to bring me the Coke I'd ordered, she apologized. For hours, she explained, she'd not been able to keep her mind on anything but Randy Belding.

The Beldings lived forty-odd miles down the coast, but Garney Belding, father of Randy, had been fishing out of St. Martins for decades, and the waitress's people were old friends of the family. Randy was in his early twenties and had a wife and small child. Father and son each had a sizable lobster-fishing boat. That morning—the morning of the day the waitress forgot my Coke—they'd had breakfast together on one boat or the other. Then Randy had set out to haul his traps. Garney was on his way out later when he saw his son's boat burning on shore. Randy was gone. It appeared he'd either fallen overboard with the engine running, or ensnared himself in the line used to lower and raise lobster traps and been yanked overboard. The boat had gone on, leaving him thrashing around in the icy bay. She had then struck the shore, heeled over, spilled fuel on a hot stove, and caught fire.

Only months before, the waitress added, Arthur Belding, brother of Randy, was rushing to a hospital to see his wife and newborn son when his van shot off a bridge and plunged into deep water. If Randy were now dead, he'd be the second son of Garney Belding to die accidentally in less than a year. As the waitress talked, the search for him was still underway. Now we knew what the helicopter had been doing while we'd gobbled our rhubarb pie. With every minute that passed, Randy's chances seemed more hopeless.

"Let's forget the Coke," I said. "I didn't really want it anyway."

For a few days, I pored over the newspapers of southern New Brunswick, but none carried a word about Randy's fate. It was as though a fisherman's death at sea was so routine it had no news value. I went back to see the Rizzis a few weeks later. They told me Randy's friends were rounding up money for his widow, and the fund now stood at $10,000.

*   *   *

Maritimers fish because they love to work on the ocean, and some do it for nothing. In an old Down Home story, one fisherman complains that catches are poor and prices low. "God, soul, and body," he says. "This is no good. This is crazy." The second fisherman says, "What are you complaining about? At least you've got work to do."

"People love to fish," David Weale told me. He's an associate professor of history and Canadian studies at the University of Prince Edward Island and a recognized enemy of all "progress" that threatens the Island's rural charm. Sitting on the back deck at his father's cottage near Red Head Wharf on St. Peters Bay, we could look beyond scrubby bushes, a delicate marsh, and a finger of sand to the mouth of the bay, dotted with buoys, and still farther to a set of brown dunes, hulking and pristine. The neighbourhood was so attractive and so good for fishing that people had been spending their summers there for at least ten thousand years, and perhaps since shortly after the last retreat of the glaciers. Off to our left, the Gulf of St. Lawrence stretched toward Newfoundland, somewhere beyond the horizon, and with Weale's binoculars I could see fifteen fishing boats messing about far offshore.

Fishing, he said, was part of the Island's seasonal philosophy of work. Traditionally, Islanders had never worked at the same job day in, day out, month after month, year after year. What was so good about that sort of drudgery, anyway? It might have been how most of the world worked, but surely it was unnatural. Surely it was more sane to change your work to suit the seasons, to do a bit of farming, a bit of teaching, a bit of taxi-driving, and a bit of fishing. Unemployment insurance was a godsend to such a system, and the whole of Island society had adapted to it. Folk cultures weren't always creative, Weale said, but they were "wonderfully adaptive." Unemployment insurance was just too tempting not to use. "If you can stay somewhere where it's pleasant, and get government pay half the year," he asked, "well, why not?"

Money is not the only reason why men choose to be commercial fishermen. As Weale said, they simply love to fish. "In the spring, they can't wait to go fishing. They can't wait to be out on the water. They're all down there on the wharf at Red Head in their pickup trucks, and they're just on needles and pins. They're that excited. Maybe it's in their blood. When you lose that sort of purpose and desire, your culture is in real trouble."

At Chéticamp in western Cape Breton, every cod fisherman who did not live right on the harbour used to own a dirty, unpainted cabin there, and each spring he moved in with his fishing gear. He fished in the morning, napped in the afternoon, and in the evening met other fishermen to banter and trade stories. He went home to his family only on Saturday, and on Sunday evening, hiked back to his cabin with the coming week's supply of bread and butter. These Acadian fishermen loved life in their waterfront huts so much that many of them neglected their farms.

To a milder degree, the same love infected the descendants of Scots and Loyalists who were friends of my grandfather Will. On Wednesday, April 9, 1919, little Charlie reported to Zoe in *The Shoreham Searchlight* that "the ice, which has been a menace to shipping for the past two weeks, has broken up, and hardly a cake is to be seen." Spring had sprung, and therefore "the local fishermen are once more haunting the favourite pleasure (?) resort, namely Port Shoreham Beach. Some are painting their boats, while others are simply looking on." The head on this story was, "PREPARING FOR FISH."

For reasons no one thoroughly understands, big schools of fish abruptly stopped coming up Chedabucto Bay, but long after there were many fish to catch, local men still looked after their boats, set out their nets and tended them, and napped and gabbed in the weather-beaten shacks at the favourite pleasure (?) resort. A cluster of wind-bashed fish huts still stands, like a tiny, abandoned village, half a mile down from the Bruce beach. The men who used these and other huts along this shore were mostly subsistence farmers, and their wives often saw their pursuit of fish as a waste of time. But the sea was wider than sheep pastures, offered more freedom than dusty barns, and smelled better than pigs. The part-time fishermen had a word for any man who was so prudent, and so fastidious about farming, that he never ventured out on the waves that marched before his eyes every day of his life. He was *dry-footed*. That meant he was a trifle cold, a bit of a penny-pincher, a fellow whose urge to make money had conquered his capacity to feel joy.

Remembering fishing with his father, my father concluded one of his finest poems, "Fisherman's Son," with these lines:

> Lord, I address myself to you: be kind;
> Mindful of how the cosmic current sets.
> Though immortality be a state of mind,
> Let there be clean firm bottom for the nets.
> When it is time for this quick flesh to die
> Let herring school through heaven's hot July.

*　　*　　*

When my wife and I, our three kids, and our black, yellow-eyed cat abandoned Ontario for Nova Scotia in 1971, we lived at first in a new bungalow near an ancient outport fifteen miles from Halifax. Every weekday morning, with a bellyful of breakfast, I climbed into the crumbling, turquoise Pontiac Stratochief that had brought us all Down Home, and while puffing on a

Rothmans, I drove through the coastal fog and under the crying gulls to my job in the city. On the way, I picked up the marine weather forecasts on CBC radio. Even more than the gulls, they told me that at last I had come to live by the sea.

The ancient outport was Prospect. As a station for European fishermen, it may well predate the birth of Halifax in 1749. When you approach it by car, you can't see it till you slip over a rise in the highway, and then, all at once, as though stage curtains have whipped apart to reveal an astounding set, the whole wild flat blue Atlantic stretches out to blank horizons and looms above a huddle of houses and a government wharf. This is Prospect. The houses and a white Catholic church sit on granite. The sea bashes the rocks, hurls spray over rooftops, and sometimes behaves as though it might just snatch the entire village, as city gutter-water snatches matchsticks and flushes them down drains. Like a painting by Alex Colville, Prospect is beautiful because it looks vulnerable and momentary before dreadful forces, and arouses awareness of the pathetic fragility of everything we make. Colville brought his paints and brushes to Prospect in the summer of 1938. He was eighteen and learning to be an artist.

A half-mile along the breezy, barren coast from Prospect brings you to a high slab of cracked granite. To get there, you follow a footpath that winds its way among bare ridges and boulders, wispy grass, creeping crowberry and bearberry, and a carpet of mushy stuff that looks like olive-green brain matter. The carpet covers dark, foot-soaking muck, and here and there someone has placed weather-beaten planks over water the colour of black tea. The path follows the sounding sea, and the beaches, littered by bony driftwood with its gray sheen, consist of creamy, flecked stones as big as basketballs. Gravel for giants. From a distance, the granite slab appears smooth and white. Up close, it's a mixture of black, gray, beige, and pink, and it's grittier than any sandpaper. You wouldn't want to scratch your arm on that rock, much less have a wave pick you up and scrape you along the surface.

The smell of the Atlantic flows in the air, and there's no sound but the surf and the chitter of birds. The worn path is proof that others know this as an exquisite spot to feel the peace that comes with being alone by the sea. On a calm, clear day here, it's hard to remember the ocean's infinite talent for murder. But just off the granite slab lie small evil rocks. Far to the west, whitecaps break, not because the wind drives them—the wind is offshore now—but for sinister, subsurface reasons. Here on the shore, at the peak of the slab, someone has anchored a homemade flag-pole in a heap of rocks. A tattered black flag, the size of a dish-rag, flutters up there, and just below and a few feet inland, an anonymous amateur historian has used black paint to scrawl old news on a granite wall: "HMS FANTOME 18-GUN BRIG SANK IN STORM OFF THIS SHORE NOV 24 1814."

The *Fantome* was in fact a sloop. Miscalculations by a cocky bluenose pilot put her aground, but Captain Thomas Sykes of the Royal Navy got his crew safely ashore in lifeboats. Not one man ended up as a mangled corpse on the giants' gravel. They were luckier than hundreds of others who have tried to sail past these knobs of rock on nights of horrors.

Four miles southeast of the granite slab, in the small, black hours of April Fool's Day 1873, the S.S. *Atlantic*, a 420-foot steamship with auxiliary sails on four masts, struck Mars Rock, Meagher's Island (now Mosher Island). The *Atlantic* was the pride of the White Star Line. Built in Belfast in 1871, she had four coal-fired steam engines, a marble dance floor, and twenty-one pianos. Her cabins boasted brass fittings and teak and ma-hogany panelling. A reporter of the day described her as "one of those floating palaces that ply across the Atlantic Ocean, mak-ing a trip to or from Europe only a pleasant episode in one's life." On March 20, 1873, she left Liverpool on a regular run to New York, and by March 31 she was off Nova Scotia and running low on coal. To pick some up, she turned for Halifax, and that was the end of her.

Before coming Down Home for good, I'd never heard of the *Atlantic*. I'd read books about the *Titanic* and *Lusitania*. And I knew about the *Empress of Ireland*, which took more than a thousand lives when she sank in the St. Lawrence River in 1906. When I moved to the Prospect Road, I had no idea I'd settled only a morning's jaunt by sailboat from the scene of one of the most hideous disasters in shipping history. My kids attended Atlantic Memorial School in Shad Bay, but until I drove round to the fishing port of Terence Bay, I didn't know what the school memorialized.

I haunt graveyards. In the one at the Star of the Sea Church, Terence Bay, a marker cryptically declares, "In memory of S.S. *Atlantic* victims, April 1, 1873." Across town at Sandy Cove, which is truly a sandy cove and a bonny setting for a lovers' picnic, I found a more thorough report. Just to the left of a hilltop cemetery, a marble sign announced, "Near this spot was wrecked the S.S. *Atlantic* April 1st, 1873, when 562 persons perished of whom 277 were interred in this churchyard. This monument is erected as a sacred memorial by a few sympathetic friends."

Like Prospect, Terence Bay is mostly a jumble of sea-whipped rocks and houses, and I wondered how the villagers had found a mound of earth big enough to hide nearly three hundred corpses. But many of those torn and bloated bodies were small. The passengers had included hundreds of women, and not one survived the wreck. Captain James Williams later wailed, "Would to God even one woman had been saved." Of all the children, only John Hindley, age twelve, made it to shore. He clung to the *Atlantic's* rigging, and while exhausted and freezing adults plopped into the seething ocean all around him, he outlasted the agony till late afternoon. The sea was so violent by then that local fishermen could no longer get their boats close enough to the wreck to rescue anyone, but as they retreated for the last time, a monstrous wave swarmed through the rigging, and the boy was smart enough to let go. The wave swept him toward the boats, and he swam the last few feet to the waiting arms of the cheering fishermen.

Some say that if you must die early, drowning is a relatively easy way to go, but victims of marine disasters don't always just fall asleep in the deep. In *Jack in Port: Sailortowns of Eastern Canada*, Judith Fingard described the wreck of the *Turkish Empire* on Partridge Island off Saint John in March 1879: "Six of the twenty-four-man crew perished, several being crushed by the unleashed timber cargo, another crushed to death in the steering gear. The captain, who had lashed himself to the rail, died as the vessel broke up, and two of the seamen, who had been recently rescued from another shipwreck, perished because they took to the mizzen-mast, which went over in quick succession after the foremast and mainmast. . . . The body of the cook was picked up 'with the right leg gone at the knee, the eyes out of their sockets and the breast crushed in.'"

For us landlubbers from Ontario in 1971, the coast of Halifax County was a sobering introduction to the realities of the sea. It taught me that Nova Scotia's licence-plate boast, "Canada's Ocean Playground," was easily the stupidest provincial slogan in the country. Terence Bay, where remnants of the *Atlantic* still lie offshore, was just east of our home near Prospect, and Peggy's Cove perched a little way west. Peggy's Cove perfectly captures the ocean's Jekyll-and-Hyde nature. Some days, the village is as pretty as a mayflower. Other days, the sea there makes you want to hide in a bank vault.

Surely Peggy's Cove is the world's most photographed community of fewer than sixty year-round residents. As an inspiration for Sunday painters, its lighthouse, church, houses, shacks, piers, and fishing boats rival the bridges of Paris. Cars, camper trucks, and tour buses from across the continent jam the parking lots in summer, and thousands of visitors scuttle like happy ants all across the strange, curvaceous plains of Devonian granite. The stone is 415 million years old. The Ice Age scraped it as clean as the inside of a sand-scoured clam shell, then sprinkled it with big boulders to create a weird lunar effect that makes you want to laugh—and to frolic right where the ocean whacks the rock with thunks that sound like muffled dynamite explosions. The thickness of the granite is immense, but the closer you get to the waves the more you feel them in your feet. The sea here, to use the memorable simile of mystery novelist Ross Macdonald, is "full of dangerous energy, like a cobra listening to music."

"PLEASE BE CAREFUL," a sign warns at the entrance to Peggy's Cove. "Swells and breaking waves may unexpectedly rise over the rocks, even on fine and calm days. Beware of slippery rocks. Enjoy the unique beauty from a safe distance. Visitors have lost their lives in the past." A second sign, mounted by the provincial government within the village, offers some natural history and then urges, "PLEASE USE EXTREME CAUTION WHILE WALKING ON THE ROCKS." Farther on, at the spot where most visitors begin the climb to the lighthouse, a third sign lies embedded in the granite. It's made of bronze, and both the typeface and the language are formal and old-fashioned: "WARNING. INJURY AND DEATH HAVE REWARDED CARELESS SIGHT-SEERS HERE. THE OCEAN AND ROCKS ARE TREACHEROUS. SAVOUR THE SEA FROM A DISTANCE." In case anyone misses this advice, an identical sign sticks to an outer wall of the only lighthouse in Canada that houses a post office, and those who retreat to the Sou' Wester for, say, seafood chowder or a lobster-and-haddock sandwich, find further warnings on their menus and placemats. Despite all the glaring admonitions, the excitement of the sea makes some foolhardy, and every once in a while, the ocean plucks someone from the granite platform and beats them to a pulp. While learning to become the Maritimes' master of the dangerous, beautiful, and transitory on canvas, young Alex Colville was here, too.

6

IN SEARCH OF MOONSHADOW

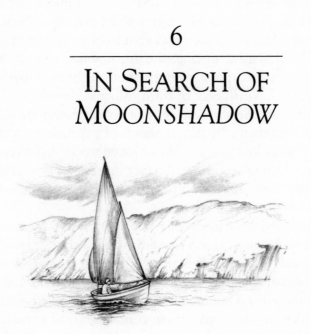

We called her *Moonshadow*, and when our children were young, she was our seagoing darling. My wife and I loved her more than any of the four other yachts we've owned, and hundreds of times I've wished we never sold her. She was a little, open boat, not quite nineteen feet long, with no cabin to offer shelter from the weather. Her designer, an Englishman, claimed to have made her seaworthy by incorporating in her hull the lines of small fishing vessels in the North Sea; in truth, *Moonshadow* did seem less like a yacht than the working boat of an extremely small-time commercial fisherman. By the standards of any racing sloop, she was a tub. She looked like an old-fashioned wooden clinker-built craft, but her turquoise hull was, in fact, fibreglass. Her gunwales and transom were made of more traditional material—thick teak—and she had brass fittings.

She was a yawl—meaning that her mainmast, which carried the foresail and mainsail, was forward, while a shorter mast bore a tiny sail well aft—and this rig was rare in a boat so small. What was also unusual about *Moonshadow* was that her rust sails were loose-footed; no boom could sweep people overboard during an accidental jibe or give them concussions. She was a centreboard boat and, with the board up, drew only ten inches of water. She had a keyhole-shaped slot for an outboard motor, and a pair of huge oars. She was curvaceous, with a pronounced sheer, and the depth of her topsides was comforting in high seas. In light airs, *Moonshadow* was ponderous, but in a breeze she sailed as an antelope runs. She was stiff, too, and when bigger yachts prudently shortened sails during squalls, I refused to reef ours and boldly romped among the fat sissies. *Moonshadow* was a lovely, tough, safe boat, with immense character. In Halifax Harbour, among the islands off Prospect, and in Chedabucto Bay, she took us to the sweetest picnics of our lives.

We sold her after three summers to buy a bigger yacht, one we soon discovered we could not afford to maintain, and a dozen years have passed since I last sailed *Moonshadow*. I feel about her as Petrarch felt about Laura. I carry a torch for her. To make matters worse, I keep bumping into *Moonshadow* look-alikes in strange waters. She was a Drascombe Lugger, the first and most popular of a line of sturdy sailboats that Honor Marine makes in Devon, England. One sunny May morning in 1983 I happened to be hiking down the coastal path near Falmouth, in the neighbouring county of Cornwall, when I came to Helford Passage. I was with a gang of Canadian travel writers, and to reach the Shipwright's Arms, where fine food and finer ale awaited us at noon, we had to take a barge-like ferry across the water. Once a smuggler's haunt, the Helford River was now as splendid a haven for small boats as I've ever seen outside Down Home, and the ferry gently picked her way through dozens of craft, all tugging at their moorings, all swaying together in the current and, in my travel-hyped imagination, all resting up before charging out into the ocean and over to Dunkirk to rescue soldiers.

Ah, but what's this, eight years after I've last seen her? Yes, it's my adorable *Moonshadow, mon petit chou!* And another *Moonshadow,* and another! That's three, no four . . . five . . . six . . . *seven* clones of my beloved. The ferry skipper keeps astern of them, and since the jauntiest feature of every Drascombe Lugger is her cheeky transom, this little squadron seems to be mooning me for having sold off one of the family. I'm in love again.

Three years would pass before I'd see her once more. In February 1986 I journeyed to a strip of sand where stubby sea grape flourished and young coconut palms swayed in the Trade Winds. It lay on the east coast of Andros, the biggest, least-known, and most sparsely settled of all the Bahamian islands. I had gone there, to a magical lodge owned by Canadians, to learn how to scuba dive. On my second day I joined a dozen other tenderfoot divers aboard a motor-driven raft that sped us out to the third-longest barrier reef in the world. There, we'd jump overboard, sink forty or fifty feet, and for half an hour, float around in what would feel like a fabulous aquarium for tropical fish. On the way out, a mile offshore, I glanced ahead, and there she was again, anchored off our starboard quarter, another gorgeous Drascombe Lugger, turquoise with teak trim and rust sails, identical to the one I'd sold, identical to the seven I'd seen in Helford Passage.

As we drew abeam of the Lugger, two men in wetsuits surfaced, clambered aboard her, and exchanged waves with my instructor. I had never used *Moonshadow* as a diving boat, but of course a Lugger was all things to all men. Minutes later, I was far underwater, eyeball-to-eyeball with a curious grouper—brown, white, and thoughtful, like a cow—but my mind was still on that boat. Seeing her was like being a man on a noisy street in an exotic city, say Hong Kong or Cairo, and spotting the first love of your life, a woman you haven't seen in a quarter-century. Though you have aged and thickened, she is as lean and quick as ever. Before you can speak, she boards a bus, the doors close, the bus goes, she's gone forever.

The problem was financial. Our new Lugger cost $2,500 in 1972, and that's what we sold her for in 1975. Used Luggers never come up for sale, and by August 1987 the price of a new one was more than $12,000, too much for our family budget. That was the month in which my recurring obsession with Drascombe boats returned in a surge of such power that for two days on the South Shore of Nova Scotia it loosened a screw in my head.

David Stevens of Second Peninsula, near Lunenburg, had phoned me. Would I like to spend Saturday afternoon with him aboard his forty-six-foot racing schooner, *Kathi Anne II*? Would a serious piano student like to watch Vladimir Horowitz practise on his Steinway? Stevens was a sailing equivalent of Wayne Gretzky. At eighty, he still raced classic gaff-rigged wooden schooners. And among those who *built* the schooners, he was also the master. Launched in 1972, *Kathi Anne II* was the most exquisite of the seventy-odd boats he'd built since World War Two. She was the one that had earned him more silver trays and trophies than he could possibly display in his modest farmhouse. After I described Stevens in *Weekend* magazine in 1973, he received the Order of Canada, and since he thought it was my story that got him his honour, he's been asking me out sailing each summer for a dozen years. (Well, who am I to destroy the man's faith in the power of the press?) When he phoned in the summer of 1987, I had not owned a boat for five years. I was so hungry for a romp on the ocean that I left Halifax two days early, just to look at yachts and poke around coastal villages.

On the first night, I stopped forty-five miles west of Halifax, at Chester. Some find Chester too charming by half, but I like it because it reminds me of novels. I can see Jay Gatsby there, strolling around in white shoes, white slacks and V-necked sweater, and a silk cravat. All summer in Chester you can smell burning firewood, much of it split by hired hands, and seaweed, roses, and pine needles. You can also smell old money from Baltimore, Philadelphia, and the investments of retired admirals, newer money from Montreal and Halifax, and the newest money of all, from West Germany. You can wonder what's making women laugh behind the manicured hedges and listen to the haunting slap of halyards against the masts of unattainable yachts.

Chester also has summer theatre. I took in *The Gin Game* that night because it starred two of the finest actors who live Down Home, both Come From Aways: David Renton, an Australian who's lived in Halifax for a quarter-century, and ex-Torontonian Anna Cameron, once hostess of CBC television's "Take Thirty" and now both an ornament and a dynamo in the cultural life of Nova Scotia.

After the play, a hit bound for Halifax, I joined Anna and her friends from the audience at the Fo'c'sle Tavern. Seated beside me was a good-looking guy with a generous moustache and considerate eyes. He was Kent Mason, a National Film Board photographer, and in Anna's opinion, "a genius in his line of work, a sheer genuis." Mason, as it happened, knew David Stevens, admired him, and wanted to make a film to capture whatever it was that enabled him to grow old with such grace, vigour, and good pride. Capped with foam, the amber beer vanished as fast as it arrived, and Mason startled me by confiding that he'd once owned a Drascombe Coaster, a boat that's a bit longer than a Lugger but flaunts the same voluptuous figure and saucy attitude. I gushed to him about my lost *Moonshadow*, and the coincidence struck me as a signal, even a directive. Dras-combe boats were almost unknown in the Maritimes, even among yachtsmen. In all of Nova Scotia, there couldn't have been more than a dozen. Mason and I, as former Drascombe owners, belonged to a rare cult. We needed a secret handshake.

The din kept increasing in that happy hole, the only tavern in Chester. As the women chattered on about *The Gin Game* and the ghastly moment when David Renton forgot his lines, Mason and I shut them all out of our minds. Only his wife realized what we were doing. She was a quiet, dark-haired woman with a lean, pretty face. As he and I put our heads closer and closer together, she knew we were selling each other on rushing out the next day to make down payments on Luggers. She also knew they couldn't afford nearly $13,000 for a boat, and as they got up to leave, she gave me a mock dirty look. "Okay, okay," I told her. "Next time we meet, no Lugger talk."

* * *

At six the next evening, I checked into the Belroy Motel in Lunenburg, the most beautiful port in Canada. A woman from St. John's, Newfoundland, teased me once by cranking up her Newfie accent a notch or two and sneering, "Ah, you poor blue-nosers with your puny Peggy's Cove. We got hunderds and hunderds of Peggy's Coves on The Rock, bye, hunderds and hunderds of 'dem." Then she turned serious. "But you've got Lunenburg," she said. "I wish we had a Lunenburg." In an article in *Atlantic Insight*, Halifax writer and CBC announcer Jim Bennet said the effect of Lunenburg on the first-time visitor is "breath-taking, all the more so because there is no good view of the place from a distance. The traveller, either by land or sea, is within its presence suddenly, and the magic can be overpowering. One Toronto baritone, between television tapings in Halifax, took a 'quick' jaunt to Lunenburg by car and was found, hours later, wandering Pelham Street in a dazed time warp, deadlines forgotten."

Lunenburg has none of the Disneyland odour of an official
Historic Village, nor the pretentious gloss of a town that no
longer has much industry except the preservation of its own
prettiness. It remains one of the major fishing capitals of northeastern North America, just as it was in the nineteenth century,
and much of its economy still spins around the well-being of its
offshore fleets and the men who sail in them. Though Lunenburg was founded in 1753, the wooden houses, offices, and warehouses—whose appearance makes you somehow remember what
you're not old enough ever to have seen—mostly date from only
about a century ago, when the port enjoyed its spurt as a boom
town. It wasn't oil, silver, gold, or diamonds that made the town
boom; it was merely the codfish that swarmed over the Grand
Banks off Newfoundland. By 1888 nearly five thousand men of
Lunenburg County were working in the cod fishery. The county
boasted 193 sailing vessels that caught cod on the banks, at least
sixty of them based in Lunenburg town.

Lunenburg is a checkerboard of narrow streets. Following a
grid pattern, houses and shops crawl all along the hills that over-
look the harbour. But if the layout is orderly, the architecture is a
jumble of bell-shaped roof lines, bulging dormers, widow's walks,
wooden scrollwork, stained glass, bay windows, and heavy cor-
nerboards and lintels.

I have never visited Lunenburg without receiving an unexpected message about how fine it is to be alive. Once, on a
summer Saturday, I went to the Boscawen Inn for lunch. Sena-
tor H.A.N. Kaulbach built the Boscawen in 1888 as a dowry gift
to his daughter, Edna Rudolph, and for those who like antique
furniture in an antique mansion, it's the best place in town to
spend a night or eat a meal. But I hate going to restaurants
alone. It makes me remember people with whom I've laughed
over dinner, in distant cities in distant times, and I wish they
were here right now and wonder if I'll ever see them again. Not
only did I have no lunch companion at the Boscawen, I had no
one even to spy upon. I was the sole customer in a gorgeous
dining room big enough for a busload of people. I sat at a table
for two by a window, ordered a dry martini on the rocks, and

looked out at the sort of noon that inspires young mothers to bare their thighs to the sun and their children to run through lawn sprinklers.

Somebody switched on a tape of a Bach piano solo. The music came to me, not too loud and not too soft, and the martini had a fine sting. A young waiter, attentive and unobtrusive, brought me three sautéed cakes, made of salt cod, mashed potatoes, and onions, as well as a local concoction to accompany them, a delicious rhubarb relish; he also served me a green salad with raw mushrooms and a goblet of white wine from Germany. Just as I decided that if a man had to eat by himself this was the place to do it, a creature moved about four feet away from my left elbow. Beyond the glinting crystal, smooth silverware and heavy, slippery linen on my table, beyond the potted geraniums at the window ledge, and just the other side of the panes of glass, a Siamese cat sneaked through grass. He was so close I could count his whiskers. Beyond him, the branches of great hardwoods clawed the summer air. Beyond them, jutted the venerable roofs of Lincoln, Pelham, and Montague streets. Beyond the roofs, and visible in a gap between buildings for only as long as it took the cat to disappear, a fully rigged schooner sailed in the path of the sun. The far schooner moved down the harbour, the near cat moved up the harbour, and on my way out of the Boscawen I met a wedding party on the way in.

The women were like garrulous birds, their voices chirpy and their gaudy dresses rustling as they moved. They smelled good, too, and the men, in their Sunday best on Saturday afternoon, looked strong and smug and content to be here rather than out on a golf course or the ocean. As I ambled back to my car, the chimes of St. John's Anglican Church began a melodious booming. The church is wooden, white with black trim and a tower suitable for a fairy queen. Now it sent "Danny Boy" down over the peaks and porches of the houses, through sunshine and shadow in the lacy trees, and all the way out to the ships and yachts that floated on the glitter of high summer. A backyard garden caught my eye. Conch shells, the kind the Bahamas diving lodge had used as a horn to summon us guests to meals, curved all around the flower bed, as bricks do in city gardens. The shells were nearly a foot long, and each was red, orange, white and purplish. Had a local skipper brought them home from the West Indies after delivering a load of salt fish in the 1880s? I didn't know. I only knew that Lunenburg was doing it to me again, making me silly.

I remembered that afternon when I checked into the Belroy Motel on the evening after my beery Drascombe conference with Kent Mason. I'd been driving all day. I went straight to my room, unpacked, shaved, poured a rum and Coke, lit a Rothmans, drew the curtains, and opened the window. A wall of alders faced me, their leaves shining in the low slant of the evening sunlight. Farther away, I could see the backs of white houses on Tannery Road and their railroad-red outbuildings; one ramshackle shed had pitched over, like a ship plunging into a sea of grass. And way off in the distance shone a corner of Lunenburg Harbour, as still as a mirror. A turquoise boat nudged a pink mooring buoy on that distant water, and when I squinted hard I knew that, as race-horse people might put it, the boat's conformation was superb and unmistakable. She was a Drascombe boat. Maybe she was *Moonshadow* herself, and maybe she was for sale.

I swallowed my drink, stepped aboard my Toyota Tercel, and navigated her along Tannery Road, leaving on my port side the one-time home of gritty Angus Walters. He was the skipper of the Lunenburg-built *Bluenose*, the greatest fishing schooner in the history of the world. Tannery Road released me on Mason's Beach Road, and soon I was only a hundred yards from the boat on the mirror. She was a Coaster, big sister to a Lugger. Seeing two Lunenburg burghers standing on the driveway of a snug pink house, I pulled over. But no, they could not tell me who, or where, the owner of that little two-master was. Until this morning, they'd never even seen her. In this neighbourhood, she was a mystery ship.

I was on the far side of the harbour from the commercial heart of Lunenburg, and getting hungry. So I drove around to the neighbourhood of big piers and ochre warehouses with gambrel roofs, found a second-floor restaurant in the waterfront museum, and sat down at another table for two at another window. I could see the Drascombe Coaster from her other side this time, but from much farther away. For no sensible reason, I wanted to keep an eye on her while the sun went down and I pigged out. My waitress looked like Natalie Wood at fifteen and behaved as though she believed a solitary diner, like a man on death row, deserved extra love. Is everything all right, sir? How are the steamed mussels tonight? May I bring you more wine? Now this is your boiled lobster, with drawn butter, potato salad, and coleslaw. *There* you go! Is everything all right? Our dessert of the day is gingerbread with loads of whipped cream. You'd like that? Good! There you go sir! Are you sure everything's all right? Is it? Thank you. Have a nice night now.

Darkness swallowed the Coaster, and I returned to the Belroy Motel. The next afternoon, I'd be aboard *Kathi Anne II*. In the morning, I saw through my back window that the Coaster had not slipped away in the night. The front of my room faced inland, and when I opened the door, Lunenburg shoved a zany picture at me: to my left, the breakfast-time sunlight of a perfect sailing day bounced off the round, silver shoulders of hundreds of Airstream trailers from throughout the U.S.; and straight ahead, from the sound system at a deserted swimming pool, came the forced cheeriness of a professional children's choir, as now—on this Day of Our Lord, August 8, 1987—it belted out "Rudolph, the Red-Nosed Reindeer."

Beyond the pool sat the offices of the community centre. Just as the ghostly choir launched into "I Saw Mommy Kissing Santa Claus," I ambled over there, asked a secretary for a key to the Fishermen's Memorial Room, entered that sacred chamber, and closed the door behind me. This, I'd been told, was the place to find the spirit of Lunenburg. The town's population still stands at barely three thousand, but over the past century or so the sea has slaughtered at least six hundred men from its fishing fleet. The names of nearly all of them are listed, under the years of their deaths, on the walls of this small room. A chart shows where more than a hundred Lunenburg vessels were lost, forty of them with their entire crews, and the locations stretch from New-foundland to the Caribbean Sea. Even down to our own time, scarcely a year passes in which the sea fails to kill at least one Lunenburg fisherman, but some years have been more horrible than others.

Under 1926 and 1927, the lists are long. Those were the years in which the August Gales destroyed six Lunenburg schooners off Sable Island, killing all of the 130 crew. In such catastrophes, nearly every family in Blue Rocks, the LaHave Islands, and other nearby outports lost a father or a son, and the grief was paralysing; but the larger Lunenburg also suffered whenever its vessels failed to return, and then sorrow spread over everything like a winter fog. Each time the schooners began one of their routine races to the Grand Banks, Lunenburg harbour was a sight of the finest kind. It was also a sight that inspired hundreds of womenfolk to start praying.

Covering one wall of the room, an eighteen-foot mural by Lunenburg artist Joseph Purcell shows Christ and the five fisher-men aboard a storm-lashed boat. The text is from the book of St. Mark: "And He arose and rebuked the wind and said unto the sea, Peace, be still. And the wind ceased, and there was a great calm." For a town of its size, Lunenburg has magnificent churches.

*　*　*

Having paid my respects to the dead fishermen, I checked out of the Belroy, drove around the corner to the Topmast Motel, and checked in. It was crummier than the Belroy, but closer to the Coaster. A middle-aged, bare-footed woman, escorted by a fat, creamy Lab, showed me a room. A house blocked the view of the boat, and I asked to see another. The second room looked as though a mixed softball team had used it for a victory bash, but no matter which way the Coaster swung on her mooring I could

see her from here in full profile. "Yes," I said, "this will do fine."
The woman looked puzzled. "The thing is," I explained, "I want
to be able to see that little green boat out there. I understand she
came into port yesterday morning. Would her owner be staying
here, by any chance?" He wasn't. The South Shore is now almost as notorious for drug-running as it once was for rum-
running, and the woman looked as though she couldn't decide
whether I was a narc or a nut.

At the edge of the water I'd noticed three rowboats. If I was to
rent or borrow one, I could easily row out to the Coaster and
check her name and home port. Maybe her owner was still
aboard, sleeping in on this Saturday morning, which was so
splendid the marvellous might happen. Maybe he'd hear me
rowing around, stick his head out of the cabin, and tell me his
wife hated sailing and he wanted to sell this very boat on this
very day. Even if nothing like that happened, however, a rowboat would enable me to sidle up to the Drascombe boat, with
her powerful family resemblance to *Moonshadow*, and caress her
curving teak, stroke her glassy flanks, and gaze into her brown
floorboards. I parked the car and started ringing doorbells. No
one answered at three houses, but at the fourth a tubby guy in
his seventies, wearing glasses and a peaked cap, came out on the
verandah. Blunt and amiable, he had a local accent as strong as
Lunenburg sausage. He didn't think it odd that a man should
want to use a stranger's punt to inspect another stranger's sailboat, but no one he knew owned any of the three rowboats. So
far as the Coaster went, he wasn't sure, but he thought she
belonged to a local man named Corkum. Tonight, I thought, I'll
hole up at the Topmast and phone Corkum after Corkum after
Corkum. The most important part of detective work is sheer
slogging.

Returning to my car, I saw an elderly, red-faced man trudging
toward the main part of town. He wore a tam and looked locally
knowledgeable. "Excuse me, sir," I said, "but do you happen to
know if the owner of one of these rowboats lives around here?"
He said, "Ah cain't tell you that, son. Ah'm from Georgia. Me 'n

the wife, we just come up heah yesterday in our trailer." He was an Airstream man, and he said that if I wanted to get out on the harbour I should report to a new downtown hotel called the Rum Runner Inn, which kept a boat for fishing excursions, and as a matter of fact he just happened to be going downtown himself, to buy a newspaper, and if I'd give him a lift, why, he'd be happy to show me exactly where the hotel was.

The Rum Runner, I knew, was across Montague Street from where Natalie Wood had brought me my lobster feast on a sea of comforting words, but it struck even me as ludicrous to hire a fishing boat with a big inboard engine just to take a peek at the Coaster. I approached a boy in a waterfront booth. He was selling tickets to tourists who wanted to cruise around the harbour in a schooner. He knew of no one in the whole town who'd take me over to the Coaster in a small boat, not even for money. Of course, if I wanted to buy a ticket for the schooner cruise, I *might* be able to persuade the skipper to alter his normal route to suit my plans. I now followed the advice of the Georgia gent.

The desk clerk at the Rum Runner was a stocky man, without flab. His hair was short, straight, and sort of blond, and he had modest sideburns. He wore blue loafers, blue pants, and a short-sleeved, open-necked shirt with pale blue stripes. I would later learn that he owned not only the Rum Runner but also the Belroy, and that until yesterday he'd also owned the Topmast. He'd just sold it to the bare-footed woman who'd shown me my room and to her husband. When I asked him if he could rustle up someone to take me out on the harbour, I had no inkling he was Gene Tanner, forty-three, founder of Deep Water Vinyl and Aluminum Siding, and Lunenburg's most hustling hotel tycoon. He seemed to be just a guy behind the counter. When I said I'd be happy to pay for a ride on the harbour, he looked confused and murmured, "Oh, heck, you wouldn't have to pay. I'll take you out. When do you want to go?" I told him I'd be back at six that night, and then I drove to Second Peninsula to join David Stevens.

Fourteen years had passed since I'd written "David Stevens,

old-age pensioner, grandfather of nine, loyal husband, non-smoker, non-drinker, milker of his own cows, raiser of his own beef, grower of his own vegetables, man of few words and much land, son of a sailmaker, brother of a sailmaker, brother-in-law of a ship's outfitter, grandson of a shipbuilder, father of a shipbuilder, cousin to four shipbuilders, and a master shipbuilder himself, also happens to be one heck of a man to face in a schooner race." Not much had changed. You could add four great-grandchildren to the nine grandchildren, and six more yachts to the dozens of wooden boats he'd built since World War Two. He had a forty-foot schooner under construction in the shed back of his house, but there was nothing new in that. Stevens and his wife had recently quit churning their own butter, and perhaps that was a concession to his having entered the ninth decade of his life, though he was still one heck of a man to face in a schooner race. Sixteen vessels had just competed during the South Shore's annual schooner regatta, and a headline in the Lunenburg *Progress Enterprise* told a story that was too familiar to Stevens's rivals: "*Kathi Anne II* sweeps trophies at Schooner Race Week."

Even while racing, Stevens is the most good-natured man I've ever known at the helm of a big sailboat, and now, with one more triumphant week behind him, the patriarch of bluenose schooner folk was as easygoing as a village barber. His amiability, however, did not dilute his authority. Aboard *Kathi Anne II*, Stevens is never anything less than the Skipper. His stature is as obvious as the power that still lives in his meaty palms and thick, old fingers, and as sure as the satisfaction in his tanned face and blue eyes when the breeze stiffens and *Kathi Anne II* heels over and leaps ahead like the flying white horse in *The Thief of Bagdad*. When Stevens surveys the waters off Second Peninsula, waters he's known since before he ever saw an airplane, his face reminds me of John Keats's description of "stout Cortez when with eagle eyes / He star'd at the Pacific."

Stevens, however, has no interest in staring at the Pacific—not if he has to get there by sailboat at any rate—nor any yearning to sail more than a couple of dozen miles from his trees, tools, cabbages, and cows. All the older people around Lunenburg knew men who sailed not for pleasure but out of necessity and did not live to come home again, and none of the survivors can ever regard the high seas as a toy. "I never liked the ocean enough to make my living at it," Stevens says. "That didn't appeal to me a bit."

Nothing made the ocean lovable except inshore races, and the fact that on certain afternoons he could gather kin and friends aboard a masterpiece of his own creation, and that then, for a few kind, clean hours, they could all sit together in her cockpit while she romped with the waves, with a warm, steady southerly and the skin-burning light of the sun and make music no one ever hears on shore. As afternoon sails go, an excursion with Stevens is innocent, like a Sunday-school picnic. No one drinks booze, and cigarettes seem so out-of-place that even I leave my Rothmans ashore. There's no hint of the hangovers, ill temper, cruel gossip, and blue-blazer pretensions that sometimes infect the crews of rich men's boats at city yacht clubs. No one curses, everyone smiles. Everyone also eats cookies, fruit, sandwiches, cheese, and bits of smoked salmon on crackers, and Stevens invites guests to take turns at the wheel of *Kathi Anne II*. She's so exquisitely balanced that, going upwind, you need barely touch a spoke to keep her long, surging hull on course.

On that last August afternoon when I sailed with Stevens, his guests included six adults and four teenagers. The adults were all sailors, and a couple had built their own boats. Two others—fit, quiet guys in their mid-twenties—were grandsons of the skipper, and one of these, another David Stevens, had served two seasons aboard the schooner *Bluenose II*. One of his jobs had been to furl topsails, and Stevens said his grandson could "go up *Kathi Anne*'s mast like a squirrel." If a squall hit us, it would be good to have such an able hand aboard, but as the day slid by, the afternoon weather fulfilled the morning's promise. The wind blew from the south for hours, as steady as a metronome, and the sun ducked every cloud that came its way. With me at the helm, we sailed on a starboard tack toward Tancook Island, where Stevens was born to a seagoing family—every family on Tancook Island in 1907 was a seagoing family—and then we charged up the

centre of Mahone Bay for a while, nipped in behind several islands, and ended up back at *Kathi Anne II's* mooring just three
and a half hours after we'd left it. It was 5:45 P.M. In recent years,
I have never stepped ashore after a superb sail in another man's
yacht without slavering again to have one of my own, even if she
can never be anywhere near as stately as a forty-six-foot schooner. Now, I had a rendezvous at the Rum Runner Inn, and my
farewells were too quick to be graceful.

* * *

Gene Tanner was waiting, and he seemed eager to escape his
hotel. We jumped into his siding company's pickup truck, and
he drove to the extreme head of Lunenburg harbour, where *Lady
Jean* lay at a dock. She was thirty-seven feet long, and beamy, a
Cape Island–style fishing boat with berths forward and below, a
roomy wheelhouse, and lots of open space aft. She was mostly
white outside, but inside she looked as though someone had
covered her with leftover paint in different shades of green. She
boasted no brass clocks, fancy controls, or mahogany panelling.
She was all business. She carried radar, hydraulic winches, and a
new diesel turbo engine. Tanner had paid $8,300 for *Lady Jean*,
and then sunk another $30,000 in her, mostly for the engine. He
used her to catch cod, haddock, pollock, and some shark, and
perhaps to show off now and then as well. Despite her heft, he
said, she was "the fastest boat on Lunenburg harbour."

He unfolded a flimsy aluminum chair, with brown and white
strips of plastic to sit on, and set it up for me near the stern. In
the pink, pearly evening, we chugged into the harbour, leaving a
row of green buoys to our port side, and soon I could see, well off
to starboard, that for the first time in the twenty-four hours since
I'd spotted the Coaster from the Belroy Hotel, somebody was
aboard her. I told Tanner it was vital that I call on her. He spun
Lady Jean's wheel, and soon the two boats were gently rubbing
flanks while I talked Drascombes with a lean man with short
black hair, a ruddy face, and a scarlet jacket. He was Robert
Corkum, and I took him to be in his early forties. The transom

of his Coaster declared *Companion, Lunenburg*, but he normally kept her along the coast, near his home at Princess Inlet. He'd just sailed her into Lunenburg for something to do during his vacation. Three years before, he'd bought *Companion* new, complete with trailer, for only $14,000. I knew that the same package would now cost me more than $20,000. *Companion* was superbly kept, and her colour scheme was identical to *Moonshadow*'s. She was not for sale.

As *Lady Jean* left *Companion*, Tanner asked, "How much time you got?"

"As much as you have."

"Are you a beer-drinking guy?"

"Oh, sure," I said, "I drink just about anything."

I thought he was going to snap open some beer at that moment, but he didn't. He turned *Lady Jean*'s bow southeast and opened her throttle. The boat roared straight out to sea, taking off so fast she almost dumped me and the aluminum chair. Though we headed for the open ocean, we shot along parallel to the harbour's eastern shore. With the lowering sun in their eyes, a man and two boys fished for mackerel from a dock at National Sea Products, one of the world's biggest fish processors. They waved, we waved, and as we zoomed past two young guys in a red rowboat who were after pollock, we waved again. The village of Blue Rocks, five miles closer than Lunenburg to the ocean's horizon in the south, slid by on our port beam. Blue Rocks in winter is even bleaker than its own name; but now, from the August sea, it looked cosy, as happy as a clam at high tide. The sun plummeted behind *Lady Jean*'s stern and drenched the bright boats and houses in splashes of burnished copper. In the evening light, *Lady Jean*'s wake reminded me of speedboat scenes on "Miami Vice." Spray from her bows flew all the way aft, and the din from her engines drowned Tanner's voice. I thought I heard him say "eastern," but I had no idea where he was taking me on this headlong voyage aboard Lunenburg's fastest boat. He seemed to be pulling off the easiest kidnapping in the history of crime.

He cut *Lady Jean*'s speed. Her bow slumped. The whole boat settled a bit, and I joined him in the wheelhouse. Tanner seemed to be steering toward the centre of a low, useless island, but as we passed a yellow and black buoy, the island split into a menacing jumble of islets, jagged traps, and dirty shoals. Then we slipped into a calm passage, and it was like slipping into a trance. A strange avenue separated what the chart identified as East Point Island and Little East Point Island, and its name was East Point Gut. It was so narrow and symmetrical it might almost have been a man-made canal. The water was silky and deep green, like bloodstones, and the islands were rafts of rock, dotted with scrawny fir and spruce. Their needles glistened in the late sunlight. I could almost grab them, and yet *Lady Jean* was gliding down the gut on fifteen feet of water. Until now, it had not occurred to me that anyone, not even a Micmac centuries ago, had ever tried to survive out here for long. But in truth, I had already entered a ghost town of the sea.

The first house I saw was rotting in a clear patch on Little East Point Island. Its roof-line sagged in a V. Thousands of salty winds had stripped off all the paint and turned the house a deeper gray than driftwood. The wreckage of a nearby lighthouse was the same colour. It had never served any navigational purpose out here, Tanner told me. It had done duty up at Lunenburg, but after its useful time was through, someone had brought it down the harbour, into the gut, and onto the island. I saw some tumbledown fish huts, too, and across the gut on East Point Island, a decrepit pier, with more buildings nestled in the trees beyond. Tanner laid *Lady Jean* against the pier, and we ambled up a slope of freshly mowed grass and into the past.

It turned out that he'd mowed the grass himself, and that he owned the ramshackle building beside the pier. We were standing in what had once been the fishing village of Eastern Points. Tanner figured there'd been as many as fifteen houses on East Point Island, and close to a hundred men, women, and children, but that was long ago. They had a big barn for their cattle, a blacksmith's shop to make fittings for their schooners, power-driven band saws, icehouses, fishhouses, a schoolhouse, wooden catwalks to smaller islands, and a general store.

"It was quite a prosperous little place," David Stevens told me later. "They kept half a dozen fishing boats in the gut. They'd go out on Monday, fish all week, and come back on Friday." Stevens was born on Tancook Island, which lies across seven miles of open ocean from Eastern Points, and he had nine brothers and sisters. The family's vegetable garden needed all the fertilizer it could get, and on Friday afternoons when the Eastern Points fleet got home, Randolph Stevens, the father, sent thirteen-year-old David over there in a primitive motorboat to pick up loads of fish guts. That was sixty-seven years ago.

Neither Stevens nor Tanner knew exactly when the people of Eastern Points had abandoned the islands, but months after my voyage on *Lady Jean* I learned a strange story that proved families were still thriving out there in the mid-1930s. I had gone to the art gallery of Mount Saint Vincent University, Halifax, to see works by a tormented wanderer from Maine named Marsden Hartley. I had never heard of him. I knew nothing of his sojourns at Eastern Points. But I happen to like both art galleries and Down Home books, and at this exhibit I bought a plump, glossy catalogue, *Marsden Hartley and Nova Scotia*. It told me more about Eastern Points than either Tanner or Stevens had revealed, and perhaps more than they knew.

Marsden Hartley's mother had died in his boyhood, and his father had abandoned him. He endured a miserable childhood and an unconventional sex life. Art scholars speculate that the loss of his father fanned his homosexual interest in German army officers. In any event, he spent decades in Germany, and it was there that he became a pioneer of abstract art. Though some see Hartley now as the greatest American Modernist of the entire first half of the twentieth century, his working in foreign styles in foreign lands earned him contempt in his own time in his own country. By 1935, after the depression had forced him to return to the States, he was a fifty-eight-year-old has-been, living in New York on sixty cents a day, and so poor he couldn't scrape up enough cash to pay for the storage of a hundred paintings and drawings. He destroyed them. Bronchitis tortured him. He had only eight years to live.

But if 1935 began as one of the worst years in Hartley's life, it ended as one of the best. For it was then, in October and November, that he found himself living with the Mason family at Eastern Points. The experience astounded him, made him feel holy, restored his creative passion, transformed his art, and equipped him spiritually to do what few artists are lucky enough to do: he used his last years to paint his greatest pictures.

When Hartley arrived in Lunenburg he intended to meet an old friend—Frank Davison, a novelist from Nova Scotia who wrote under the name Pierre Coalfleet—but he missed him by a day. Lunenburg bored him. Taking a taxi-driver's advice, he went along the coast to Blue Rocks, where he boarded with Libby and Leander Knickle for seven dollars a week. It was there that he met some Masons, who regularly crossed more than a mile of ocean, mined with jagged rocks and killer shoals, to get from Eastern Points to the mainland. If Hartley liked the Knickles, he adored the Masons. It was as though he had at last found the family he'd lost half a century before. To his friend Adelaide Kuntz, he wrote, "I fell in love with the most amazing family of men & women . . . veritable rocks of Gibraltar in appearance, the very salt of the earth." He persuaded the Masons to take him in for the same price he paid the Knickles and later wrote that Eastern Points was the most elevating experience of his life.

The father, Francis Mason, looked and sounded "like a great Shakespearian actor or a dark angel of Blake's." Just watching Papa Francis say grace made the artist feel honoured to be among the Masons. The mother, Martha Mason, was a powerful saint. The daughter, Alice, was a gentle giant, with "an Amazon body." She could carry a double armful of firewood as easily as if it were toys. The boys were Donny, thirty-one, and Alty, twenty-eight. They, too, were giants, and noble savages. They walked like bears, Hartley wrote, and yet they were loving, and as gentle as lambs. They were "divine" when drunk, shy when sober. They had wild beauty, sweet characters, and fierce looks that hid tender natures. They were good, warm playmates, and completely humble. The whole family was like rivers, no, *oceans* of loving kindness, and "all of them look like cinnamon bears, & are terrifyingly powerful & so quiet & childlike. I feel as if I had found my chosen people."

Hartley returned to New York City in November, but, for love of the Masons, made his way back to Eastern Points in July 1936. He felt calm, and he painted well. Then, on Saturday night, September 19, during a gale that had whizzed up from Florida, Donny, Alty, and their smaller cousin Allen tried to come home from Blue Rocks by rowboat. They never made it. Their punt, without oars, turned up twenty miles away, and within a few days the local undertow gave back their mangled bodies. Now, Hartley shared the crippling grief of Francis and Martha Mason. He regarded them as archangels on earth, "and I never expect to see or know anyone more thoroughly beautiful in every possible way." A year before, he had noticed a touch of Christian martyrdom in the hard life of the Masons; now he saw that, even in the face of unbearable loss, the religious faith of Francis Mason did not waver. The artist would never forget that.

To console the Masons, he stayed at Eastern Points till December, and though he could never bring himself to make the trip back to the islands, he saluted the family in *Cleophas and His Own: A North Atlantic Tragedy*, in which he gave each Mason a French-Canadian name. The manuscript was a flowing, tearful mixture of prose and rolling poetry, a celebration of the Masons' saintliness and a dirge for their drowned. More important to the art world, Hartley also returned to Eastern Points in his painting. In his last years—he died in 1943, at sixty-six—he painted a series of dark, thick, menacing images of dead fish and birds, lobster buoys and nets, storms, rope, starfish, and schooners sailing under skies that yawned with violence. These paintings are full of symbols and religious allegories. Working from memory, Hartley also painted the Masons—singly, in groups of two or three, and all together in *Fishermen's Last Supper*. He made them look stoical, tragic, victimized, the toys of hideous fate, and yet enduring, and somehow triumphant. They are square-shouldered, block-shaped, big-faced, big-fisted icons, and it is these works that justify Marsden Hartley's claim on immortality.

* * *

"Hey, look at that," Tanner said. A field mouse hustled through the grass he'd cut. "And look at *that* little fellow," he chirped, proudly pointing at a toad. "This island's just alive with animals. There's pheasant, loads of deer, even moose." The existence of moose on East Point Island was a tall story, but deer could have swum over from the mainland. And anyway, Tanner was so boyish and excited about his island wilderness that it was easy to forgive any boasts he made on its behalf.

For $75 at a tax sale, someone had picked up an abandoned house across the gut on Little East Point Island and had fixed it up for summer use. It had new roof shingles, freshly painted green walls and white trim. Among the crumbling gray wrecks, it was like a fashion model in a nursing home. A handful of buildings still stood over here on East Point Island, and one of the biggest had also been restored as a summer home. It was empty right now, however, and so were all the other houses. Someone had been trying to renovate the tiny schoolhouse where Hartley had watched Papa Mason during a Sunday service: "I could see the holiness and wanted to see it, it came from his face over me, and I wanted it that way." In another house— one that Tanner had sought but failed to get—plates still stood on the kitchen shelves. He said they'd been there so long they were stuck to the wood.

The houses rose from different heights and faced different directions. Footpaths connected them, and remnants of paths wandered into the wilderness. "There are no highways on the island," Hartley wrote, "and where the people live on the inner side, only a thin path made day in and day out by the few feet that walk over the spine-like rocks, more like the vertebrae of prehistoric animals than anything else." When he first arrived in November 1935, he marvelled over "deep forests & the trees all hanging with grizzly moss," and these descriptions were as ac-

curate in 1987 as they had been more than half a century earlier.
Beyond the houses, I stared into a ravine, a hairy green valley of
entanglement and shadow, and it seemed to plunge far below sea
level. The illusion was so powerful that I didn't doubt Tanner
when he told me that often, while fog, wind, and rain punished
Lunenburg only five miles to the north, the sun singled out Eastern Points for special consideration and bathed it in heavenly
light and semitropical warmth. "It's another world out here," he
said. "Really."

The waterfront building he owned had once been the general
store, and it looked as though it was half warehouse and half
residence. We entered through an empty room whose white
walls still bore signs in mint condition: "Wrigley's Spearmint
Pepsin Gum," "Goodrich Rubber Footwear," "Salome, The Classic Egyptian Cigarette. In handsome metal cases to fit the
pocket." We moved into a plain, rangy living room with nothing
in it to excite any antique collector. I sat down on a couch, and
Tanner, remembering that I was a beer-drinking fellow, emerged
from his kitchen with two cold, sweating bottles of Keith's ale.
He had enough beer to satisfy a convention of truck drivers, and
much of it was crammed into a refrigerator. "You mean you've
got electricity out here?" I marvelled.

When Eastern Points had been a year-round settlement, a
power company had strung underwater cables out from the
mainland, and the islands were still part of the provincial electricity system. Whether or not the convenience of electricity
gave the islanders a taste for mainland comforts and amusements
they could not resist, it was not long after the power arrived that
the people began to move away. Some stayed longer than others.
"I bought this place from an old fellow who gave up fishing only
a year ago," Tanner said. "His name was Herbie Corkum." Another Corkum. If I owned Robert Corkum's *Companion*, and if I
lived in Lunenburg County, I'd sail to Eastern Points every
summer.

By the standards of coastal Nova Scotia, the evening was
freakishly warm. We were comfortable in short-sleeved shirts,
and the icy ale was as good as it might have tasted at noon in

Jamaica. I downed three bottles while Tanner told me he'd gone to Ottawa in his early twenties; worked like a dog there, putting down water mains; got into a business of his own, installing storm windows, doors, and siding; married an Ottawa woman; and in 1970 brought her home to Lunenburg. "When she first came here," he said, "she couldn't even eat fish. But she wouldn't go back to Ottawa now for all the money in the world." We felt we knew each other pretty well by the time *Lady Jean* rocketed us up to Lunenburg harbour and into the sunset. Diving birds plucked fish off Blue Rocks. We hurtled past a lighthouse with a constant red light, while far astern and just above the horizon a full, pale, and carefree moon sailed along. The sky was blue above the moon and pink and creamy below, like bedding for a baby girl. I had good dreams at the Topmast that night, but none was as wondrous as the real day had been.

*   *   *

The next morning I took the coastal highway into Halifax. I tried to keep my eyes on the road and floating boats at the same time, and at the head of St. Margarets Bay, within twenty minutes of the city, I saw another Coaster dancing at her mooring. I pulled the Toyota over to the shoulder, quizzed a couple of cottage-owners, and soon found her owner. He was Phil Donham, a writer, and he showed me his haulout apparatus for the boat, confided that he'd rather have a Lugger, and explained that he'd recently picked up this Coaster, secondhand, for a mere $7,000. And no, she was not for sale. I was the eighth guy this summer to spot his boat from the road, come down his driveway, and engage him in Drascombe talk. I had left my gray car up on the highway and walked down, but Donham's gray car was in his driveway, and our boat conversation unbalanced me. I said good-bye and then tried to jam my key into the doorlock beside his driver's seat. He watched my brief struggle. He thought it was extremely funny. Next summer, dammit, I'll have me a *Moonshadow II.*

SAINT JOHN:
CITY OF TURBULENT SPIRITS

I first saw Saint John when I got off a bus on King Street just before a murky d. wn in September 1954. I was twenty and was bound from Toronto to Sackville, New Brunswick, for my last year at university. King Street was still the bedraggled commercial centre not only for the city but also for outports and towns all around the New Brunswick and Nova Scotia shores of the Bay of Fundy. Writing for *Maclean's*, Ian Sclanders, a Saint John man who'd long since moved away, said, "This odd, broad, steep, slightly drab thoroughfare has no tall or very distinguished buildings. It is only a fifth of a mile long. Yet it holds a special place in the history, heart and business of a whole rugged salt-encrusted region." As a college boy on King Street, I knew none of this. Nor did I know about Saint John's reputation as a wretched, smelly burg, dying on its feet. I only knew I was hungry and had two hours to kill between bus rides.

I shared a lunch counter with meaty dockworkers. I downed coffee, spongy toast, and a soft-boiled egg, and then strolled to the waterfront spot where, 171 years before, British ships from New York had dumped fourteen thousand Loyalists from the American Revolution. I didn't know much about that, either. As the sun climbed somewhere, the air turned from black to dark gray, and stayed that way. The seagulls on the pilings at Market Slip were twice as big as the ones I'd sailed among on tame, tideless Toronto Harbour. These were monster gulls— brown, white, fierce, and tatty—and the stench of rotten fish mingled with wraiths of fog. The harbour was the colour of dung, and Saint John was the most romantic place I'd ever seen. I sent a postcard to a girl I'd left behind, in Toronto. As things turned out, we got married exactly one year later. Her name was Penny Meadows.

Three children, two grandchildren, a dozen jobs, a dozen homes, and thirty-two years later, we showed up in Saint John together. Two of our children were now older than I'd been on the morning I'd mailed the postcard. Since then, I'd been back to Saint John only once, and only overnight. Penny had never been there before, but it made her feel both comfortable and elated, and she wondered why it had long suffered such a vile reputation.

* * *

Movie star Donald Sutherland tells a story about his boyhood in wartime Saint John. His father was an air-raid warden, and one night he told the boy he was going to a town meeting to discuss the purchase of a warning siren. When he returned, little Donald said, "Hey, Dad, are we gonna get a siren?"

"No, son, we're not," Mr. Sutherland explained. "You see, we figure that if the Nazis come over the city, it'll probably be foggy out. They'll never see us, and they'll fly right by."

"But what if the sky's clear, Dad?"

"Well, they'll still fly by because they'll look down at Saint John, and they'll think they must have bombed it already."

Donald Sutherland is not the only one who remembers Saint John as a dirty, fog-bound wreck. For decades it endured a reputation as the ugliest city in eastern Canada. Visitors denounced its hills, its fog, and the ramshackle way its dismal houses clung to grim rock. The hotels were so bad that even the most exhausted travellers, arriving by steamship, hopped the first train to Montreal. For many, Union Station typified all of Saint John, and according to George Nestler Tricoche, a British writer who came to town in the Moaning Twenties, the station was "the most unattractive, uninviting, inconvenient, blasty, dreary edifice of the kind east of Montreal."

From the age of sail to the arrival of Sputnik I, what industry there was in central Saint John was mostly coal-fired and spewed soot on the city. As the use of coal sank, the stink from the Irving pulp mill rose. Poet Carl Sandburg wrote, "The fog comes on little cat feet." In Saint John it came on big, smelly feet, more than a hundred days a year. With sloping streets, silent wharfs, grim slums, greasy mist, grimy Victorian stone, and a smell of decay that was almost as powerful as the foul odour from neighbourhood mudflats, Saint John in the early 1950s was a perfect location for a movie about Jack the Ripper.

Those who love the city cannot avoid its bad old reputation. They invariably explain its current charms and virtues in terms of its past blemishes and vices. How miraculous that such a dump should now be "The Greatest Little City in the East!" That's Saint John's official slogan, and on a fine, fogless afternoon in June of 1987, the boast was believable. At an outdoor table at Market Square—the $100-million waterfront development that opened in 1983 and has helped revitalize old Saint John—I gulped Moosehead Ale and munched shrimps with a fellow who'd spent all his life in the city. I was so close to the spot where I'd dawdled at dawn thirty-three years before that I could easily have clouted it with an empty beer bottle, but the scene was as different from what I remembered as Nice is from Pittsburgh.

Market Slip, where we sat, had once been a ghost pier, with rotten wharfs underfoot. Now, all along the slip, a juicy garden of red-white-and-green sun umbrellas blossomed outside eateries and grogshops. The most cheerful waitresses in the Maritimes smoothly hustled their beer-laden trays among the parasols, and a gang of geezers belted out country music from an elegant gazebo. Grounded in shallow water, a tarted-up tug served as a tourist-information office. Armies of visitors streamed in one door of Barbour's General Store, a museum featuring nineteenth-century merchandise, and out the other. Families flowed across the neat park that marked the spot where all those desperate Loyalists had once huddled. Girls in their summer dresses met boys in their summer heat at the town clock—a marvellous piece of wood sculpture, with chunky life-like, life-size gents sharing a circular bench with flesh-and-blood Saint Johnners. Balloons bobbed and jiggled, and the harbour glittered. The sun shone, the breeze blew, the gulls flew, and my friend said, "This really is the greatest little city in the east, but you know, it used to be the arsehole of the world."

"Hesitantly, like a man admitting he puts ketchup on his omelettes," poet Alden Nowlan wrote, "I admit that I belong to that little band of eccentrics who feel something very much like love for Saint John." The little band, however, did not include

Colin Mackay. Born in Rothesay, a swank suburb of Saint John, Mackay was president of the University of New Brunswick from 1953 to 1969. Though he trots around the globe to promote international causes, his home is now back in Rothesay, and as president emeritus of U.N.B., he has an office on the Saint John campus. It was there that he told me he hadn't relished the idea of semiretirement in the port. "When I came back to Saint John," he said, "I was just appalled. I was quivering with trepidation."

Mackay is tall, gangling, energetic. His hair is long and gray, and the lines that bracket his mouth are deep. His eyes are quick but kindly, and he's an eloquent, hyperactive talker. If comedian Steve Martin were to lose twenty-five pounds and gain twenty-five years, he'd look something like Colin Mackay.

In his youth, Mackay said, Saint John wasn't just economically stagnant, it was intellectually dead. As president of U.N.B. he'd fought proposals for a university in Saint John. Now, sitting there in his U.N.B. office, he realized that "this place should have had a university." On a per capita basis, Saint John had been the richest city in Canada during the 1860s, but then the decline began. By 1900 "things were getting worse and worse. Everybody was going west, *everybody*—the lawyers, the school-teachers, all the natural leaders, and there was no university to train new ones. There was no leadership. All that was left was the ragtag."

During the Great Depression, "it was awful here, simply awful. Everything was bust. There's a sepia photo you should see. It shows the old Market Slip and the warehouses on the water, and there's one or two trading schooners in there, but on all the downtown street space, you can see only a couple of men. Saint John looks like a ghost town. . . . And there was no cultural leadership. . . . Fredericton had its parlour Bolsheviks, but growing up in Saint John, you didn't even know what a Marxist was."

The 1950s were little better. To Mackay, King Square, at the top of King Street, symbolized everything that was then wrong with Saint John. City Hall bumf now calls King Square a green island of calm in the city's heart, but Mackay remembers it as a gray island of the dying. The old folks who sat there had "a vacant stare. There was an air of hopelessness about them as there sometimes is among elderly Métis, Canadian Indians, and the old in African villages. It was as though they knew they'd all lost, that they were part of some dismal failure. There were an awful lot of them, but now I'm not so conscious of being surrounded by old wrecks. I don't sense that anymore." Saint John, it had turned out, was not such a bad spot for a man with a vigorous mind to have his office, "and the physical rebirth of the city has helped tremendously."

Another man who remembers Saint John well before its physical rebirth is Arthur Doyle, political historian and alumni director for U.N.B. A wide-smiling fellow with a lean face, Doyle is a quintessential Maritimer in three respects. He dotes on gossip, especially political gossip, and thinks it's fine that "Maritimers are really nosy as hell." Second, he loves to spin yarns. Third, he'd choose New Brunswick if God gave him the following choice: to live in Calgary on a million dollars a year for the rest of his life, coming Down Home only for short visits, or to live in New Brunswick till he dies, earning just enough money to enable him to get by. Doyle's U.N.B. job keeps him in Fredericton, "but my roots and soul are in Saint John," and he regularly goes home. As a teenager, "I was always trying to get a tan, but now I love the fog."

In the early fifties, the mouldering, soot-caked buildings of old Saint John seemed as changeless as gravestones. Doyle's father, a plumber who'd somehow prospered in real estate, told the boy that the man who beat the odds by making money in Saint John did not build a fine new house. He bought a fine old house. "You *bought* one of *these* houses," Arthur Doyle explained. He himself lived till he was four in a house built in 1834, with a stone fireplace in the basement, a house that was still standing in 1987. He grew up in a place built in 1878. It had curved bannisters, high ceilings, double parlours, and four fireplaces.

Doyle remembers his father saying, "Saint John is the only city in Canada where there hasn't been a single significant change in fifty years. The same factories that you see here now were here at the turn of the century, and the foundries, the waterfront, the docks, the warehouses, the office buildings on Prince William Street, they're all here, exactly as they were then. It is as if the clock stopped in 1900 and has remained stopped ever since." Among the cities of the Maritimes, Saint John was the most dramatic symbol of the Golden Age that was lost forever. It was an antique that still worked, but just barely.

*   *   *

By the 1760s, French authority was finished in North America, and the Saint John River and harbour were safe for exploitation by British colonials. Simonds, Hazen, and White, hustlers from Massachusetts, moved fast to set up a trading operation at the river mouth. Exporting beaver pelts and pickled fish, trading boards and shingles for West Indian rum and molasses, and ferrying goods for pioneers up and down the river, the company had ten good years. It was a harbinger of the city's economy. Saint John would always thrive and languish as its foreign trade thrived and languished. Its commercial health would always depend on laws passed, trade decisions reached, and wars declared in distant capitals.

The American Revolution throttled the business of Simonds, Hazen, and White. They had chosen the side of loyalty, and rebel forces raided their little settlement, burned the local fort, and briefly imprisoned William Hazen and James White. In 1778, however, the British put a stop to the Patriots' bullying by erecting Fort Howe and filling it with troops under Major Gilfred Studholme of the Royal Fencible Americans. Fort Howe still offers the finest view in Saint John. It sits at the head of the harbour on a blob of the oldest rock in the Maritimes—limestone formed in North Africa more than a billion years ago and welded to North America by a collision of continents—while far below, ships load potash, conventioneers carouse at Market Square, and cars beetle along Main Street and over the Harbour Bridge.

Studholme was there to greet the Loyalists when they arrived in 1783, cleared the hill that became King Street, pitched tents and crude shelters made of hurricane sails, and started to squabble over land grants and political power. Within one year, he issued nearly two million feet of boards and a million and a half shingles. Within two years, his soldiers were breaking up a club-swinging, rock-throwing, election-day mob outside a King Street tavern and throwing ringleaders in jail.

From even before Saint John's incorporation as Canada's first city on May 18, 1785, it was a town of prickly, fist-shaking losers, people who felt cheated, betrayed, abandoned, and shabbily repaid for everything that their loyalty to the Crown had cost them. A sense of unfairness, a feeling that the British government owed the Loyalists much more than it gave them, festered not only at Saint John but in every Loyalist settlement from Shelburne, Nova Scotia, all the way to Niagara in the west. If Loyalists had anything in common, it was mostly hatred: hatred for the rebels who'd persecuted them, hatred that spawned an anti-Americanism that, among some, has survived even to our own time.

British historian A.L. Rowse met U.N.B. history professor W.S. MacNutt in 1960 and later wrote, "I have run up against the old United Empire Loyalist sentiment against the United States. A Loyalist historian, Highlander MacNutt is quite shocked by my pro-Americanism." MacNutt saw more thuggery than heroism among the patriots, and his opinion did not mellow with age. In the last essay he wrote before he died in 1976—exactly two centuries after the Declaration of Independence—MacNutt had things to say about the rebels that might well have infuriated any American reared to believe in the glory of the revolution:

Gangs of vigilantes, mouthing slogans of liberty . . . moved through the countryside to force compliance on all and sundry. Neutrality could be just as obnoxious as avowed enmity. Plunder became commonplace. . . . Unprotected women and children were . . . stripped of their belongings and driven from their homes. The observation of a Georgian lady that "the scum rose to the top" was applicable everywhere as the badge of a revolutionary carried with it a license to plunder. Bullying and dragooning became normal features of life. Seldom has this systematic terror of the American Revolution been presented in popular accounts . . . Admittedly there was no guillotine, but there is opportunity to speculate on the relative merits of tarring and feathering as against the compulsory and liberal doses of castor oil administered by Mussolini's *squadrone* in Italy.

Though the Loyalists at Saint John had a common loathing for the beastly rebels, it did not unite them. From the moment they arrived, there was a rift between soldiers and civilians. The soldiers had spilled rebel blood, knew they could never go home, and felt their sacrifice was greater than that of any civilian. Moreover, the countryside was a shock to everyone: rocks, humps, swamps, and tangled underbrush cursed the terrain, and the soil was poor. Squabbles erupted over land grants. The first arrivals drew big lots, only to see them split, and split again, with each shipload of Loyalists. Some had expected to move up-river immediately, but since their titles weren't clear, had to linger for months at the river mouth while their savings vanished. In short, the city was born disgruntled, if not outraged.

The oldest part of Saint John is a peninsula. In the 1780s, a barrier of forest and rock stood between Upper Cove, around what's now Market Square, and Lower Cove, farther south. Political attitudes divided the two coves as neatly as spruce and limestone did. Ex-soldiers and dissatisfied businessmen lived in Lower Cove and expected it to become the commercial centre of the city. Upper Cove was home to an instant aristocracy that included the attorney general, solicitor general, other backers of colonial authority, land agents, and town directors who supervised the distribution of lots. Upper Covers managed to hog the best waterfront property, and Lower Covers saw them as crooks. Upper Covers denounced Lower Covers as blackguards who deserved to be hanged and tagged them with the supreme Loyalist insult: rebels.

Though many Saint John Loyalists detested one another, they shared a contempt for John Parr, the governor of Nova Scotia, who lived in Halifax. Before the creation of New Brunswick as a

separate colony in 1784, Parr Town, as old Saint John was first
called, came under his jurisdiction. He was a fat, Irish-born
army officer—hard-drinking, quick-tempered, and resentful of
the way the Loyalists made work for him. "All our disturbances
and disagreements in the province originate at the River St.
John," he complained, "where there are many turbulent Spirits,
who are full of groundless complaints, lies and false representa-
tions, and their Agents replete with gross partialitys." Saint John
would never be free of turbulent spirits.

When New Brunswick got a governor to call its own, he
turned out to be another Irish-born army officer: Thomas
Carleton, an authoritarian who prized order over democracy and
allied himself with the Loyalist élite. The turbulent spirits of
Saint John would long resent him as the man who stole the
status of capital from their city and gave it to Fredericton.
Carleton called an election for the first legislative assembly in
New Brunswick in 1785, and rum-fuelled Lower Coves launched
a polling-day attack on an Upper Coves' hangout on King
Street. It was then that the redcoats came down from Fort Howe
to squelch the riot and jail its leaders.

The Lower Coves won the election but not the power. In a
shameful piece of rigging, an official "scrutiny" disqualified
enough of their votes to guarantee an Upper Cove victory.
Carleton had wanted an assembly of "worthy and respectable
characters," and when uppity Lower Coves complained about
the crooked election results, he and his pet legislators passed
laws to suppress freedom of expression. For the next half-
century, a Loyalist oligarchy, a snotty Family Compact, would
run New Brunswick much as it pleased, and it would run it from
Fredericton. Saint John would not gain the right even to elect
its own mayor till 1853.

It would never enjoy the perks, polish, or pretentiousness of a
capital. Nineteenth-century Fredericton was pleased to call itself
the Celestial City, a reference to heaven drawn from John
Bunyan's *Pilgrim's Progress*. But Saint John dreamed of becoming
the Manchester of America or the Liverpool of America, and as

late as the mid-twentieth century one of its officials was urging it
to emulate Detroit.

From its birth, Saint John would be home to crass "men of
trade." It would be a city of money-men, moguls, merchants,
and manufacturers, of shippers, gamblers, promoters, and
profiteers. It would be a city of industrial might and industrial
decay, of sudden fortunes and sudden turns of poverty, of brief
commercial glory and long commercial calamity. Saint John
would also be a Lunchpail City: home to millworkers and foundry workers, to carpenters, coopers, and cordwainers, to
deckhands, dockhands, and factory hands, to mobs of violent
union men and hordes of Famine Irish. It would be a city of
barrels and barrows, wagons and drays, steam whistles and spewing smokestacks, red lights and Irish cops, hard drinkers and soft
touches. Saint John would be as warm-hearted as it was two-
fisted.

It would also be a city that, like the rioting Lower Covers way
back in the election of 1785, loved to take over its own streets.
In 1914 much of Saint John loathed its streetcar company and
supported the trolleymen who'd gone on strike. Following a
strikers' parade, on a night of what the press called primitive
savagery, a crowd of ten thousand boiled around at the foot of
King Street. Some of those among this "Howling, Frenzied Mob
of Strike Sympathizers" managed to capsize two streetcars, smash
every window in the company offices, knock out the city's electricity by pouring cement in a dynamo, and drive a cavalry
charge back up King as fast as it had come down. Though the
violence horrified respectable Saint John, it was merely an unusual expression of a usual custom.

For Saint John had always loved a parade, and its parades had
long had a habit of turning nasty. It now claims to be the most
Irish city in Canada, and in the mid-1800s it was the scene of
the deadliest clashes between Catholic and Protestant Irish anywhere in the Maritimes. When the Orangemen marched into
the Irish North End on the Glorious Twelfth, everyone expected
bones to splinter and blood to spurt. Even when parades failed to

incite violence, they were loud, spectacular, and witnessed by just about everyone in town. Only a year before the trolleymen's strike, the city's unions organized a huge Labour Day parade to demonstrate working-class solidarity. With bands blaring and banners waving, printers, carpenters, teamsters, plumbers, and other tradesmen marched around town, and thousands of townsfolk lined the streets. Parades were a city tradition, a way for people to show whose side they were on, and when the trolleymen marched, the spectators showed they were on their side by sabotaging company property.

Labour violence was already familiar to Saint John; longshoremen had terrorized scabs as far back as the 1880s. But this was also a city in which even an event as loving as New Year's Eve could turn violent. Rockets zoomed, steamships hooted, bands played, and the crowds *marched*. On New Year's Eve 1910, hundreds of people attacked a streetcar, ripped off a fender, bashed in a headlight, and snapped the trolley pole. Though the vandals were mostly youths, the middle-class bystanders apparently felt that battering a streetcar was an admirable way to welcome 1911, and the company must have been meat-headed not to have foreseen the worse destruction to come. For as historian Robert H. Babcock put it in 1982, "the social and cultural traditions of Saint John were such that collective violence against a widely perceived 'enemy' was by no means unthinkable." This was no Fredericton. It was still the home of turbulent spirits. Saint John would never be sissy, and it would always be, above all else, a seaport.

*   *   *

In the late 1700s, nine tenths of everything New Brunswick imported, including livestock, grain, and flour for Loyalist settlers, flowed through Saint John. Since Britain denied American traders direct access to the British West Indies, Yankee goods also passed through the port. In 1788, just three years after the city's incorporation, it had a fleet of sixty square-riggers for the West Indies trade. Not only in Saint John but also up the river and in nearby Bay of Fundy coves, shipbuilding was beginning to flourish. Saint John exported thousands of barrels of fish each year, as well as furs, deerskins, and masts for the Royal Navy. Still, the little port languished till the early 1800s, when decisions in London, Washington, and Paris enabled it to ride tides of warfare to a bonanza that lasted forty years.

Saint John had much to thank Napoleon for. During the Napoleonic Wars (1803–1815), he choked off England's supply of timber from Baltic countries. A nation without timber would be a nation without ships. For the most crucial raw material in her war for survival, the mother country now turned to her North American colonies, and wood quickly replaced fur as the great staple that moved east across the North Atlantic. The New Brunswick economy became a timber economy, and Saint John revelled in a gigantic share of the trade.

Meanwhile, the Americans, still neutral in 1807, responded to wartime trade blockades in Europe by imposing an embargo on all foreign-bound vessels in U.S. ports, and this, too, spelled profit to Saint John. The embargo enraged New England merchants, who promptly turned to smuggling. To entice Yankees to send cargo to Saint John for trans-shipment, Britain declared it an open port. Now goods from the U.S. bound for overseas flowed into the city, and so did goods from Britain bound for the U.S. To get to Saint John, U.S. trading vessels dodged U.S. warships, but after that, cruisers of the once-reviled Royal Navy escorted them into the harbour.

Smugglers used a motley collection of boats, some as small as canoes, to carry U.S. flour to British New Brunswick and British manufactured goods back to the U.S. Moreover, with respect to trade between New Brunswick and the "enemy" in Maine, the War of 1812 was a Gilbert-and-Sullivan war. Loaded with food, tobacco, cotton, and naval stores—all smuggled out of New England—U.S. vessels dropped into Saint John for "repairs." To carry the goods abroad, the city needed its own ships, and the shipbuilding boom coincided with a house-building boom.

By the 1840s it was clear that the juice that war had injected into the shipbuilding and timber trades had been good to Saint John. Only twenty-five hundred people had lived there in 1803;

now, the population stood at twenty-five thousand. The official-
ly chartered city that had really been a village was now the
biggest town in the Maritimes. Its fleet of locally owned ocean-
going vessels was the biggest in all British North America, and
in 1841 Saint John accounted for a fat proportion of the more
than 800,000 shiploads of timber that the northern colonies sent
to Britain.

But if no one yet foresaw the death of the age of wooden ships,
Saint John already knew that timber exports were a shaky foundation for its future. The trade went in cycles. It mushroomed
and collapsed again and again, and each collapse ruined merchants and threw lumbermen and mill hands out of work. No
city was more aware of the crucial protection Britain granted to
commerce in colonial timber, nor more terrified of free trade.
The British Commons rejected proposed changes in the
preferential timber duties in 1830, and the moment Saint John
got the news, the people celebrated in the streets and lit a huge
bonfire in King Square.

If the timber business made Saint John a boom-and-bust sort
of town, it also bred a boom-and-bust sort of man. No one has
described the lumbermen of early New Brunswick better than
Donald Creighton in *The Dominion of The North*:

> With their dislike of the drab, continuous work of the farm, their
> impatience at the puritanical restraints of society, their love of rum,
> of gaudy finery, of uproarious companionship, the lumbermen were
> the *coureurs-de-bois* of the nineteenth century; and they swaggered
> about the streets of Saint John with the same jaunty and insolent
> assurance that the returned fur traders had once shown in
> Montreal. . . . [They] came to represent freedom, and quick
> wealth, and rich and varied experience for the entire community.
> In the autumn they drew the restless young farmers' sons away to
> the camps; and in the spring they brought their easy-going, hard-
> drinking standards to the ports.

These profane swashbucklers from the deep woods, who enlivened the streets of Saint John every summer for decades, were
New Brunswick prototypes. "I have a theory," says former U.N.B.

president Colin Mackay. "It's that, more so than Nova Scotians, New Brunswickers have a sense of humour. We are quite different, and it was the timber trade that made us different. Much more than Nova Scotia, we've been a boom-and-bust economy. So we make $100,000, spend $200,000, and end up in jail, or flee to the United States. New Brunswick lawyers are forever absconding." At least some New Brunswick businessmen were less discreet and more flamboyant than Down Home tycoons are today.

"Look at Saint John," Mackay continued. "Boom and bust. Bust and boom. My grandfather lived in a magnificent home in Saint John. It had mahogany doors, heavy mouldings, the whole works. A MacLeod had built it, but he went bust before he got a chance to live in it. So my grandfather picked it up for $12,000. This sort of thing didn't happen in Nova Scotia. When men made quick money in New Brunswick, they wanted to show it off while they still had it, and if you couldn't build a bigger home than your neighbour, then you tacked on a bigger verandah. A lot of these men were cheery, amusing rascals. Beaverbrook comes out of that same mould. You know, even Mr. K.C. Irving can be very amusing at times. He's a strange man, but he has a sense of humour most people don't know about. . . . Anyway, the thing to remember about the New Brunswicker is that he knows, from a young age, that life is a joke."

Life was no joke to the Irish who came to Saint John in the mid-1840s, and their arrival was no joke to the port. Its condition was feeble. A disastrous fire, probably set by a turbulent spirit, had destroyed much of the town in 1841. Moreover, Britain had at last turned toward free trade, dismantled preferential duties on colonial timber and returned to Baltic markets. As if this weren't dreadful enough for Saint John, slumps in international trade also sapped its economy. In one of the earliest waves of the Maritime exodus, skilled workmen went west by the hundreds. The city was therefore ill prepared for the greatest wave of immigration in its history. It was already home to thousands of Protestant Irish—Loyalists and their descendants were now a minority—but then came the Famine Irish, mostly

Catholic, mostly poor, thousands of them diseased, emaciated, half-starving, or dying.

Their first stop in the New World was Partridge Island, the quarantine station that sat at the mouth of the harbour, often smothered in bone-chilling fog. Partridge Island would later be known as the Ellis Island of Canada, and its most zealous lover in 1987 was Harold E. Wright. A bouncy, bespectacled history buff, in his early thirties, Wright told me he'd collected 33,000 items of historical interest out there. His obsession with the island is so powerful that in the Christmas season he chooses to live there as a substitute for the regular keeper of the lighthouse. His girlfriend isn't exactly a Partridge Island artifact, but her grandfather had been a Partridge Island lightkeeper. Wright's research has revealed some gruesome facts. Between May 2 and November 1, 1847, the quarantine station's "most infamous years," nearly fifteen thousand Irish landed in New Brunswick, and some twelve hundred died on Partridge Island and in Saint John. On June 21 no fewer than twenty-five hundred were in quarantine; island hospitals could accommodate only two hundred. The military sent tents, but most of the immigrants were too weak to erect them. The dying lay on bare ground, and rain quickly exposed hastily buried corpses.

The tide of Irish to New Brunswick was so huge that Lieutenant-Governor William Colebrooke urged Britain to "stay the accumulating torrent." Though thousands of Irish moved inland, thousands more lingered in the depressed port. The last thing the established poor wanted in Saint John was an invasion of new poor. The city was so hard-up it often couldn't afford to light its street lamps, and up and down its dark, poverty-struck neighbourhoods, crime and religious hatred flourished together. The Irish Catholic ghettos of the Portland wharf district and York Point were clutters of shabby tenements, so filthy and crowded they might have shocked even a Charles Dickens, and the badly trained police faced a surge of muggings, beatings, and robberies. Smart people never entered those neighbourhoods, but gangs of armed Orangemen did. On the Glorious Twelfth in

1849, at least a dozen men died in street warfare between Catholic and Protestant Irish. Better times ahead would mellow religious differences, and Saint John was now on the threshold of its brief Golden Age.

*   *   *

An awkward mutt of a ship hit the water for the first time at Marsh Creek, Saint John, in 1851. One observer called her "square as a brick fore and aft, with a bow like a bulldog." Thirty-eight feet amidships, she was spectacularly beamy. Her keel was 184 feet long, and she looked more like a gigantic garbage box than a swift vessel. Some said her timbers were merely pieces of hackmatack that had been lying around James Smith's shipyard after the completion of real ships. Others sneered that she was "James Smith's folly." She certainly behaved that way at her launching. Like a monster duck that did not take to water, she initially refused to slide down the ways. Then, before anyone got a line on her, she rushed into the water, shot across the waves, and embedded herself in mud. As the tide fell, she slumped over on one side, and in the two weeks that it took workmen to free her, her weight twisted her keel. The people of Saint John thought she was hilarious, but they soon learned to adore her. She turned out to be the biggest, fastest, and most famous clipper packet in the world. She was the *Marco Polo*, and though she spent most of her life carrying passengers and cargo for owners in Liverpool, she remained a fabulous advertisement for shipbuilding in Saint John.

Ships usually took between a hundred and a hundred and twenty days to sail from Liverpool to Australia, but the *Marco Polo*, on her first voyage Down Under, made the run in sixty-eight days. She carried 950 passengers, thirty crew, and thirty working their passage. She returned to Liverpool in seventy-four days, sailing up the Mersey River with a sensational banner strung between her biggest masts. It said: "The World's Fastest Ship." By 1854 the boast of her owners, James Baines and Company, was: "Hell or Australia in Sixty Days." Over the next decade, she carried thousands upon thousands of British on emigrant runs to Australia, and on one of these voyages, as late as the 1860s, she beat the steamer *Great Britain* by more than a week. The years of the *Marco Polo's* glory were precisely the years of Saint John's glory.

The city was cocky at mid-century. In all of British North America, only Montreal and Quebec City had bigger populations. With more than thirty-one thousand people in 1851, Saint John was bigger than Halifax, bigger even than Toronto. Its shipbuilders were about to prove themselves the most dynamic in the colonies, and its merchants dreamed of being kingpins in a trading empire stretching around the world.

The suspension bridge opened in 1853. One hundred feet above the Reversing Falls, it soared across to the west bank. A marvel of contemporary engineering, it was also a statement of progress, a tangible promise that Saint John would move onward and ever upward, and the model for illustrations for promotional schemes for decades to come. Also in 1853, five thousand tradesmen and others paraded through town to celebrate the turning of the sod for the ambitiously named European and North American Railway. The festivities were more lavish than any the city had ever known. The parade was a mile and a half long, and one of the horse-drawn floats was a small fully rigged clipper ship. Linking Saint John to the Gulf of St. Lawrence at Shediac, New Brunswick, the railway would bankrupt the company that built it and dump debt on the provincial government; but no one knew that when the lieutenant-governor's wife was turning the sod to the accompaniment of a seventy-gun salute.

Not railways, but shipbuilding and international trade were the foundations for a wave of prosperity in the port, and their thriving was once again the gift of distant turmoil. The Australian and California gold rushes, along with the Crimean War, stimulated world trade in the 1850s and boosted shipbuilding. The Civil War and trade reciprocity with the U.S. kept the local economy bubbling in the 1860s. Rising freight rates fattened bank accounts as cargo-laden Saint John vessels slipped past Partridge Island and headed out for British, European, American, and West Indian ports. As early as 1851, Saint John boasted fifteen saw mills, employing more than five hundred men, and the first cargo of every Saint John vessel was Saint John lumber. During the 1850s and 1860s, a dozen local ship-yards launched more than two thousand wooden sailing vessels. In the best years, shipbuilding employed more than five thousand men and boys. Old-timers would later recall that you could get a ship rigged and outfitted in Saint John during its Golden Age as easily as you could buy a man's suit. More than eight hundred vessels listed Saint John as their port of registry in 1874, and local boosters declared that the fleet Saint John owned was three times bigger and costlier than the Spanish Armada had been.

By 1867, when Canada was born, Saint John was not only a city of shipbuilding and trade; it was also one of the new nation's hives of manufacturing. Visitors called it a pushy, commercial town that favoured bluntness over pretentiousness. It lacked courtliness and gentility. "The Halifax merchant is often indo-lent, always easy," a reporter for the *British Colonist* wrote in 1864. "The Saint Johnian is eager, ardent, and untiring. He gives all his life up to business. He opens his shop or his office at an early hour, he risks more, speculates more, loses more, makes more; he fails in business oftener, but after failure he always manages to rise again and make another fortune."

In 1867 Saint John celebrated its wealth by erecting what is still the finest market building in Atlantic Canada. The City Market is 394 feet long and 80 feet wide. It is open, roomy, friendly, generous, a late flowering of the Golden Age, and a working symbol of the city's history and character. It operates under a royal charter. Its purpose is commerce, and its construc-tion is the work of shipbuilders. The hand-hewn roof timbers form perfect half-circles. Together, they look like a wooden ship under construction, except that she's upside-down and a city block long. Twenty trusses and forty knees support the roof, all dovetailed, and fastened with wooden pegs. Each year, some two million shoppers pass between the iron gates and wander among rows of merchant stalls on the indoor street.

You can buy antiques, junk, wood carvings, sweaters, firewood, Christmas trees, and Kung-Fu books in the market, but most people go there for food. You can buy fresh food from New Brunswick and exotic food from the far side of the world: lychees in syrup from the Orient, maple syrup from Albert County, the finest olives from the Mediterranean, the finest honey from the valley of the Saint John River, bananas and banana bread, Cheshire and Cheddar, kiwi fruit and rhubarb, grape leaves and beet greens, knockwurst and swordfish, California plums and Bay of Fundy scallops, and, in season, local asparagus, squash, fiddleheads, turnips, new potatoes, tomato plants. . . . Fish or fowl, brown eggs or red sirloin, cold cuts or hot peppers, sauerkraut or succotash, the City Market has it. It's open six days a week, and if I lived in Saint John, that's where I'd go for all my groceries.

The market, however, is more than a market. It's also a club. John G.L. (Lorne) Enright, deputy market clerk, says a gang of retired lawyers, judges, businessmen, and sea captains hangs out there. "Their wives send them here for a pound of hamburger," Enright says, "and it takes them all day. They run into their friends and solve world problems." Moreover, knowledgeable celebrities have always visited the market. One of its merchants regularly shipped local cheese to Lord Beaverbrook in London, and old-timers insist that, during a royal visit, the future King Edward VIII kept slipping out of his suite in a nearby hotel to stroll by himself in the market. "Pierre Trudeau, Ed Broadbent, Joe Clark, they've all been here," Enright boasts.

An affable, ruddy, curly-headed fellow in his mid-fifties, Enright is the captain of the market. His bridge is a cabin that's high above the indoor street at its eastern end and overlooks flags and food right down to the western gates. The office is like a hockey broadcaster's gondola, and it's so small two people can barely sit in it without bumping knees. But Enright loves it in there. His forebears were Irish, like those of more than half the people of Saint John, and it's right that a fellow who describes himself as "pure Irishman" should be running a place that's such an essential part of the city's flavour. He remembers coming to the market with his parents when he was four, and at twelve "I worked here with Mrs. Peacock in the centre aisle, delivering flowers. Just about every kid in the city worked here. . . . Well, in 1966, I was appointed deputy market clerk. [The clerk is the mayor, but that's a legal nicety.] I've spent my life in the market, and there's no other place I've ever wanted to work."

The heads of a moose and the last caribou shot in New Brunswick sit on the roof of his office because "I'm supposed to be looking after them for a guy I know." There's a big, brass bell up there, too. To begin and end the day's business, Enright opens a window, reaches out for a rope, and yanks it to ring the bell. But on Monday, February 2, 1976, he did an unusual thing. He rang the bell to clear the building shortly after lunch. The Ground Hog Storm was galloping lickety-split off the ocean and toward the city. Since the market was now exactly one century old, Enright wasn't sure how safe it would be. When the storm struck, he was walking around in there by himself. "You could hear everything creaking all over the place," he recalls, "and I kept looking up at the roof. When I went outside later, my car was lifting off the pavement. It was a '71 Ford, with a V-eight engine. The storm was that strong. But we only lost a chimney here. The market, she stood it. She stood all the storms, just like she stood the fire when she was one year old."

No Canadian city has ever suffered a fire as devastating as the holocaust that wrecked the heart of Saint John on the night of June 20, 1877. The *Marco Polo* would sail on till breaking up on the coast of Prince Edward Island six years later, and the townsfolk would recover their cockiness for a little while; but later, the great fire would be remembered as the curtain that closed on the Golden Age of old Saint John.

*   *   *

Saint John was a wooden city, and in June 1877 it was a *dry* wooden city. By Wednesday the 20th, when the temperature nudged 80°F, the town had basked in six straight weeks of strangely sunny weather, and the millions of shingles that sheathed its buildings were like tinder awaiting a match. Hay and straw filled livery stables and barns. Warehouses stored lumber, tar, canvas, clothing, gunpowder, and oil. The head of the harbour was a warren of skinny alleys and rickety fences that ran among sawmills, tenements, shacks, sheds, and shanties. That's where the fire started, at York Point in an Irish ghetto near the northern boundary of the city. Sparks from a lumber mill ignited a pile of hay shortly after 2:00 P.M., and a stiff wind from the northwest, unusual in June, drove the fire to Market Square and from there all over the Saint John peninsula.

The fire tore southeast, gobbling up block after block after block. It leapt across streets, raced among schooners, and generated such intense heat that some houses, even before the main blaze reached them, just burst into flames. Sucking up air, the firestorm created a terrifying wail. Along the harbourfront, the blaze stopped only when it reached the water and had nothing left to demolish. On Sunday, June 24, the *Saint John News* contemplated the devastation inflicted by "the devouring element," "the fire fiend," and "the red-eyed monarch":

> A pile of broken mortar-marked bricks, a jagged section of brick wall, a stone basement with a heap of ashes within, or a chimney standing like a sentinel in the desert, is all that remains of thousands of homes in which men, women and children lived, of factories in which hundreds earned their daily bread, of churches in which the people worshipped, of shops in which trade was carried on. Ruin to left of us, ruin to right of us, ruin in front and rear, ruin everywhere. The head aches, the heart swells, the bosom heaves, the eyes fill with tears and refuse to gaze on the evidence of the misery of twenty thousand people. Few such scenes have ever been witnessed.

The fire killed eighteen people and injured dozens more. The *News* sounded almost boastful about it. Under the headline "OUR GREAT FIRE," the paper declared on June 22: "Two Thirds

of the City in Ruins" and "Four Fifths of the Property Destroyed." Damage was estimated at $28 million, a gigantic
amount in the 1870s, and insurance covered scarcely a quarter of
it. Historians figure the inferno wiped out sixteen hundred
buildings. The Customs house, city hall, post office, churches,
banks, businesses, docks, warehouses, factories, and hundreds of
houses all disappeared within ten hours.

Not three days after the fire died, however, and while smoke
still rose from the rubble, workmen were clearing the streets,
property owners were tidying up their land in preparation for
construction, and a Mr. Lewis, a blacksmith, had already erected
a frame for his new house. Lumber was flowing into town, and a
new city — a city of brick, stone, wider streets, and tougher fire
regulations — was about to rise from the wreckage. More than a
century later, Saint John boosters would brag about Market
Square, the tasteful renovation of the waterfront, and the
smartening-up of nearby streets, and they'd lay claim to "the
most dramatic comeback of any downtown in Canada." But the
modern comeback, satisfying as it has been, was not as dramatic
as the Victorian comeback. In the first year after the fire, Saint
John erected no fewer than thirteen hundred buildings, and
hundreds more went up in the year after that.

The rebuilding of old Saint John was glorious evidence of the
city's wealth, resilience, and confidence, but it was also like laying a red carpet for a monarch who never showed up. Saint John
proved its prosperity just when it had begun to lose it. The
miraculous rebirth drained the city of capital that might have
helped it to cope with cruel economic and technological
changes. Historians still argue over the precise mix of circumstances that shoved the city into its decline, but a worldwide
depression shrank lumber markets in the 1870s, and even before
the fire, unemployment ravished parts of the city, and the exodus was underway. Steel ships and steel rails conquered wooden
ships and canvas sails. After Confederation, Saint John found
itself on the edge of a political and economic system that looked
inward and westward, not out to sea. Power lay in central
Canada, and local industries succumbed to ruthless and better-

financed competitors from Montreal and Toronto. The federally financed Intercolonial Railway bypassed western New Brunswick, sucked trade away from Saint John, and favoured Halifax. In the first five months of 1880, thirty local businesses rolled over and died. Some suggest that if Saint John was a boom-and-bust city, this bust lasted right down till the 1960s.

But the city stagnated in pieces, not overnight, and market conditions sometimes kicked life back into its industries. On June 30, 1967, to celebrate Canada's hundredth birthday, the Saint John *Telegraph-Journal* published the boyhood memories of sixty-five-year-old Harrison MacElwaine. The Saint John of just before World War One, he recalled, was far from lethargic. Indeed, it was a boy's heaven of industry, street life, and chances to make mischief. He and his buddies sneaked into a tannery, a lime kiln, a grist mill, cotton mills, jute mills, saw mills, brickyards, shipyards, and factories that made soap, shoes, nails, axes, and locomotives. In the streets they marvelled at a bear who waltzed for money and another bear who wrestled every man who paid his owner a dime. The boys followed Italian organ grinders with trained monkeys, the iceman with his yellow wagon, clothes-hawkers who wandered the streets with mountains of coats and suits on their shoulders, a fabulous one-man band, a medicine man who flogged Doctor Banyan's Elixir, and a knife-sharpener who sometimes deigned to put a razor's edge on the boys' jackknives. The urchins of Saint John harassed door-to-door fish and fruit peddlers, waylaid skinflint junkmen, gorged on molasses that leaked from Barbadian puncheons on the docks, set illegal street fires to celebrate neighbourhood weddings, and rode horse-drawn sleighs in winter, paddlewheel steamers in summer, and open trolleycars to Seaside Park.

They heard military bands in King Square and German bands on street corners. They watched Labour Day parades, mile-long circus parades, jugglers and dancers in tents, careering horse-drawn fire engines, ship launchings, shuffling prison chain gangs, dog fights to the death, and when the Irish cops dragged suspects from taverns, fights that made saloon brawls on television half a century later look like tussles among pantywaists.

MacElwaine's boyhood chums haunted the City Market, a hobo jungle, a gypsy encampment, blacksmiths' shops, livery stables, sail lofts, the masted harbour, and when they were sly enough, even saloons full of hard-working, hard-drinking, open-handed dockworkers, teamsters, foundry workers, factory hands, and shipyard blokes.

"It was in the saloons, especially the one on Water Street," MacElwaine wrote, "that I found the men with the sheath knives on their hips, the sailors, the hardy adventurers of the strange places of the world, brawny, hairy-chested rovers of the Seven Seas, hoisting a foot to the brass rail to lean on the long bar in good fellowship and talk casually of Singapore or Zanzibar or Australia, of shipwrecks and sealing and whaling, of storms at sea and this ship and that, and the strange sea monsters they had encountered. Their very clothing brought the salty tang of the sea to my nostrils as I crouched below the level of the bar."

*   *   *

As flack for the Greatest Little City in the East, Joel Levesque works for Mayor Elsie Wayne, and along with the voters of Saint John, he sees her as the greatest little cheerleader in the east. After the famous fire, a woman wrote to a local newspaper to argue that what Saint John really needed was a woman mayor, and in 1983, 106 years later, the city finally got one. With Levesque at her side in her eighth-floor corner office, which offered a sweeping view of the harbour, Her Worship told me exactly why the little city below was so great. Levesque, who had placed her third — behind The People and The New Downtown — on his list of "50 Great Things About Saint John," murmured his endorsement of her opinions, and every once in a while dropped a fact she'd forgotten to brag about. An earnest guy in his thirties, Levesque had a trim dark moustache, pale cheeks, baggy knees in his gray suit-pants, and a love of Saint John that seemed untinged by public-relations phoniness.

Mayor Wayne was fifty-five, and her hair was short, straight, and as white as the teeth in her generous smile. Her glasses were thick, and the lens bevelled at the edges. The temples were gold, and her gold earrings held red stones. She wore a dark blue suit and a white blouse with a high collar. She was all business, all crispness, all pride in her city. Remembering 1985, Saint John's bicentennial, she said, "Our slogan was 'We're two hundred years proud,' and the people *were* proud. They were never proud before." Levesque said, "We used to be a dirty, dull, gray little city. The rest of the world knocked Saint John, and Saint John agreed. All that's changed." Describing the new spirit of the townsfolk, Wayne talked as though she had uncorked a magnum of champagne, or released a genie: "It had been capped for so long. Now it was released."

* * *

K.C. Irving, eighty-eight in 1987, was twenty-second on Levesque's list of great things about Saint John, but on lists of the richest men in North America he invariably hovers among the top ten. Business journalists calculate that the empire he founded and still owns includes roughly four hundred companies, employs 25,000 people, and reaps $2 billion a year in sales. Estimates of Irving assets have run as high as $8 billion, but no outsider can be precise. Neither K.C. Irving nor any of his sons — James K., Arthur L., and John E. — ever releases such figures. Nor does anyone else in the Irving clan or management gang.

Irving owns fleets of trucks, buses, coastal vessels, and ocean-going ships; newspapers and broadcasting companies; pulp and paper mills; and vast tracts of New Brunswick forest. Thousands of Irving gas stations sell Irving products in eastern Canada. Off Saint John, Irving tankers hook up to an Irving deep-water terminal — the first of its kind in the Western Hemisphere — and then an Irving pipeline brings the crude oil ashore to an Irving tank farm, where it awaits its turn to enter the Irving oil refinery, the biggest in Canada. Just above the Reversing Falls, steam, smoke, and fumes come tumbling out of a dozen chimneys at an Irving pulp mill that dominates the view of the river and sometimes the smell of the city. As Levesque drove me across the bridge over the falls and into town, he rhymed off the names of all the Irving-owned industries and properties we passed. He did this for hundreds of yards, and later, as we drove out Bayside Drive toward the east side of the outer harbour, he nodded at the Courtenay Bay neighbourhood, where seven shipyards had flourished more than a century before and the *Marco Polo* had endured her comical launching, and he reverently announced, "This whole forebay, it's all Irving." After that we passed Irving's Saint John Dry Dock, and Irving's Saint John Shipbuilding, prime contractor for a multibillion-dollar programme to build frigates for the Canadian navy. Compared to K.C. Irving, I thought, J.R. Ewing of "Dallas" is a two-bit hustler.

Saint John, Levesque told me, was really "Irvingtown," and not just because Irving industries dominated the city economy. It was also because K.C. Irving had chosen Saint John as headquarters for Irving operations far beyond the borders of New Brunswick. The Irving men were Saint John men. No, they were not models of corporate citizenship; their industries had made air putrid and rivers scummy. But if a Come From Away were so bold as to complain about the stink from the Irving pulp mill, a local might rebuke him with, "Yeah, but it's the smell of money." If the stranger continued to badmouth the Irvings, Levesque said, "he might get a knuckle sandwich."

Everyone in Saint John, he continued, "either works for Irving, or once worked for Irving, or has a relative who works for Irving." Mayor Wayne's father, Paxton Fairweather, had managed K.C. Irving's first gas station in Shediac, New Brunswick. Levesque, as a teenager, had worked part-time at a busy Irving station in central Saint John, and every Christmas the mighty K.C. himself — lean, lanky, bald, and bony — had dropped round in his blue Ford, with Mrs. Irving at his side, to offer season's greetings to "the boys." On one Christmas Eve, he showed up while the station's phone was ringing. The call was from a man whose car was stuck in snow and ice at a church more than two miles away. Could someone please send a tow truck? Levesque started to explain that the station had no truck, but Irving interrupted him to find out what was going on. Then, at seventy years of age, one of the richest men in the world observed Christmas Eve by paying cash to one of his own gas stations for two bags of road salt, putting them in his trunk, and driving through a blizzard to help free a stranger's car. "You can bet that fellow became a lifelong Irving customer," Levesque said. "You know, just about everyone in Saint John has at least one K.C. Irving story like that."

*　*　*

"There's something so familiar here," my wife, Penny, said. "What *is* it?" We were strolling around on streets that Loyalists had named more than two centuries before: Queen, Princess, Prince William, Duke, Charlotte, Mecklenberg, Germain, Carmarthen, Pitt, Leinster, Orange. . . . Surely we had seen these musty buildings before — but where? Was it in an old photograph, a book about Victorian architecture, a movie about nineteenth-century Boston? Nearly all these houses, shops, and office buildings had arisen together during the amazing building boom that followed the fire, and now, 110 years after the last ember had died, Penny and I explored the neighbourhood, and we smelled something that was neither fire, fish, fog, nor the Irving pulp mill up the river. It was our own childhood in the Toronto of forty years before, a Toronto in which milk, bread, and junkmen still moved around town aboard horse-drawn wagons.

A native of Saint John might find it neither flattering nor credible that in 1987 the city reminded us of Hog Town in 1947, but this part of town — unlike other Down Home cities, and exactly like Toronto in the glory days of its pro hockey team after World War Two — was mostly made of brick and stone. That had been the lesson of the fire. I have never been able to see the faded lettering of a commercial message, hand-painted on a brick wall, without remembering the bicycles, ball games, knee-scabs, and Orange Crush bottles of my Toronto boyhood. Now, on the rosy walls of old Saint John, I could make out "Shamrock Plug Tobacco," "John Foster, Family Groceries," and "Delicious Refreshing Coca-Cola."

There was something old-fangled about the window displays of the smokeshops and corner groceries. The proprietors had jammed in so many packages of goods, with different labels, that the displays looked like quilts or jigsaw puzzles. Some were dusty, as though they'd been pieced together when your mother was still buying Rinso. Then there were the children in the streets. When Penny and I were kids, the automobile had certainly arrived in Toronto, but it had not yet conquered the streets, where the odd parked car was still an intrusion on children's territory. It got in the way of games. Streets, lanes, and driveways were built for vehicles, but they *belonged* to youngsters. Now, on this warm sleepy Sunday evening in June, children of old Saint John were playing a kind of baseball on Queen Street, before it sloped down to Courtenay Bay. They were swinging like Tarzan out toward Sydney Street on a rope strung from a branch in Queen Square, and they were hiding and pouncing on one another, like cats, in back alleys, doorways, and staircase cubbyholes. They were playing everywhere except in playgrounds, and that's how life had once been for us kids in Toronto, too.

But the neighbourhood was intriguing for reasons that had nothing to do with our memories. For this was where the big boys had once worked and lived and kept their families. It was home to bankers, insurance-company owners, lumber magnates, an early oil tycoon, and owners of fleets of trading vessels. Men who manufactured beer, biscuits, brass, and leather goods resided in this part of town. So did sea captains, importers, exporters, grocers, wholesalers, building contractors, hardware merchants, surgeons, lawyers, politicians, a printer and publisher, a photographer, a druggist, a manufacturer of gravestones, and New Brunswick's first professional undertaker. Some of these characters built houses not just as dwellings but as ads for their wealth and individuality. They imported architects from Boston — which is why the brick row houses on Germain Street remind some of Beacon Hill — and from New York as well. They insisted on the finest stained glass; family crests in terra cotta; family initials carved in stone above front doors, or etched in door glass; patterns of fruit and flowers worked into exterior stone work; and at one house, rooftop gargoyles that spat rainwater.

The main business thoroughfare in the nineteenth century was Prince William Street, and here, too, the burghers of Saint John made playful use of stone to celebrate the city's prosperity. At Chubb's Corner, for instance, a row of stone faces gazed down at us from above the third-floor windows, and we learned later that these were probably likenesses of the workmen who put up the building, of the mayor of the day, and of Mr. Chubb himself. A local paper had hoped "no more of our buildings will be adorned by such buffoonery." But more than a century later, clusters of stone grapes decorate the entrance to what was once a liquor shop; the faces of two Indians and of Mercury, god of commerce, stare at the street from what was once the post office; and a bunch of gargoyles, one of them frozen in the act of spewing coins, leers at passersby from what was once a Bank of Nova Scotia.

In the corner of an old folks home that used to be the big and beloved Admiral Beatty Hotel, we found the Creole Café. Our window overlooked King Square, with its sidewalks in the pattern of a giant Union Jack. A sound system brought us jazz by Louis Armstrong, and we ate Cajun chicken wings, Cajun barbecued ribs, and Toulouse St. Gumbo.

By straining a bit, I found historical irony in our dinner. If men like Admiral Beatty, who served under the Union Jack, had not exiled the poor Acadians in the 1750s, none of them would have ended up in Louisiana where they perfected Cajun cooking; and if American enemies of the Union Jack had not exiled the poor Loyalists nearly three decades later, there might never have been a Saint John in which to explore the architectural legacy of a Victorian heyday by the sea and find such satisfying surprises as the Creole Café. The architectural legacy survives because of another irony. So much of what was once affluent Saint John remains because, for more than half a century, Saint John was not affluent. The decay of commerce meant the preservation of buildings; progress got no chance to smash down character.

On our last day in town, we were snooping around Market Square in cold rain when nastiness erupted at Loyalist Plaza. Since delegates were arriving at the nearby harbourfront hotel for a convention of the Canadian Nuclear Association, the Conservation Council of New Brunswick had organized a demonstration to oppose construction of a second nuclear power plant at Point Lepreau. More than two hundred people had gathered to wave placards, listen to speeches by anti-nuclear leaders from away, and release hundreds of helium-filled "No to Lepreau" balloons. But job-hungry trade unionists, who dislike enemies of construction projects, launched guerrilla warfare on the crowd.

A hundred-odd hardhats charged the gazebo where the speakers had gathered. The assault force tore placards from the hands of demonstrators, jabbed the balloons with knives, pens, and lighted cigarettes, yanked microphone wires, and drowned out speeches by chanting "Yes to Lepreau" and "Go home, hippies." No one was hurt. The violence was not so bad that the redcoats had to come down from Fort Howe to restore order. Yet it seemed appropriate that, on our last day in the once and future port, turbulent spirits were again on the loose.

8

FREDERICTON: PAMPERED PET OF OLD NEW BRUNSWICK

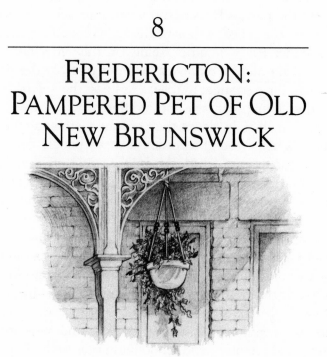

It is the day of rest, and the summer morning is as flawless as an egg. With my belly full of French toast and sausages, I stroll out of the Lord Beaverbrook Hotel and straight into the orderly magic of the part of Fredericton where the rich folks live. The people are still in bed, or maybe they're in church. Scarcely a car moves under the voluminous elms on the sun-splattered avenues, and no mower buzzes or laughter rings in the park-sized backyards. I'm a stranger in town. As I pass the porches of wooden castles, plump cats eye me indifferently, roll over, stretch, and, yawning hugely, flaunt their creamy teeth and pink, pointy tongues. When I round a corner, a yappy poodle berates me. I hear the twittering of little birds, the wind off the river as it shuffles high leaves, and a solitary Sabbath-breaker at work on his house with a hammer. But that's all. Fredericton was "an old man dozing by the river," Bruce Hutchison wrote in the 1940s. On such a morning, nothing seems to have changed.

On riverside land, bowling-green flat, this neighbourhood seems to be infested by the spirits of its long-gone luminaries: stalwarts of the high church, exploiters of high sinecures, and stars of high education; bishops, knights, and lieutenant-governors; merchants, colonels, lawyers, and surgeons; poets, painters, and premiers; and schoolmasters as well, along with an affluent whoremaster or two. Most were Loyalists, descendants of Loyalists, lovers of the Union Jack, and haters of the Yankee rabble. Their houses stand as monuments to their individuality, and in some cases, their eccentricity. If the New Town in Edinburgh is the home of splendid stone uniformity, Fredericton is the home of splendid wooden variety. For a long time now, it has been pleased to call itself the City of Stately Elms, but if disease ever takes the elms, the town might try the Gingerbread Capital of Canada.

The gingerbread is anything but drab. Shingles, clapboard, doors, trim, and shutters wear not only the traditional white and black, and white and forest green, but also the colours of cream, burgundy, chocolate, maple sugar, mushrooms, *crème caramel*, fiddleheads, snow peas, wax beans, the dark sliding river, and this morning's limpid sky. I think of wedding cakes and ice cream. Some of the houses sport brass coachlamps at their doors, wrought-iron railings, hanging flowerpots on their verandahs, trellises for roses, and a boat in the backyard. Ah, the gardens! What lush messes some of them are.

Mary Pratt remembers the gardening philosophy of old Fredericton. A superior artist, she and her husband Christopher Pratt, another celebrated painter, have lived for a quarter-century at the mouth of the Salmonier River, St. Mary's Bay, Newfoundland. Her husband and her four children are Newfoundlanders, raised in the land of fog, bog, and barrens; but St. Mary's Bay, whatever its virtues, is not the valley of the Saint John River, and part of Mary Pratt is forever Frederictonian. Born Mary West, the daughter of a Tory lawyer who became the province's attorney general and a judge, she grew up on the right side of the river, here on the streets I'm now wandering in these minutes before the churches release their worshippers. She wrote to me recently, and as a painter, she recalled the neighbourhood in colours and patterns:

"Whenever I think of Fredericton, I see its sidewalks, pink; its roads, purple; and its lawns, flat and bluish-green." Lawns were "rolled and shorn with impressive regularity." Hedges were clipped neatly, but not exotically. "No topiary birds or teacups. There were some of these oddities in a little park in Fredericton Junction, and they were considered 'not quite nice.' In fact, gardening was kept within the limits of the possible, and any poor Johnny-come-lately who didn't understand that flowers must seem to grow in clumps — scattering themselves discreetly under trees and apparently with wild abandon in beds and borders, artlessly arranging themselves without the pressure of human discretion — well, just let him try marching his tulips in lines, or planting his geraniums, alyssum, and lobelia in patriotic patterns. He would be subjected to the amused scorn of those intrepid believers that all must look 'natural.'"

This pretentiousness irritated little Mary West. Since "the natural look" was harder to achieve than "the fake look," wasn't the fake look more truly natural? But as an art teacher told her later, "Art is not reality." In any event, four decades after Mary's childhood, I am sloping along the streets of her memory, and I find that the thin red line of tulips remains a rarity, and in garden after garden the natural look still holds sway. It is perfect for a neighbourhood that somehow manages to look orderly and jumbled, extravagant and subtle, graceful yet bizarre.

I pause at the white picket fence of 634 George Street, where the natural look dominates a yard big enough for three croquet games. The house is 154 years old and as English as a cricket bat. It's Georgian in style and, rare for these streets, made of red brick. The trim is white, the shutters dark green, and since it was here that the young Charles G.D. Roberts fell victim to the urge to write poetry, the place can fairly claim to be the birthplace of English-Canadian literature.

It was in this house that Roberts was living when, at eighteen, he finished *Orion*, and according to Lorne Pierce, editor of the Ryerson Press for forty years, this one poem proved that "at last a singer had come who proved that one might sing the new songs of the Dominion with the grace and charm our elder poets in Britain possessed." It was here in the shade of this same yard, in a time when English poets were public idols, that Roberts, his first cousin Bliss Carman, and the other teenage poets of Fredericton's small aristocracy used to gather to marvel over Tennyson, Swinburne, Matthew Arnold, William Morris, and D.G. Rossetti, author of *The Blessed Damozel*. Now, more than a century later, with my hands on the fence, I listen for echoes. Did those romantic youngsters — descendants of Loyalists in an Empire-loving village that had housed British regiments for eighty-four years — speak with English accents? I survey what the garden holds: big, rambunctious blossoms, folding deck chairs, a table with parasol, and a shuffleboard court. In the heart of what other Canadian city would I find a Georgian rectory with a white picket fence and a shuffleboard court? Time is a shifty force in Fredericton.

Like an Edwardian-age visitor with little on his mind, I drift farther in the tranquil buzz of the riverside morning. I chance upon 83 Shore Street, boyhood home of Bliss Carman, the most lyrical and celebrated poet in Canadian history. In June 1929, when Carman was sixty-eight, a brain haemorrhage killed him as he stepped out of a cold shower in New Canaan, Connecticut. Ten months later, his first cousin and fellow poet Theodore Goodridge Roberts, youngest brother of the great Charles G.D., lovingly recalled this same Carman home: "A small house which faces inward on its own garden of lawn and elms and lilacs and turns a windowless back on the street. But in those days there was nothing in Shore Street for even a poet's house to turn its back upon. Grass grew there between the earthen footpaths and the earthen roadway; the kindly neighbour's various livestock wandered there, grazing or grunting; all the little front gardens were full of flowers and bees and butterflies, all the backyards of scratching poultry, and all the trees of singing birds."

And this morning? The 147-year-old house is white with green shutters and red roof shingles. Though a few windows open on the street these days, the true front of the building, with its French doors, still faces a secret garden. Lupins and tiger lilies bloom there under enormous elms, and the narrow street-side garden is crowded, dishevelled, and once again full of flowers and bees and butterflies. The road is paved now, and the livestock and poultry are long gone, like the golden-haired poet himself. In his memory, the Imperial Order of the Daughters of the Empire, none of whose hundreds of branches was ever more staunch than Fredericton's, has put a plaque on the house. It bears his words: "Earth to my mother earth, spirit to thee."

Mary Pratt's mother belonged to the I.O.D.E. chapter that installed that brass plaque, and Mary passed this house every day on her way to school. Once a week, she walked the family dog to Carman's grave and thought about life being short and art being long. "Bliss Carman was a hero," she recalls. "Shop girls slept with slim volumes of his poems under their pillows. . . . On hazy days, his 'Fair the land lies, full of August / Meadow island, shingly bar' seemed as much a part of the land as the Saint John River."

From Carman's house I can see the river he loved, and I wander across Waterloo Row to the Green, once called the College

Common. Flanking the Saint John River for hundreds of yards, it is a gift to us connoisseurs of Sunday walks. Though the Saint John is mightier than the puny streams of England and no thatched cottages hide among the wooden mansions of Waterloo Row, you can't wander along the Green without thinking of British villages. It was here, under earlier willows, that Victorian author Juliana Horatia Ewing — whose children's stories provided the symbolism later used by Brownies in their rituals — wrote sugary verse and sent it home to *Aunt Judy's Magazine* in England. Her husband was a major in the British Army, and they lived on Waterloo Row from 1867 to 1869, when Canada was a baby and Carman and Roberts were boys. "The tenderly romantic spirits of [Juliana] Ewing and the girl queen still brooded over this little, colonial, Loyalist, provincial British North American town," Theodore Goodridge Roberts wrote in 1930, "infusing a gentle and sentimental glamour as of prayer books with markers of purple ribbon, church parades of little redcoated garrisons, and transplanted English parsons and English fairies. It was an enchanted atmosphere."

Feeling somewhat enchanted myself, I leave the manicured sward and on black, spongy soil push my way through head-high grass till the river laps at my shoes. It smells muddy, warm, soapy, so different from the cold kick of the ocean breezes that roil the Bay of Fundy eighty miles to the south. Nothing moves on the Saint John except a black schooner, and she just sways at her mooring. On a morning when the water's as placid as a swan pond in London, it's hard to imagine that this same river sometimes brings to Fredericton the thundering destruction you associate with avalanches: for a couple of centuries now, floods have periodically wrecked houses and barns, drowned farm animals, wiped out crops, and swept through all of downtown Fredericton. The spring floods brought ice, and ice jams created more floods, and sometimes the huge blue oceanbound blocks smashed down big bridges and swept the pieces along with the rest of the river rubble.

"The spring flood was a time of great excitement," Mary Pratt says. "Fathers would stand on the river banks, their legs apart, their arms folded over their chests, their braces visible over their neat white shirts, their ties flying in the wind. . . . Great chunks of ice would grind by our house, floating down from Edmundston, Woodstock, Florenceville, etc. The sloshing, banging, and scraping would continue for about a week, and then — oh, bliss! — we would be allowed to wear short socks."

If the river is tame on this July morning in 1987, and free of ice, it's also free of traffic. It is a ghost river. Once, it was Fredericton's highway to the wide world, the route for exports and imports, the last leg of travel for immigrants and visitors, the pipeline for incoming news. Once, the river swarmed with canoes, bateaux, scows, sloops, schooners, brigs, barques, tugboats, and steamships. Once, in the 1860s, it boasted more than thirty steamships, and each year tens of thousands of passengers sailed on steamers between Saint John and Fredericton. To modern Fredericton, however, the river that gave the city its reason for being has become little more than a nuisance. For one thing, it's polluted. For another, it has forced the construction of expensive bridges, and yet it still slows down people who want to get places fast in their cars.

I return to the Green, catch an errant soccer ball on my right instep, and drive it back to five guys at a goal-mouth. They give me a cheerful round of applause. A lethargic game of mixed softball is underway just downriver, but I turn upriver on the footpath and soon meet a middle-aged couple with a dog. The man wears a cream safari suit and Tilley hat. The woman's slacks are paddy green, her blouse purple, and she's slung a white sweater over her shoulder. They tell me the dog is a female Airedale and needs to be clipped. "Yes," the man says, "she gets rid of her wool." All three are fit and genial, and Fredericton is coming out to play.

Two young women, one in silky yellow jogging shorts and the other in silky scarlet shorts, approach me from behind and sweep by on my left and right, and as they pull away in front of me, I observe their bouncing curls, rhythmic elbows, and the backs of their smooth, plump thighs, and I think of what local booster Frank H. Risteen wrote in 1897 about the typical marriageable

Fredericton girl: "The Celestial girl is both useful and ornamental. She is a flower by the dusty wayside. She is ice-cream in August and sunshine in April. She is a ripple of laughter on the river of time. In short, she is the frosting which Heaven has spread o'er the dreary plain cake of earth."

I follow the two jogging ripples of laughter up the river of Time to Christ Church Cathedral, and then stretch out on the holy lawn. The cathedral is both cosy and grand, intimate and splendid. A fine Gothic pile of gray stone, topped by a trim steeple that soars nearly two hundred feet above the grass, it's the most *English* building I've seen outside the United Kingdom. It's largely a copy of a medieval church in Norfolk. After the cornerstone was laid in 1845, the mother country's Society for the Propagation of the Gospel marvelled that not only in the colonies but in Britain as well "no such work has begun since the Norman Conquest, that is for seven hundred years."

I hear organ music inside and the voices of choir and congregation rising sweetly in a final hymn of praise. Even before the music dies, the front doors swing open, and two dowagers emerge, unfold a card table on the grass, and set up a plastic cannister with a spigot. Then the minister comes out on the steps, and as the worshippers stream out to the table for foam cups of pink lemonade, he greets each of his flock. He has an energetic style, a trim beard, and a ruddy, amiable manner. His cream cassock and green stole reach almost to the ground. I mosey over for a shot of lemonade. The dowagers remind me of Peggy Ashcroft and Margaret Rutherford. The whole scene has so much pure Sunday morning in it that somebody should be filming it. The river slides by. The elms, maples, and oaks loom benignly over old folks, young parents, and kids in their Sunday best. After a while everybody drifts away, waving, chatting, climbing into cars. The minister tells me I'll be welcome at Evensong, tonight at seven, and I'm tempted.

A summer Sunday in Fredericton makes you want to reform. I really should go to church. I should impose some order and discipline on my life. I should write more letters to friends and relatives, pay bills on time, look after my property, grow flowers, quit smoking, start jogging, take up chess, keep a basset hound, do civic good. Being a proper Frederictonian might not be at all bad.

"The placid Celestial citizen is at peace with all the world," Frank Risteen wrote for the local tourist committee in 1897. "The tranquil river flowing by his door is a mirror of his mind. He is content with his lot, for, if he is secure from sudden attacks of affluence, he is equally safe from the withering disaster that comes from reckless speculation. He is liberal in thought — conservative in action. Perched upon a pinnacle of judicial impartiality, he calmly listens to the evidence as to the doings of the outer world, and then takes time to consider. Whether rich or poor, bond or free, the name of Fredericton is inscribed upon his heart and he carries with him his love of the fair old elm-shaded city to the end of his earthly days."

* * *

Lord Beaverbrook gave Fredericton a fine playhouse in 1963. Almost a quarter-century later, children of Saint John were going door to door, gathering nickels and dimes, to help pay for the renovation of a tumbledown theatre so their city could at last boast one decent spot to stage shows. Yet the people of Saint John (115,000) outnumber those of Fredericton (44,000) by more than two to one. Among New Brunswick's cities, Fredericton has always been the pampered little darling, accepting treasure as its right, like the prize courtesan of an Oriental potentate. Arthur Doyle, the lanky, garrulous alumni director for the University of New Brunswick, likes Fredericton well enough, but at heart he's a Saint John boy. While discussing differences between the cities, he says, "Saint John has had to pay for every goddamned thing it ever got." Not so, Fredericton.

Fredericton's first victory over Saint John occurred when they weren't much more than ramshackle camps for frightened, angry, and sometimes starving and freezing refugees from revolutionary America. Loaded with Loyalists, ships sailed in 1783 from New York for Nova Scotia, which still included today's New Brunswick, and by year's end they'd dumped more than fourteen thousand at the mouth of the Saint John River. About nine thousand spent the winter of 1783–84 right there at Parr Town (later Saint John), and more than a thousand, mostly disbanded soldiers and their families, found themselves facing the murdering winter upriver at St. Anne's Point (later Fredericton). Conditions there were even more grisly than at Parr Town, and the Loyalists felled by that first winter lie under gravestones with indecipherable lettering, in a small clearing downstream from where I admired the comely joggers. In the spring of 1784 the flood of Loyalists north of the Bay of Fundy was so great that Britain established the new colony of New Brunswick and appointed Colonel Thomas Carleton governor. Parr Town had petitioned to become the capital, but Carleton and the British government preferred the riverside plain at St. Anne's. This was the first time little Fredericton grabbed a prize that big Saint John craved. It would not be the last.

Once Carleton saw Fredericton, the waggish Frank Risteen wrote in 1897, "he seems to have had no further use for Saint John." Fredericton, near the heart of the province, was invulnerable to coastal attack. It was as far upriver as sizable vessels could sail. Moreover, Fredericton was full of ex-soldiers who'd been trained to be orderly and obedient, while Saint John had already been naughty, and if not quite rebellious, certainly disrespectful of colonial authority. And rowdy Saint John was perhaps too commercial to be the capital of what the founders of New Brunswick dreamed would one day be "the most gentleman-like province on earth."

In many minds, two hundred years later, Saint John remains tough, grubby, and unfavoured, while Fredericton remains polite, clean, and highly favoured. Poet Alden Nowlan knew both cities and loved them well. "Fredericton is the last stronghold of civility," he wrote in *Guide to Atlantic Canada*. But "gentleman-like" was "not a description that anyone would apply to the roughneck, rollicking, and intensely Irish city of Saint John." Is there another pair of rival cities in English-speaking Canada in which an essential character difference stretches right back to the days when the first houses replaced tents and lean-tos?

In 1880 the wooden legislature in Fredericton burned down, and Saint John, in a futile effort to reverse almost a century of history, offered to build a new one within its own city limits. The provincial assembly defeated the proposal, and in 1882 Fredericton got its handsome stone Second Empire Revival legislature. For little Fredericton, it was a gigantic construction job, at one point employing more than one hundred and fifty stonecutters, masons, blacksmiths, and other tradesmen and labourers, but the bill was footed by all the people of New Brunswick. These, of course, included the people of Saint John, who had recently rebuilt their own city after the horrendous fire. In Fredericton, the legislature remains a major architectural ornament, next only to the nearby cathedral.

The cathedral was like the legislature in two respects: Saint John, a city of more than 25,000 people, wanted it; Fredericton, an unincorporated town of 4,000, got it, and got it largely as a gift, this time from Britain. Governors in British North America had hoped the Church of England would discourage the democratic ideas that had fanned rebellion in the thirteen colonies and encourage a loyal, stable, conservative society. By 1840 the Church of England knew it needed new bishoprics in the colonies, and in 1843 New Brunswick became a bishop's see. Now it needed a cathedral and a bishop.

He would be the Reverend John Medley, a London-born, Oxford-educated Tractarian. Tractarians promoted the symbolism and mystery of the early Church, its Catholic aspects, and the idea that clergy were intermediaries between man and God. But Saint John swarmed with Irish Episcopalians, and they were sworn enemies of Irish Catholics. They were also evangelicals who stressed Protestantism, personal salvation, the life of the spirit above ritual, and the power of congregations. Medley and his cathedral would end up in the capital, and he would become known as John Fredericton.

Under ecclesiastical law, the seat of a bishop had to be not a town but a city. Queen Victoria solved that little problem for Fredericton. In 1845 she simply declared it a city for ecclesiastical purposes. Saint John had been a legitimate city for sixty years, and now it was outraged. In the *Morning News*, a Saint John man wrote: "I was astonished to observe what a place they have chosen for the site; to say nothing of the situation of it, the ground is a perfect mire, and I should not be surprised to see the whole concern sink — that is, if it ever floats at all. It is the opinion of many persons that the Cathedral should be built in St. John."

But that was not the opinion of the Church of England. Moreover, Bishop Medley was so good at gathering donations in the Old Country that Frederictonians had to put up only £4,000 of the £16,000 it cost to erect and furnish their gorgeous Gothic cathedral. When fire melted its eight bells in 1911, their replacement didn't cost Fredericton a nickel. Financier James Dunn — born in Bathurst, New Brunswick, and now, at thirty-six, building his fortune in London — not only paid for their replacement but also threw in another seven bells. One weighed nearly two tons.

If Fredericton had the cathedral, it also had the military. Nova Scotia could defend itself with naval power, but New Brunswick was vulnerable to overland assault by Yankees. Right from its birth, Fredericton was a garrison town: the most important link between Halifax, the Maritimes' headquarters for British naval and military power, and Quebec City, key to the St. Lawrence. For the eighty-four years following 1785, regular units of the British army lived in Fredericton. The townsfolk witnessed the arrival of such famous outfits as the Grenadier Guards and the Royal Scots Fusiliers. Floating past the military compound in canoes, the locals listened to regimental bands in the evening. At the very core of their city sat the barracks, officers' quarters, guard house, and parade grounds that still give Fredericton its smell of history. After the last of the British regulars left in 1869, the young government of Canada decided to establish its own infantry schools. Both Moncton and Saint

John bid for the school designated for the Maritimes, but once again Fredericton won the prize. The school opened in 1884, and as W. Austin Squires wrote in his history of Fredericton: "Thus Fredericton, after a lapse of fifteen years, once more had a garrison. The sound of the bugle, the music of the Infantry Corps Band, the shout of the Sergeant-Major echoed through the compound as in days of yore, and young ladies' heads once more responded to the sight of handsome officers and marching men in scarlet tunics and tight trousers."

Then there was the university, another juicy spin-off from Fredericton's status as capital. As early as 1785, seekers of office and favours abandoned Saint John for the new capital, which soon boasted an élite of educated Loyalists, officials from Britain, army officers, lawyers, and clergy. They wanted their sons to get a good education, and the College of New Brunswick was granted its charter in 1800. It became King's College in 1829, and thirty years later, just before Bliss Carman and Charles G.D. Roberts were born, the University of New Brunswick. It would not deign to open a branch plant in smelly, blue-collar Saint John till 1964, 105 years later.

* * *

Lord Beaverbrook, child of Newcastle, New Brunswick, filled in whatever blanks in Fredericton's cultural life had been left empty by government, the military, the church, and the university. He treated the town as a rich, doting father might treat the only daughter he ever loved. To crack his whip over the assorted institutions he gave to town and gown, he regularly descended upon Fredericton. He did so in a style that some, including the Presbyterian preacher who'd fathered him, might have regarded as extravagant to a devilish degree. He had quarters in the Lord Beaverbrook Hotel and an apartment next door in the Beaverbrook Art Gallery. Sometimes he took over the university president's house on Waterloo Row, the president fleeing to a bungalow on the campus. Arthur Doyle says, "He used to have his maroon Rolls-Royce flown over, and a uniformed chauffeur who'd hop out to open the door for him. Beaverbrook wore black shoes, black silk socks, black suits, dark ties, and white collars. His face always seemed to be tanned, and he had brown spots on the backs of his hands."

Describing the eighty-one-year-old Beaverbrook in Fredericton in 1960, British historian A.L. Rowse referred to "the little black dynamo" and the "wide boyish grin on his frog-face." Rowse recalled Beaverbrook's cheerfully confiding, "I make my money in Britain, I spend it over here." And so he did. One of his earliest gifts to U.N.B. was a library, which he named after two of his New Brunswick–born cronies who became prime ministers: Bonar Law of Britain and R.B. Bennett of Canada. Opened in 1951, the Bonar Law–Bennett Library now houses the provincial archives. High over the main entrance and just legible among tree branches, you can still read the Latin inscription, "NE DERELINQUAS ME DOMINE." It means, "Do not abandon me, O Lord." The choice of wording was apparently that of the mortal lord, not of the grateful, financially strapped university.

When the notoriously acid British journalist Malcolm Muggeridge visited Fredericton in 1963, he decided, "In New Brunswick Lord Beaverbrook is his own personality cult." He noted the bronze statue of Beaverbrook just upriver from the Lord Beaverbrook Hotel; the Beaverbrook Art Gallery and the Beaverbrook birdbath just downriver from the hotel; the Beaverbrook Playhouse, "completed but not yet opened," just opposite the hotel; the nearby Beaverbrook Skating Rink; "and on a pleasant eminence, the buildings of the University of New Brunswick, also borne down with the weight of massive and various Beaverbrook endowments." Remarking that overdone adulation of "some saint or sage or poet" usually has the excuse of being posthumous, Muggeridge mischievously added, "How extraordinary then, to find a case in which someone still living has been memorialized to a degree which might have been considered excessive if accorded to Napoleon in Corsica, or to Shakespeare in Stratford-on-Avon."

Muggeridge went so far as to compare Beaverbrook to Joseph Stalin: "The one hacked and killed his way into history, the other has tried to buy his way in — a more comical, and infinitely more innocuous procedure." Since history, like fame, was a wayward mistress, "the sacrificial offerings of flesh and treasure piled up on its altar are frequently disregarded." In the long haul, Muggeridge concluded, Beaverbrook would scarcely merit a footnote in the annals of world history; but meanwhile, among Frederictonians, the very mention of his name produced "the same faint twinge, the same perceptible lowering of the voice, as among his journalistic employees."

Muggeridge's deliciously irreverent remarks appeared in *Maclean's* in 1963. Nothing the magazine printed in the early 1960s drew more outraged letters from readers — except Pierre Berton's assertion that if his daughter were to engage in premarital sex, he'd rather she had it in bed than in the back seat of a car. Though the abuse of Berton was national, almost all the attacks on Muggeridge came from Fredericton. Mayor William T. Walker, noting that *Maclean's* was a product of hateful Toronto, wrote, "It is articles, actions and attitudes such as yours which apparently provided the name 'Hog Town' for Toronto, and which perpetuates the same." In its "Mailbag," *Maclean's* printed only one defence of Muggeridge. Margaret Walls of Dartmouth, Nova Scotia, said she'd lived in New Brunswick for forty years and that Fredericton's *Daily Gleaner* — run by Brigadier Michael Wardell, an Englishman with a black eye patch who'd worked for Beaverbrook on Fleet Street — "would have you believe that Frederictonians love Lord Beaverbrook, Loyalist descendants, the I.O.D.E., and God — in that order."

If Fredericton was not amused by the *Maclean's* article, neither was Beaverbrook. Muggeridge worked for the Beaverbrook press, and when he lashed A.L. Rowse's new biography of Shakespeare in the *Evening Standard*, Rowse complained directly to the lord with whom, three years before, he'd chummed around in Fredericton. In a conciliatory letter, Beaverbrook told Rowse, "Just about the same time, I read an attack on myself by the same author, published in a Canadian magazine. On the whole, I have more right to complain than you." He promised that never again would the *Standard* allow Muggeridge to review a book by Rowse. He also fired Muggeridge.

But in New Brunswick, a quarter-century later, it's clear that Beaverbrook *has* bought a kind of immortality. In a pretty park in central Newcastle, a cairn holds his remains and supports a bust. Beaverbrook-in-bronze gazes through a gap between small buildings to the glittering Miramichi River. A businessman wanted to erect another building in the gap but, as one shop-keeper told me, town councillors said no because "they didn't want to spoil his lordship's view." Meanwhile, over in Fredericton, town and gown continue to enjoy all the baubles and benefits that Beaverbrook showered upon them. Like cultural institutions in much bigger cities, Beaverbrook's art gallery, Beaverbrook's playhouse, and the Beaverbrook-bolstered university now suck up subsidies from distant taxpayers who don't get much out of them. But as the more sour critics in the less pampered towns of New Brunswick may well ask, "So what else is new?" Fredericton gets what Fredericton wants. It's the capital.

*   *   *

Some Frederictonians have always believed that they were better than other New Brunswickers. The town was the creation of people who felt they'd paid for their loyalty to the Crown by being driven from their homeland by Yankee scoundrels. Loyalists were more loyal than thou. Though few talk out loud these days about the superiority of their Loyalist blood, Frederic-tonians know their town still boasts qualities its founders trea-sured. It has a whiff of gentility about it. In Saint John some see it as anaemic, but many Frederictonians regard their city as an oasis of culture and refinement, surrounded by a territory of foul-mouthed woodsmen, French-speaking fishermen, and coarse men of trade. Even Frederictonians concede their town is smug, but they do so smugly, as though they know it has plenty to be smug about. Outsiders detect a certain prissiness in Fredericton as well. A.L. Rowse, fresh from Britain, called U.N.B.'s venerable Alfred G. Baily "a master of local lore" and "a rather prissy character of some distinction," as though you could not be one without being the other.

Fredericton's respectable Christians have not invariably been warm, generous, and open-hearted Christians. When the Society of St. Andrew erected a bonny statue of Robert Burns on the Green in 1906, bluestockings objected because many believed this greatest of all Scots poets had been a boozer and lecher. When the New Brunswick government arranged a state funeral for Charles G.D. Roberts in 1943, a dean of the cathedral refused to conduct the service because Roberts, once the very symbol of Canadian literature, had been a womanizer who'd run out on his Fredericton-born wife. When the story spread that Fredericton's favourite folksy barber had refused service to a black, the U.N.B. poet and scholar Fred Cogswell preserved the incident with these lines: "The snow has pitied you and made you fair, / O snow-washed city of cold, white Christians, / So white you will not cut a black man's hair."

More boisterous New Brunswickers sometimes see Frederictonians as a reserved crowd compared to the gang in, say, a Newcastle or a Saint John drinking joint. On a sweaty July night in 1987 I went to the River Room in the Lord Beaverbrook Hotel to witness an instant-poetry contest — "Ready, set, create," the master-of-ceremonies ordered the two dozen contestants, and punched his stopwatch. They had thirty minutes to perfect their masterpieces. Later I told one of the losers that I found it odd that the judges had chosen, as the top three entries, poems about elbows, fidgeting, and vomit. He was a beefy guy in his thirties, with thick, black hair and a walrus moustache. I took him to be a truck-driver, but he gave me a business card that identified him as a "psychic consultant" who read leaves and cards "At Your Place Or Mine." You never know who you'll meet in Fredericton. "That's right, old lad," he muttered. "Elbows, the fidgets, and gag. What does that tell you about Fredericton?" I wasn't sure, but something other than his Moosehead Ale was giving him a bad taste. He was from Campbellton, on the north shore of New Brunswick, and his blood was Acadian and Anglo-Irish.

Though Fredericton strikes some as a trifle stuffy in a British way, it is also polite in a British way. Television celebrity Gordon Sinclair once complained that during a coast-to-coast tour, Fredericton was the one city where no one recognized him. He was wrong. Frederictonians knew who he was all right, but they were too courteous to buttonhole him. Fredericton is still so loyal to the Crown that townsfolk turn out for every official royal visit as though the *Daily Gleaner* had announced the Second Coming; but during the summer that Prince Charles trained in New Brunswick to be a helicopter pilot, he wandered around Fredericton, unshaven — and unbothered. When he went to a symphony at the playhouse that Beaverbrook had given the town, when he went to a Johnny Cash show at the Lady Beaverbrook Arena, nobody demanded either a kiss or an autograph. Fredericton's status as a political, religious, educational, and cultural capital has meant that for a city with a population that's only one sixty-ninth that of Toronto's, it has seen more than its share of celebrities. This has not made it a groupie capital. Groupies are not polite.

There's something British, too, in Fredericton's affection for its eccentrics. The town grows them as skilled truck farmers grow prize vegetables. "You can be absolutely bonkers and still be accorded a place in the community," said Alden Nowlan. "If, for example, you walk around quacking like a duck, you will become known as Quack-Quack, and it will be said that nobody is a true Frederictonian until Quack-Quack has quacked at him. Eccentrics are a protected species, partly because it is a university town. The legends that surround Quack-Quack, the Fox, the Overalls Man, the Guardian of Virgins and the rest of them, invariably include the claim that 'he was a Rhodes Scholar.' Sometimes it's true."

* * *

It's Saturday morning, and hundreds of Frederictonians have followed their noses downtown to Boyce's Farmers' Market. Crossing the parking lot in the salivating throng, I notice a graceful blonde with a fine face. She's sitting by the open back door of a station wagon, with her tanned legs nicely crossed, and she's selling decorated pillows. A bearded, bespectacled, tweedy chap lopes by with his arms full of leaves. "The beet greens look good," she chirps, and he says, "Oh, I just love 'em. A big platterful, with butter and pepper and vinegar. I just love 'em." Do they know each other? It doesn't matter. Like gossip, the love of fresh food is social glue in Fredericton.

"Fiddleheads, salmon, and capers," Mary Pratt recalls. "We had that meal at least twice a week in May and June. Sent into the backyard to scale the salmon, I would hold the knife, blunt side against the fish, and pulling smartly against the scales, I'd send them spraying into the air — little chips of silver against the dark green of the grass. We thought everyone ate salmon, and asparagus, and the sweet Jerusalem artichokes, dug up after the winter. We had no notion of luxury living, and when the shad, and new beets, and samphire greens appeared, they were simply *expected*. There was never any marvelling at the goodness of this food. Spring lamb. Strawberries. New peas, splayed from their crisp pods into an aluminum pot held in my lap, in the sun on the front steps." In later years, in the lean country of Newfoundland, Mary Pratt would build her national reputation with exquisite paintings of food on her kitchen counter. Like the Dutch masters, she had come from rich land.

One reason why Governor Carleton chose Fredericton as the capital was that "the country above it is incredibly fertile." Now, more than two centuries later, as I snoop around the market, the legs of the display bins look as though they can barely support the loads of glistening tomatoes, peppers, and "English Cukes — Seedless! Burpless!" At the Harrison Farm Market stall, a barker harangues the crowd: "Come on, come on. Get your local potatoes. New potatoes, new potatoes. You've been hollerin' for 'em all winter. Don't go home without 'em." The market sells leather goods, knitwear, wooden knick-knacks, jewellery, and used comic books, but mostly food, food, glorious food, enough international goodies for a U.N. cocktail party. On one counter, a quart basket of strawberries sits beside an entire pig, split lengthwise. Where are you, Mary Pratt?

I find Goofy Roofy's, an L-shaped breakfast counter that's open only on Saturday mornings and seats only a dozen people. It serves the market crowd, local and visiting celebrities, the occasional unwary tourist, and indeed anyone brave enough to endure the chattering inquisition of its zany proprietor. She is Ruth Chapel, a Czech by birth, an authentic Fredericton eccentric by avocation. The boss of Goofy Roofy's is not a Quack-Quack, but she is one of a kind. She's a small, feverish, middle-aged woman with short, curly hair, a friendly glare behind her glasses, and a quick, wide mouth. Like her waiters, who serve a few tables outside, she wears a red T-shirt with white lettering that blares, "I'm a Goofy Roofy Gobbler." She rules with the power of her personality and curiosity, firing out orders to her tiny kitchen, slapping breakfasts down on the counter, wise-cracking, badgering, bantering with everyone in the joint who's not cringing for cover.

"Where you from?" she demands of strangers. "What are you doing here? Are you sharing? Are you polite? Always be polite, especially at home. It's very important. Always say, 'Please.'" When a girl orders coffee, Ruth pounces. "You didn't say 'Please.'" The girl blushes but fights back: "Well, you didn't say, 'Excuse me, *please*, would you like some coffee?'" Ruth leans across the counter, stabs her own chest with a forefinger, and yells, "I'm the one who's doing the testing around here." The girl wilts. "*One* egg!" Ruth says to a fellow who's just ordered. "You can't have *one* egg. It messes up the system. They come in flats of twenty-four." A man from Colorado sits down, cameras and light meters dangling from his torso. "Why are you wearing all that photography stuff?" Ruth asks. "It's just to attract attention, isn't it?"

Ruth tells me how thrilled she was to be on Peter Gzowski's radio show, not once but twice, and I order Smoked Gzowski — toast, and eggs scrambled with vegetables and smoked salmon. Before I've finished it, and without ignoring any of her other customers, she has extracted as much of my life story as I've ever told any stranger at 9:30 A.M. But we are no longer strangers. She says I remind her of her father, from whom her mother was divorced when Ruth was three. What a terrible shame it is that I'm travelling alone, without my wife. Do I know that Goofy Roofy's was directly responsible for bringing together three couples who later got married? For that matter, do I know that this young woman, whom Ruth has just seated by my left thigh, is "the Atlantic women's body-building champ," and why don't I ask her out to dinner tonight?

The champ, a regular Goofy Roofy gobbler, is eating elder-berry pancakes. She's amiable enough, but I sense she's not in-terested in a dinner date with a Ruth Chapel nominee old enough to be her father. She has blonde shoulder-length hair, not much makeup, smooth, clear cheeks. She strikes me as prettier than she is muscular, but then her jeans and yellow sweatshirt hide all those ropy, rippling, prize-winning sinews. Her name is Denise St. Pierre, and though she looks fresh out of high school and ready for a Miss Teenage contest, she tells me she's a divorced woman of thirty. I'm still old enough to be her father. Denise normally works out for three or four hours a day, but in "the season" — the three months before a big competition — she spends up to seven hours a day perfecting her body. Now she's after the national title. She probably wouldn't have time for a candlelit dinner anyway. This breakfast will have to do.

During the intimacy of our final coffee together, she confides that before bad publicity about Premier Richard Hatfield's private life amplified the ancient whispering about him, he, too, was a regular Goofy Roofy gobbler. She seems to miss him. Later, another chronicler of the society at Goofy Roofy's tells me that when Hatfield bellied up to the counter one fine Saturday morning, Ruth told him he should do something about his teeth, that no premier of New Brunswick should have such yellow choppers. Only a Somebody would have such gall, but as an English traveller complained about Fredericton in the nineteenth century, "Every snub-nosed youngster who runs to stare at you around the corner thinks of himself as the son of Somebody."

* * *

Suburbs, malls, and satellite villages hem in the tight old capital. Since the 1940s, when Fredericton was still home to a mere ten thousand-odd people, the population has more than quadrupled. The town's area, which now includes villages on the north side of the river with histories of their own, has expanded to fifty square miles. Despite this, some of the character of the old town survives because, even with respect to government gifts it once resented, Fredericton was lucky. In 1800 the government gave nearly six thousand acres to the College of New Brunswick. Reserved land and the river surrounded the town, and in 1852 a local editor complained that the endowments to church, college, and military had prevented development, leaving Fredericton "as naked as a rock on a common." But the limits forced it to grow in a neat, compact way, and the chief enchantment of today's Fredericton is that you can easily explore its most historic elm-draped avenues on foot.

Richer Frederictonians live here on the south side of the river, on "the Flat" where I took my magical walk and the slopes that surround the university a little way inland. This is the Fredericton that Charles G.D. Roberts meant when he wrote, "My city, Fredericton. . . . A jewel in a dream." A U.N.B. administrator told me, "More people actually live on the north side now, but most south-siders either don't know this, or don't care. More people live in India. So what?" A lot of low-level bureaucrats and working-class folks live "on the wrong side of the river." After Joseph Daigle, member of the legislature for Kent South, won the Liberal leadership in 1978, he needed a home in the capital. Fredericton backbiters, even within his own party, sneered, "He bought a house across the river. Now what does *that* tell you?"

South-side Frederictonians with high incomes live in three social circles: professors, senior bureaucrats, and Old Fredericton Families, locally known as OFFs. But not every OFF truly comes from an old Fredericton family. The *old* sometimes simply means monied. Certain merchants, car dealers, and real-estate developers have earned their pile since World War Two, in the decades when the university and the bureaucracy together created thousands of safe jobs. Though many OFFs can indeed trace their roots back to the first Loyalists, a few are descendants of Jewish and Lebanese immigrants. Speaking of OFFs, a knowledgeable Frederictonian told me, "About fifteen really run this town. These guys buy their cars, insurance, office space, and building supplies from one another. They fish together, and they go to the Y together. The Y is a big thing among OFFs. When handball got fashionable, they easily raised a million bucks to build courts. OFFs are also big in the United Way, and the Chamber of Commerce. They tend to be Rotarians and YMCA presidents. Professors don't become presidents of the Y."

The university crowd holds its own cocktail parties, and so do the senior bureaucrats. OFFs don't think much of professors or bureaucrats. Professors don't think much of bureaucrats or OFFs. In short, one professor happily advised me, "there really isn't a hell of a lot of interaction." This layering of Fredericton society depresses newcomers who can't shoulder their way into any of the three solitudes, but it is not as cut and dried as it seems at first.

My professor friend, who asked that I not print his name because "this is a very small town," said: "Between Fredericton and Saint John, or any other goddamned city in the Maritimes, there's a sharp contrast in the sheer per capita volume of middle-aged yuppies. What we've got here are these two-income families. The husband's a prof, the wife's got a good job in the civil service, or vice versa, and they're each pulling down maybe $50,000 or $60,000 a year. They drive upscale Hondas, or Audis, Volvos, or maybe a Mercedes, and they usually have a second car. It's a station wagon. They have exactly two kids, and a house on the hill. They travel a lot, on business and pleasure, and they have nice tans in winter. Their kids go to the Y, and they spend lots of money on clothes. Naturally, they support the Playhouse and the art gallery."

But if Fredericton is a city of cliques, yuppies, and cross-river snobbery, it is also the city of Goofy Roofy's, Quack-Quack, Alden Nowlan, and, on occasion, a loving kind of style. When Nowlan died in 1983, poets, fiction writers, editors, scholars, and cronies from his newspaper days joined his wife, Claudine, and his son, Johnny, at the funeral in the chapel of the ancient U.N.B. Arts Building. So did Premier Richard Hatfield and a fair number of other Frederictonians. Pallbearer Jamie Stewart played an Irish lament on a flute he prized, then snapped the instrument over his right knee. Like Nowlan, it would sing no more. The bagpipes skirled, and out at Forest Hill Cemetery — where the poet's grave gaped, a few inches from Carman's and a few feet from Roberts's — Walter Learning, then artistic director of Theatre New Brunswick, read a Nowlan poem to the funeral party.

What happened next was described by Ralph Costello, president and publisher of the Saint John *Telegraph-Journal*, in his own paper on July 3, 1983:

Alden Nowlan was not going on his final journey without a proper toast from his friends, not while his son was alive and breathing — so a bottle of Jamieson's finest was produced and a loving cup went the rounds of the pallbearers before Johnny sent the bottle itself crashing into the coffin which had just been lowered into the grave.

With that, Johnny's coat was flung to the ground and he picked up a shovel. Strangers would not bury his father.

And that is why on a warm June afternoon three grave diggers stood in the background, and watched bemused, as Johnny Nowlan and soon all the pallbearers and others in the funeral party shoveled dirt into the grave of Alden Nowlan, writer, poet, and humanist, dead at fifty.

It's not every day that a newspaper publisher covers a poet's funeral, but then Nowlan was not an ordinary poet, and little Fredericton is not an ordinary city. Nowlan knew that. He once asked, "And where else could you meet the premier, the mayor, a poet, and Stompin' Tom Connors walking arm-in-arm at 4 A.M., or drive past a wild black bear on the way to work, and attend a reception for the Dalai Lama that same afternoon. That has actually happened in Fredericton which, in addition to everything else, is a city of almost surrealistic surprises."

THE SEDUCTIVE MYTH
OF THE PERFECT ISLAND

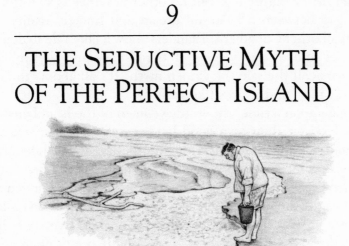

Prince Edward Island may well be the saddest province in Canada. It's not sad all the time, of course, and your typical Islander doesn't walk around looking as though a truck has just killed his favourite dog. But no other province is so tortured by the gap between a beautiful dream and homely reality. More than all other Canadians, Islanders allow a fairy tale to dominate politics and distort visions of their homeland destiny. Some scholars call the tale the garden myth. It's all about "the Island way of life," and it goes like this:

Once upon a time, the sturdy yeomen of the Island grew their own food on their own good land, exported vegetables to the United States, and carved out prosperity, independence, and happiness for their wives and children. Farm families not only turned the Island into the Million-Acre Farm, the Garden of the Gulf, and Canada's Garden Province but also founded a loving society. Everyone cared for everyone else. Everyone had a powerful sense of community. Folks built pretty churches and cosy schoolhouses, and in a land that was as pastoral as the people were peaceful, even the horses were happy. Politics was feisty but fun, merely a theatre to create characters worth talking about on long winter nights. The Island was really a northern Eden, and seas protected it from troublemakers, tricksters, and seducers from away. It was a world with few strangers and no problems. The Island's secret was self-sufficiency, and the people who made it self-sufficient were the fellows on the family farms. Farmers were better than other people.

The dream whitewashes history. For one thing, the Island was never an independent kingdom. When it ceased being a colonial territory of the French, it became a colonial territory of the British, and after that a junior partner in Confederation. Far from being prosperous when it joined Canada, it was almost bankrupt, and federal handouts began at once.

For another thing, Islanders were not invariably paragons of loving kindness. Alexander and Lucy Woolner Macneil, for example, were a decidedly chilly pair. The maternal grandparents of Lucy Maud Montgomery, whose *Anne of Green Gables* spread the dream of the Island way of life around the world, they raised her almost from infancy. Alexander was an irritable despot who couldn't resist humiliating the child, and his wife was reserved, narrow-minded, and carping. Lucy Maud, on the other hand, was warm, impulsive, imaginative, and romantic. If she was everything that her grandmother was not, she was also everything that Islanders either undervalued or mistrusted.

The qualities they treasured were stern: frugality and an ox-like capacity for work. Anyone who did not work much was not worth much. Island history professor David Weale has described "work heroes" who were like modern sports heroes: "Whether you were the best man with an axe, or the best man with horses, or the first to have the crop in, or the woman who hooked the most rugs over the winter, or the one who made the best chow or mustard pickles, or the one who set the best table for the minister and his wife, a reputation for diligence and industry was coveted by virtually all."

Thriftiness was next to godliness. Sir Andrew Macphail (1864–1938), a celebrated doctor, essayist, and professor at McGill University, once said his Island-born mother could trace the recycling of a shred of cloth backward for sixty years. Remembering his boyhood on the Island, Macphail also said, "Exuberance of language was strictly checked." But if Islanders were miserly even with words, this was rarely true when it came to gossip. Along with the famous sense of community went intense nosiness and intense pressure to be like everyone else.

It was as hard to have a cherished secret on the Island as it was to be a girl rebel, and Montgomery found something stifling and coercive in the local obsessions with work, thrift, and gossip. In *Anne of Green Gables* she invented a little redhead whose immortal charm lay in her having the spunk to challenge the boring values of a claustrophobic society. Anne may be everyone's favourite fictional Islander, but as David Weale points out, she is also "the girl from away, and was created not because she was like the people of Cavendish but precisely because she was so unlike many of them."

Many were bigots. Differences of class, politics, religion, and ethnic background often inspired Charlottetown men of the

Victorian era to beat one another bloody in the streets. If society in the capital of the garden was as gentle as the dream suggested, why was it that in 1890 Mayor Dawson seriously proposed treating drunkards with the cat-o'-nine-tails? During a byelection in the Belfast neighbourhood in 1847, Irish Catholics and Scots Presbyterians attacked each other with fists, clubs, and rocks. The mayhem continued all afternoon, and when it was over, at least three men were dead or dying, and scores of injured lay writhing. Religious friction was so raw in 1885 that, when the Grey Nun nurses at Charlottetown Hospital offered their services during a smallpox epidemic, the city rudely turned them down.

Eight decades later, religious bigotry coloured the debate over the merger of St. Dunstan's University and Prince of Wales College, and as recently as the mid-1960s both the rift between Catholics and Protestants and the vigour of local racism appalled Come From Aways who were settling in Charlottetown. Happily, religious friction has largely disappeared from the town. Charlottetown has grown more tolerant, and the Come From Aways have helped. The Confederation Centre of the Arts, opened in 1964, the University of Prince Edward Island, and a burgeoning bureaucracy have brought squads of outsiders to the Island, and whatever their sins in the eyes of native preachers of the Island way of life, they've broadened some minds.

Wariness of outsiders, another Island characteristic that the fairy tale excludes, has sometimes blossomed into full-fledged hatred. In the 1760s, the British government divided the colony into sixty-seven 20,000-acre properties and awarded these by lot to friends and hangers-on in London. For a full century, the mess this giveaway created made Island politics complex, virulent, and occasionally murderous. The land issue aroused such violence in 1865 that Lieutenant-Governor George Dundas called in redcoats from Halifax to protect rent-collectors. Islanders have long seen this tumultuous period as a David-and-Goliath battle between little tenants who loved and deserved the land they nurtured and big landlords who raked in rent while loafing in England. The landlords were not Come From Aways. They were Stay Aways, and everything was all their fault.

In truth, however, much of the fault lay not with bloated bloodsuckers in the mother country, but with greedy hustlers among a crafty, home-grown élite. The real exploiters of the horny-handed sons of the soil were often land-grabbers among the Island's own bigshots. But the ruling fable says Islanders are always good guys, while the bad guys are invariably from away. More than a century after the absentee landlords ceased to be a problem, Islanders found new villains in "the feds" and in imported experts who rashly tried to foist their foreign ideas on the Island way of life.

Far more than evil outsiders, it was a succession of provincial governments—of Islanders elected by Islanders—that undermined the dream. It was Islanders who presided over the introduction of improved highways, shopping malls, suburban sprawl, rural electrification, consolidated schools, farm mechanization, crop specialization, promotion of heavy tourist traffic, and bribes to get outsiders to build ugly factories on Island soil. Island governments have done all this, says political scientist David A. Milne, "while cynically or muddle-headedly offering the public a tonic of pastoral communitarian rhetoric and heritage boosterism." For decades, premiers have talked up the Island way of life while unleashing a tide of modernization that could only destroy it. To many Islanders, however, the enemies remain "outside experts."

At the heart of the dream lie the family farm and the belief that even though farms may be falling like ripe apples in a hurricane, farming remains the very essence of the Island's character and that farmers are more noble than city folks. Between 1931 and 1976, the number of acres in farmland dropped from 1.2 million to 730,000, and between 1941 and 1976, the number of farms dwindled from 12,230 to a measly 3,677. Farmers are now only a small part of the Island population, but such is the power of the dream that, as David Weale told me, "every election is really an election about the family farm." This mystique has skewed legislative power in favour of rural areas, kept municipal governments weak, led to an underrating of urban problems, and otherwise defied reality.

A change in the style of farming now threatens to denude the Island even of its famous red soil. As farmers relied more and more on machinery and manufactured fertilizers—when thirty thousand horses vanished, so did a lot of manure—their expenses rose faster than income. They had to expand or quit, and those who expanded were often whip-sawed by the food corporations that bought their produce and the farm-equipment companies that sold them what they needed to grow it. Caught in this squeeze, many farmers abandoned mixed farming for specialized production of, say, potatoes, hogs, beef, or dairy products. Some altered their cropping systems and tore out hedgerows to accommodate big machinery. These changes, along with the heavy use of inorganic fertilizers, not only reduced the soil's fertility but also made it easy prey for erosion by wind and water. Such developments would have broken Lucy Maud Montgomery's heart.

*   *   *

She hated change on the Island. As late as 1919, she told her friend George Boyd MacMillan by mail that she still resented seeing automobiles "in that haunt of ancient peace. . . . I wanted to think there was one place where the strident honk-honk of the car horn could never jar the scented air." Visiting Cavendish in the summer of 1918, she said, "I got a blow in the face." Someone had cut down the "school woods," and that "wide green beautiful hill of plumy spruce and fir was now an abomination of desolation of stumps. The schoolhouse sat on its crest wantonly, indecently naked. The whole sight was obscene. If I had the power I would have spitted the author of the outrage on a bayonet."

More recently, tourism has dealt many Islanders a similar blow in the face, and it has become hard to reconcile Montgomery's Island of quiet rural bliss with the fact that each summer, thanks to intense government promotion, close to 600,000 visitors buzz around a province of only 124,000 residents. Though fears that tourism would turn the garden into a huge Coney Island have not come true, the industry has nevertheless littered the countryside with hokey museums, dumb funlands, and cheesy rides and gimmicks. Moreover, sociologist Judith Adler has argued, it's all very well for an outside expert from a big city to argue that Island beaches are nowhere near their saturation point, but "an Islander feels a loss when discovering three hundred cars parked at a beach he once shared with only a few neighbouring families."

Some feared in the 1970s that tourism might turn noble natives who wrested a living from God's sea and soil into sucks of visitors with bucks, forelock-tugging toadies with their hands forever outstretched for tips. The Island, however, has never been a promising breeding ground for servants. All island peoples treasure self-sufficiency and independence, and though Prince Edward Island as a whole has never had either, some of its farmers, fishermen, and farmer-fishermen once enjoyed both. Many Islanders still believe the best things in life come from not having to jump whenever some honcho snaps his fingers. They not only dislike having bosses; they even dislike *being* bosses. Their attitude is ideal for "one-man, one-brat lobster fishing," often with a wife helping out on the boat as well.

Stomping around among workers at his little brewery outside Charlottetown, Island industrialist Billy Rix grumbled, "I know what these guys are thinking. They're thinking, 'As soon as I've saved enough fuggin' money to buy me a fuggin' lobster boat, I'm going to quit workin' for that sunnuvabitch Rix.'" A man who's scheming to buy a lobster boat probably would not make a good caddy or bellhop.

At North Rustico, I heard an old story about a conversation between a local fisherman and a waggish Yankee tourist. The town lies just inland from the magnificent dunes of the North Shore. For more than a century, ever since families first came to beach lodges by train from Montreal and Boston, tourists have flowed through North Rustico. Back when the flow was still a trickle rather than a flood, when the roads were all dirt, red dirt, a cocky American noticed a barefoot fisherman weeding his garden. "That's quite a pair of shoes you got there," the tourist cracked. As quick as snapping the tail off a boiled lobster, the local replied, "Yessir, they're made of the same material as me arse, and y'know, I've had that for sixty-five years and I've only worn but one hole in it."

Stories about Islanders taking no guff from strangers don't mean the natives hate visitors, but they are a symptom of the Island's schizophrenia about the tourist industry. Islanders want tourists' money, and many accept the government line that tourism makes a fabulous contribution to the provincial economy. But they don't want the wooing of tourist hordes to undermine farming and the Island way of life. When zealous tourism promoters tried to ban the use of manure near roads that served a lot of tourists, they failed. The people backed the spreaders of real manure.

One of the more questionable features of the garden myth concerns its quaint political life. Island political campaigns may well have been funny, picturesque, and boisterous, but when it came to greed, cynicism, and two-bit corruption, they often made the politics of even New Brunswick look clean by comparison. During a crucial byelection in First Kings, for instance, the rumoured price per vote was $100, but some held out for new bathrooms and paved driveways. Locals claimed to have seen whole convoys of trucks, said to be loaded with expensive liquor, rumbling into the riding at night. Such bribery characterized a campaign not in the bad old days at the turn of the century, but as recently as 1966.

Some argue that, even now, the old-style, patronage-ridden, boss-follower politics of rum, paving, and pay-offs is far from dead, but in the past twenty years a new political force has arisen. Fed up with Grits and Tories who offered more grants and entertainment than policies and solutions, Islanders formed groups outside the traditional parties to fight for what they wanted. Concern over education, the environment, social problems, civil liberties, farm crises, the use and ownership of land and, indeed, just about every aspect of Island living, spawned at least a

dozen councils, commissions, and associations. These organizations, publicized by television coverage, became the Island's
most effective political opposition in the 1970s, and their vigour
still gives the whole Island an air of town hall democracy.

If no other province has quite the same political atmosphere,
it's because no other province endures so painful a chasm
between the imagined grace of yesterday and the destructive
facts of today. One more warehouse on the outskirts of Toronto
makes no difference to the character of Ontario, but the Island is
so small that its people can easily see what every new parking
lot, mall, or factory does to the farmland of the dream.

More than all other Canadians, Islanders fret over the future
of their province. In the winter of 1987–88 they were stewing
over what a tunnel or causeway to the mainland might do to the
precious Island way of life. They wanted the link, and they
didn't want it. They are like that. They want to preserve pastoral
bliss while enjoying fast cars on paved highways, varied shopping in colossal supermarkets, saunas and Jacuzzis, overseas
vacations to cure cabin fever, fine restaurants and the money to
patronize them, live theatre and lots of movie houses,
Vancouver's choice of television channels and Mississauga's
standard of living. Many Islanders seem to want the best of
Manhattan in a rural paradise. They want it all. They can't have
it all, but trying to calculate the perfect mixture of what they
can reasonably expect to get is a never-ending torment.

* * *

Part of the Island way of life—the truest part—is the sheer
beauty of God's little acres in the Gulf: the exquisite melange of
red soil, blue ocean, Irish-green slopes, and tree-lined lovers'
lanes; of ponds, streams, ferns, nooks, dunes, and bluffs; of sea-
washed blankets of sand, and wind-tossed mobs of white, pink,
purple and yellow blossoms. When sunshine leaps back into a
vale after a summer shower in the evening and the shadows are
long on the rinsed grass, a holy radiance settles on the Island,
and even strangers understand the power of the dream. This is
the Island that's remembered by its people when they're far from

home, the lost paradise that obsessed one of author George Galt's grandfathers as he lay dying in Massachusetts. The old man had met and married his wife, another native of the Island, in Boston. He'd spent the rest of his life down there and become a loyal American citizen. "My grandfather rarely spoke of his early life," Galt wrote in *Trailing Pythagoras*, "but in the year before he died, at the age of ninety-two, he rose from his bed several times and said desperately to his wife, 'I've got to get to the Island.' He was ill and weak, and she was able to restrain him."

Barbara McAndrew also felt she had to get back to the Island. Remembering visits home during the eight years that she and her husband Jack spent in Toronto, she told me, "Every time the plane banked to come into Charlottetown, we cried. Every time the plane took off from Charlottetown, we cried. And every time it sailed into that yellow cloud over Toronto, we cried again."

Homesickness runs in her family, as it does in mine. One of her great-uncles was Robert Harris, an Islander whose career as an artist kept him in distant cities most of his life. During Christmas in Paris, bells of street donkeys reminded him of superior bells on sleigh horses back home. During Christmas in Montreal, spindly evergreen limbs in the churches reminded him of superior spruce branches in churches back home. Blank, gray skies of London reminded him of superior blue skies back home. Compared to the Island, no city was ever quite up to scratch. Though Harris ended up in Montreal, he never stopped going home. In the last years of his life, he could barely walk, and yet he made his painful way each summer to a cottage colony that overlooked his beloved Charlottetown. "I don't know of any town in Canada," he wrote, "that looks anything like as nice."

Another eminent victim of homesickness was Lucy Maud Montgomery. At thirty-seven, in 1911, she married Reverend Ewan Macdonald and moved with him to Ontario. Like Robert Harris, however, and like tens of thousands of expatriate Islanders to follow, she went home each summer, and every time, the beauty of the Island floored her. In a letter to a friend in 1924, she said, "Some old gladness always waits there [at Cavendish] for me, and leaps into my heart as soon as I return. The evenings there were wonderful. A pale silver moon shone in the sky. The roads were of that brilliant red peculiar to Island roads on a dewy evening after sunset. There were exquisite views of ponds and drives and harbour all bathed in opal dust.

"A certain part of my soul long starved mounted up on wings as of eagles. I was at home—heart and soul and mind I was at home. My years of exile had vanished. I had never been away."

More than half a century later, Island historian F.W.P. Bolger said that Montgomery, while lathering the Island with such praise, wrote things that "seem so eternally true that they should be repeated almost like daily prayers are repeated."

Montgomery the writer, Harris the painter, and Andrew Macphail the medical man all wrestled with the classic Island dilemma: how to reconcile full commitment to the Island way of life with personal ambition. None succeeded. Through her writing, Montgomery came closest; but she, too, eventually found herself moving far away, to what she called "smug opulent Ontario." Macphail celebrated the life of the Island farmer in his writing, but he also confessed that, as a boy on an Island farm, he "worked thinking only of escape." These three famous Islanders talked and wrote about the wonders of the Island way of life and returned summer after summer after summer. But they settled in central Canada, and that's where they died. They were Island parallels of my father.

*　*　*

But some do come home to stay.

Jack and Barbara McAndrew gave up $193,000 a year in Toronto to return to the Island and scramble to earn $33,000, but they have nine cats to console them, as well as a spunky red dog whose eyes have what Islanders call "that sooky-baby look," and three hundred caged doves, pigeons, quails, and other show birds. Every morning, the birds awaken the McAndrews at six. Jack started with pheasants, to train his dog Gunner as a retriever, but a year later he had these hundreds of other birds, and Gunner still wasn't trained. Though Jack has been shooting wildfowl since he was in short pants, forty years ago, Barbara says that when it comes to killing the birds he raises, he's something of a sooky-baby himself. As fast as they breed, which is very fast, he gives them away. When a hen is on her nest, Island women say "she's gone clucky," and the McAndrew birds are forever going clucky. "Look at that," he says proudly, cushioning a pale blue egg in the hand that's signed God knows how many sharp show-biz deals. "Yup, three bucks an egg."

Jack names the birds after Canadian celebrities, many of whom appeared on television shows he produced. As he examines rustling heaps of gray feathers, he says, "There's Don Harron, and there's Maureen Forrester, and Liona Boyd. Is that Brian Mulroney? No, it's not." He hints that any minute now a Harry Bruce may be hatched, and it's flattering to be in such company.

I had not seen the McAndrews for nineteen years, but I happened to be staying at the Charlottetown Hotel, and they lived only a few miles away. It was a sunny summer Sunday, a morning that was so full of classic Island tranquility and so radiant a cliché that I wanted to leave the city to see if I could find Anne of Green Gables trotting up through the decades in a surrey with the fringe on top. "You just come out the Trans-Canada to Cornwall," Barbara told me by phone, "and then you take number nineteen down to Meadow Bank, but don't cross the West River, just keep right, and then a white husky dog will take a run at your car from your right, but that's not our dog. We're on your left just where he runs out—he never fails—and you'll see a plastic rooster in our drive." Fifteen minutes later, the husky charged, I turned left past the rooster, and Jack came out to greet me.

The yard was a small, messy park, crowded with trees. Gunner, a Nova Scotia Toller, chased two cats up a trunk, but neither the animals nor Jack seemed to regard the romp as anything more serious than a routine game to promote fitness. Everything looked friendly and unkempt, including Jack. His dark thicket of beard might have housed hummingbirds, and his heavy eyebrows showed straggles of gray. His eyes were large, luminous, as deep a brown as Black Magic chocolates, and they still shone with opinion. He might have been one of the revolutionary intelligentsia in a movie about Czarist Russia. He grinned at me, held out his hand, and said, "Nineteen years, and I still owe you that punch in the nose."

An old joke from a funny time, the punch deserves background, and so does Jack. Born in Dalhousie, New Brunswick, and schooled partly in Halifax, he was still a boy when his father, a travelling salesman, moved his family to Mount Edward Road, now well inside the sprawl of Charlottetown. Suburbia seeps across the countryside, and good roads to the city suck business out of fading villages, but in Jack's youth Mount Edward Road was still farm country, and, he recalls, "it seemed to be on the edge of everything." He was a country boy from a hard-up family. To help out at home, he routinely strapped a gun to his handlebars, and with a pack of sandwiches from his mother, bicycled off to bag black ducks, pheasants, and Hungarian partridge. His gun was "an Ivor Johnson, single-barrelled, double-gauged shotgun," and he remembers it as a man who raises pacers and trotters remembers his glossiest, fastest, and most money-making pony. In the fall, Yankee hunters paid the kid as a guide because "I knew where the birds were." He also knew where home was. No matter where Jack went, he'd never shake his love of the Island.

By the mid-1960s he was working out of Halifax—where he'd met and married Island-born Barbara Tuck—as chief of the Outside Broadcast Department, the Atlantic Region, the Canadian Broadcasting Corporation. "I kept cooking up story assignments," he said, "just so I could come back home to the Island." I wanted to shake his hand. Getting employers to send you Down Home is a family tradition among us Bruces. As general superintendent of Canadian Press in its Toronto headquarters, my father used to schedule annual meetings of the Atlantic division in early fall. That way, he made sure he got Down Home at CP's expense in late September and early

October, when the beauty of The Place was at its most spectacular. In 1963 I persuaded *Maclean's* to send me Down Home from Toronto to write about Robert Stanfield's chances of becoming prime minister. In 1968 I persuaded *The Star Weekly* to send me Down Home to write about how Mount Allison University was weathering flower power. In 1970 I persuaded *The Canadian Magazine* to send me Down Home to write about what happened after an oil tanker leaked her cargo in black blobs that fouled the Bruce beach. Now, one Alexander Bruce —son of Harry, grandson of Charles—works in Toronto for the *Globe and Mail* and regularly persuades the paper to fly him Down Home for stories.

The faster Jack rose at the CBC, the more he resented the cultural imperialism of his superiors in Toronto. The Maritime stories they wanted seemed always to be clichés, features about *Anne of Green Gables*, Highland games, national parks, and fishermen in slickers and rubber boots. When he suggested more original stores, CBC headquarters in Toronto insisted they were "not representative of the region." He learned to hate those words. It infuriated him that CBC ignoramuses, more than a thousand miles inland, could make rulings on what was representative of the Maritimes. Snarling in his beard more than two decades later, he said, "They were turning me into a Maritime nationalist. They wanted only the most stereotyped stories from down here. If you didn't have a seagull shittin' on the lens, they just didn't want it."

He quit the CBC and settled down in Charlottetown with Barbara and their two boys. By the time of the punch in the nose, he was director of public relations for the Confederation Centre of the Arts and a stringer for the *Globe and Mail*. Early in 1969 he was telling *Globe* readers about ways in which Island cabinet ministers had blown $10 million on a boondoggle that a mesmerizing Norwegian-born promoter had talked them into. The fellow's name was Jens Moe, the politicians had all been members of the Tory government of Walter Shaw, and the recently victorious Liberals had gleefully called a royal commission to get to the bottom of the whole affair. Getting to the bottom of it could only mean revealing cupidity, stupidity, or both on the part of the hated Tories. Jack called me in Toronto, where I worked as a columnist for *The Star Weekly*, to tell me what a hilarious piece I'd get out of the hearings.

I had never heard of Jack McAndrew, but neither had I been Down Home for a while. I told my boss, Peter Gzowski, about this real smelleroo of a political story on the Island, and he said sure, go ahead. When I reached Charlottetown, dense snow choked the streets, and the temperature hung at zero Fahrenheit. Gossip was relieving the Islanders' midwinter cabin fever, and it was all about Jens Moe, the Tory fumblebums, and what was now known as the Georgetown fiasco.

Moe had proposed that, in the little port of Georgetown, the government help him set up Bathurst Marine, which would build fishing trawlers, and Gulf Garden Foods, the biggest food-processing plant the Island had ever seen. When the plant wasn't handling cod, haddock, sole, shark, or even whale, why, it would freeze vegetables and TV dinners and, my friends and fellow Islanders, there would be jobs forever. The marine yard opened in 1964, the food plant opened in 1965, they both closed in 1966, and Jens Moe vanished from the Island.

No one could figure out where $10 million of taxpayers' money had gone. That wasn't much by the standards of development bungles in other provinces, but the Island was home to only 110,000 people, and the per capita penalty was roughly $91. In Ontario, with its population of 7.5 million, a blunder that cost $91 a head would have been a $682-million scandal. Gulf Garden Foods owned the biggest industrial plant on the Island, and there it sat, in a seacoast village, and, as a Charlottetown lawyer told me, "If you can't afford to go to the Alps, and you want to hear a really beautiful echo, just go down to Gulf Garden Foods." He must have been a Liberal.

Every Toronto journalist who parachutes into a Down Home town to write a story should be so lucky as to have a Jack McAndrew helping out. He introduced me to lawyers at the hearing, gave me background on witnesses, loaned me his entire *Globe* file on the Georgetown farce, and invited me home to dinner. The McAndrews' high-peaked house was faced with warm, red stone, and when the lights twinkled through the stained-glass windows at night and the iron fenceposts jutted through billows of snow, the place looked ready for Christmas-card photography. It had been designed in 1892 by William Critchlow Harris, master of architecture in the High Gothic Victorian style—brother of artist Robert Harris, whose most famous painting was *The Fathers of Confederation*, and another great-uncle of Barbara Tuck McAndrew. The house was on West Street, where a premier, mayor, chief justice of Canada, wine merchant, sea captain, and four lieutenant-governors had lived. The street skirted the harbour, and Jack, while walking inland to his job at the Confederation Centre, spent anywhere from five to fifteen minutes, depending on how many friends he stopped to chat with.

The McAndrews had crates of Malpeque oysters, the best in the world, and while we swallowed a dozen oysters each, Jack boasted about his clam chowder. It had bacon bits in it, and onion, potato, haddock, lobster, and cream. It was a superb chowder—possibly even as good as the chowders I myself was destined to concoct in Nova Scotia—and pretty soon, Barbara brought out boiled lobster and melted butter. I met the boys, Shawn and Randy, and the family's first Nova Scotia Toller, an earlier Gunner, and I kept thinking, *If an art-centre flack, who freelances on the side, can live like this in Charlottetown, within a few miles of the best beaches in Canada, why am I keeping my wife and kids holed up in smelly old Toronto?* Three years would pass before we'd move to bluenose country.

The morning after the McAndrew feast, I interviewed Walter Shaw, the cagey, eloquent ex-premier whose Tory government had been accused in 1966 of fighting a crucial byelection by vowing, "If it moves, give it a pension; if not, pave it." At eighty in 1968, he was still leader of the Opposition, and despite the Georgetown disgrace, still popular. The royal commission investigating the affair, he growled, "isn't going to do anyone any good. You can appoint a royal commission to investigate anything. You could appoint one to investigate a church, and what would they find? They'd find the janitor stole a few light bulbs, and an elder got drunk one night, and maybe the minister said the wrong thing, or something."

Comparing the disappearance of $10 million to the disappearance of a few light bulbs struck me as so comical I put Shaw's statement in my column, and evidence at the hearings equipped me to skewer his whole gang of former cabinet ministers. I glued my facts together with sarcasm to make a one-page piece that *The Star Weekly* headlined, "Fiasco in Prince Edward Island: how to blow $10 million in a few easy steps." By the time this appeared, I was back in Hog Town, thank God. I do not like to ponder my possible fate had I lingered in Charlottetown till the day the Grit machine shoved photocopies of my column—on a page bearing the image of my face—into the letterboxes of every house on the Island and tucked thousands more under windshield wipers.

My first indication of how some Islanders felt about the column came in a letter from an Island-born woman in Saskatchewan. My hunch was that she was the homesick daughter of a member of the Shaw government. She said I was a peanut head and a pea brain and asked if, when I was born, my mother had "crawled from under the porch" and bitten me. She also felt no one would blame Toronto for the fact that my wife and I lived there because that "poor, dirty, stinking city has enough against it now." She hoped that if I ever went swimming at an Island beach, a lobster, a *big* lobster, would "grab onto your ————." She closed in red capital letters, with the offer of "a punch in your big ignorant nose" and the wish that I and mine would all rot in hell. Why? It was because I had "a poison pen."

While the Island-wide distribution of my column made me think of enemy biplanes dropping leaflets on tired soldiers— urging them to surrender because their leaders had betrayed them and slackers were seducing their wives—it made fuming Island Tories think only of bloody revenge. For the first and only time in my life, I endured denunciation in a provincial legislature. My byline had been appearing in national magazines for eight years, but an outraged Tory politician speculated that Harry Bruce did not exist. The name was a front for some dastardly Liberal hack, and Island politics being as intimate as they were rancorous, Jack McAndrew was a prime suspect. As a naive interloper from Hog Town, I had not known that he was a Liberal speechwriter. Nor had I known that he was so thick with the Grits that he was about to run for them in a federal election. (He lost to Heath MacQuarrie.) The punch was coming.

My column had derided Leo Rossiter because, as fisheries minister, he'd had a lot to do with the charming Mr. Moe and the ludicrous Gulf Garden Foods. When Jack appeared at a party where many Tories drank much booze, Rossiter asked him if he was the dirty so-and-so who'd put all that crap about him in the Toronto paper. Jack started to explain that he had indeed covered the Georgetown story for the *Globe*, but that, actually, the guy who'd written the offensive *Star Weekly* column was a Toronto journalist named Harry Bru—Whap! Rossiter's big right fist caught Jack full in the face. Down went the publicity director for the Confederation Centre of the Arts, for the full count. Life is so gentle in the Eden of the North.

* * *

Around the time of the punch, the Confederation Centre promoted Jack from publicity director to producer, and he began to deal with Canadian stars such as Anne Murray, Gordon Lightfoot, Edith Butler, and Nancy White. Barbara caught on at the Charlottetown *Guardian* ("Covers the Island like the Dew"), which paid her all of $65 a week to run its women's pages and write a daily column. In 1975, however, Jack was appointed Chief of Variety Programming, CBC Television, Toronto. He took the job partly because he wanted the experience of "playing with the big boys. So I went up to Toronto, but I went with the intention of coming back. I'd give it five years."

By 1980 he was once again fed up with the CBC. Peter Herrndorf was vice-president and general manager of the English Service Division, and "I had a fundamental difference with him." Herrndorf, he felt, had persuaded the corporation to sacrifice drama, music, and variety programming to the cause of becoming "a purveyor of information, and I say you find the soul of a nation in its artists, not in panel discussions on freight rates and free trade."

Herrndorf offered him the corporation's best job Down Home, the CBC's regional directorship for the Maritimes, at Halifax. This was a plum Jack had wanted for years, but taking it now would have appeared as his endorsement of the CBC's policies of stripping its regional operations of money and clout. "Frankly, I was terrified broadcasting people down here would think I'd become one of the hated *them* up there." For the second time, he quit the CBC.

He set up shop in downtown Toronto as an independent producer and soon put together a series in Los Angeles featuring stand-up comedians, and a string of shows starring David Bowie, The Band, The Police, and other world-famous rock groups. In Cuba he worked with Harry Belafonte and Liona Boyd on a series arising from an international festival of classical guitarists. His reputation as a writer-director-producer was high, and Barbara was pulling in $43,000 a year as editor of an insurance-company house organ. The McAndrews, in short, had only one problem in 1983: eight years had passed since they'd left the Island.

"I ran into two guys on the Island who had a little film company," Jack recalled, "and they said they wanted to expand into video, and, 'Are you interested?'" The upshot was that the McAndrews came on home, and so did their sons, grown men by now. Shawn is a graduate in theatre arts from Ryerson Polytechnical Institute, Toronto, and Randy is a cameraman. Like sons of some lobster fishermen, they both work for the family business. Jack is the boss of Video Atlantic, but he's also up to his ears in two sister firms, Points East Productions and Media Concepts, an advertising outfit. In the summer of 1987 he was taking $25,000 a year out of the business, about a sixth of what he'd been earning in Toronto four years before. Meanwhile,

Barbara, working upstairs on a word-processor in their home in Meadow Bank, was barely making $8,000 a year as a freelancer. "We're just working our ass off," Jack said.

It was he who found the house, but she had mysterious knowledge of the place before she even saw it. "He brought me out here to see it at six in the morning," she said, "and I had this instant sense of *déjà vu.*" It turned out that her great-uncles, the Harris brothers, had known Long Creek, just across West River, all their lives. Their father and his brother-in-law bought a farm there in 1858. The Harris family did not settle at Long Creek, but Robert and William often visited their cousins and painted and sketched the fields and river that Barbara now sees out her southern windows. Moreover, before moving to Meadow Bank, she already owned some of those same works. "They just hung themselves on these walls," she says. "Look at this one. It shows the ferry landing that was right down there a century ago!

"When I look out that window, coming back is all worthwhile. Our Toronto friends thought we were totally insane, and even some of our dear, close relatives. Some people took our decision as a rebuke. We had somehow looked down our noses at Toronto. Of course, Toronto thinks it's the centre of the universe anyway. You drop off the end of the world at Mississauga."

Jack, too, talked a lot about why they had come back and why it was that, for him at any rate, Toronto would always remain inferior to the Island. But all his talk came down to only one thing: "I was at the top of the heap. I was making lots of money, and might have made a whole lot more. I had offers from Los Angeles and New York, but if I wasn't living at home, it made no fundamental difference to me where I was living. There's *home,* and then there's just all the rest of it."

10

HALIFAX: THE BEST TOWN I'VE EVER KNOWN

Penny and I celebrated the last of our thirteen lucky years in Halifax by going to the Carleton Hotel on Hallowe'en night and taking a second-floor corner room that offered a matchless view of what may well be the biggest, weirdest, and—for those who hate crowds—the most unnerving annual party in all Canada. In recent years, the Halifax Mardi Gras has blossomed into a scheduled mob scene in which close to forty thousand men and women, most of them in costume, mill around, squash against one another, and scream their lungs out on two short city blocks. They squeeze into a dozen deafening bars, where the staff sport wild costumes of their own, and by three in the morning they've left Argyle Street as a sea of smashed bottles, fast-food garbage, and scattered barf.

The build-up to this monumental bash begins a few days earlier when the bars advertise their costume contests. Then, in the hours before the invasion of downtown, costume judges visit offices, banks, and shops to choose the best-outfitted staff. Just before dark, police block off motor traffic at both ends of Argyle Street. By nine o'clock, when Penny and I elbowed our way through the bar-bound swarms in the Carleton's lobby, thousands of costumed students from the city's universities had flooded Argyle. The bedlam had already begun.

The short street where the hysteria swirled is one of the most historic in Halifax. Late in the eighteenth century, when the city was young, mansions and willow trees lined both sides of Argyle, and men of the social standing of Richard John Uniacke had townhouses there. A gigantic Irishman, he was imprisoned as a possible agent of Yankee rebels in 1776, but later earned a law degree in Dublin, returned to Halifax, built up the biggest legal practice in the province, turned into the staunchest of Tories, and became the exceedingly rich attorney general of Nova Scotia. When his son killed a merchant in a pistol duel, old Uniacke had the unsavoury duty of presenting him to the court on a murder charge. Young Uniacke was acquitted. Just along from the attorney general's house, on the other side of

Argyle, was fellow Irishman Richard Bulkeley's home, now the core of the Carleton Hotel, where Penny and I gaped down at the Hallowe'en turbulence.

Bulkeley witnessed the birth of Halifax. When Colonel Edward Cornwallis, governor of Nova Scotia, founded the city in 1749, Bulkeley was his right-hand man, a dashing young officer who'd served as a king's messenger and was already rich enough to bring to the wilderness a mountain of baggage, three thoroughbred horses, and his own butler, groom, and valet. Though other British officers escaped Halifax as quickly as they could, something about it intrigued Bulkeley. He was still there in 1758 when the British not only captured Fortress Louisbourg from the French but also dismantled it, stone by stone. The cut stone had come from Normandy. The spoilers hauled it off to Halifax, and Bulkeley, who had recently been married, used some of it in the construction of his mansion. As a crippled old codger, he was Judge of Admiralty and held court in his house. Press gangs kept nabbing locals for the Royal Navy in 1798, and in an early scuffle between civil and naval authority, Bulkeley caused a ruckus by summoning nine captains to his private courtroom and tongue-lashing them for flouting the law.

By 1908, when Henry Ford boasted that his new Model T was "stronger than a horse and easier to maintain," the house had long been a hotel, and my aunt Anna, then a girl of fifteen, stayed there briefly with her grandmother Tory. Aboard the *Malcolm Cann*, the little steamer that ran out of Guysborough, down Chedabucto Bay, past The Place, and on to the rail connection at Mulgrave, Anorah Tory suffered such dreadful seasickness that she cried, "Oh, Anna, tell Captain Durkee to please take me home again." But she loved to visit Halifax, and especially to stroll in the Public Gardens, which looked as British as Big Ben (and still do). The Carleton, Anna remembers, was cosy, quiet, and reasonably priced, all in all an entirely suitable place for a mature lady from the sticks to stay with her teenage granddaughter.

When Penny and I reached our room, I poured us some rum, opened the windows, and let the Hallowe'en din roar in from the street. Within our walls lurked rock quarried in Normandy in the early 1700s, and amid the mob on Argyle stood the Five Fishermen restaurant in a building that had once housed an art school promoted by Anna Leonowens, heroine of *Anna and the King of Siam*. Just across Prince Street, and so close I could easily have beaned its white wooden backside with a candy kiss, St. Paul's Church loomed in the darkness. The first Church of England cathedral in Britain's overseas colonies, St. Paul's boasts a font topped by a carved dove with outstretched wings that dates back to the time of Charles I and witch-burnings. St. Paul's is "the mother" of the Anglican communion in Canada and the oldest building in Halifax.

Now, however, on Hallowe'en, tipsy Lucifers, vampires, and witches swirled about "the Westminster Abbey of Canada" and lolled against its wrought-iron fence. Man-sized skunks, bunnies, chickens, bears, blind mice, Mickey and Minnie Mouses, alligators, werewolves, bees from outer space, the lion of Oz, and abominable snowmen cavorted with World War One air aces, roaring Viking warriors, Arthurian crusaders, Swiss yodellers, Arab sheiks, Dutch dairymaids, Picasso clowns, Emmett Kelly clowns, blinking robots, peaceniks, terrorists, cowboys, convicts, zombies, astronauts, sailors, Mounties, ballplayers, moonies, and redcoats like those once seen around here every day. Monks, Roman senators, Batman, Quasimodo, Don Quixote, Darth Vader, the Planters Peanut Man, a couple of Zorros, and the only Groucho Marx I've ever seen in a red-and-black lumberjack shirt, they all ogled nuns, belly dancers, geisha girls, the Queen of Hearts, Miss Liberty, a female Paul Revere, two *big* girls in diapers who sucked on baby bottles, six singing babes in pink tights, dozens of witches who'd dressed for seduction rather than flying on broomhandles, and a pair of curvaceous gams, sheathed in black, jutting from a four-foot paper pumpkin.

I ventured into the street.

"Did you see the guy with the flies all over his face?" I heard a six-foot vampire, with a stake in his chest, ask a five-foot Charlie Chaplin. "Yeah," Chaplin replied, "and what about the dork with his eyeball hanging out?"

"Come on," said a drunken student, dressed somewhat like a pirate, "do I look like a mermaid?" He was trying to gaze deeply into the hard eyes of a pretty young woman who was wearing a short fur coat, net stockings, and stiletto heels. "No, honey," she said, "but you don't look like no pirate either." Klondike Kate reeled by, leaning on Merlin, who had a stuffed parrot on his shoulder, and she squealed, "Here I am, hanging onto this man, and I don't even know him." Raggedy Ann saw me taking notes. "You a reporter?" she demanded. "Yes, I guess so." She waved a hack saw in my face, and asked, "You want your beer opened?" A monstrous Smurf gave three uncostumed teenagers a jolly greeting just as a bottle of booze slipped from one boy's hands and smashed on the pavement. "Fuck off, Smurf," the boy said. I'd had enough.

By dangling my key over the heads of the surging mob at the entrance to the Carleton, I informed a bouncer that I had a room, and he managed to clear a path through the creatures. Upstairs, Penny and I closed the windows, but the street noise still filled the room. A baseball fan told me the next day that, from half a mile south, the din from Argyle Street was like the roar of Yankee Stadium as he'd approached it from blocks away during a close World Series game.

I wondered what the ghosts of Bulkeley and Uniacke thought of this outlandish bust-up, and I was glad Aunt Anna was not with us. Penny and I had planned to spend the night at the Carleton, but while Hallowe'en was spectacularly entertaining, it was also oddly depressing. We missed our nest. At 2:30 A.M. we picked our way through the shards and stinky spills on Argyle Street and strolled past a few lonely young drunks, up Spring Garden Road, beside the Public Gardens, and into the neighbourhood of Dalhousie University. By five to three, we were under the covers in our own bed.

* * *

If war were all there was to history, Halifax would be the most historic little city in North America. Britain created it in 1749 to counter the menace of Fortress Louisbourg, a French possession in those days. Thus, the city was born in the expectation of war, and it soon became a creature, a byproduct, a servant, an exploiter, victim, parasite, sweetheart, and hag of war. It was not exactly a warmonger, but for its merchants the mongering was always best in wartime. That's when Halifax was fat and lewd. It was a fortress, a depot, an implement of war. For generations it echoed to the sounds of drums, fifes, marching men, signal guns, sham battles, and the piercing tweet of the bosun's pipe. For generations it had one overriding purpose: to serve as North American headquarters for British troops and the Royal Navy. For generations the military treated its civilians as nuisances, intruders, or when the navy's press gangs were on the loose, as future cannon-fodder.

The city was only nine years old when, in May 1858, British brass gathered in the Great Pontac hotel for one of the most historic military banquets in Canadian history. The host was James Wolfe, later the commander of the British forces that took Quebec, and his guests included forty-six senior army and navy officers, mostly from Britain but also from New England. Some would one day find themselves fighting on opposite sides in the American Revolution, but for now they were all boozing and gorging together before achieving the final conquest of Fortress Louisbourg. Wolfe's bill for the night listed twenty-five bottles of brandy, fifty of claret, and seventy of Madeira; fortunately, the carousers had three days to recover before setting sail on the mission that would smash French power on the northeastern seaboard of North America. Wolfe, along with victorious regiments and warships, spent another year in Halifax and then sailed for Quebec and the battle that completed the conquest of New France. News of Quebec's fall reached Halifax in late September 1759, and the celebrations lasted for days. Each night, thousands of lighted candles appeared in the windows of houses.

Three years later, British forces that had captured Havana sailed into Halifax with loot worth hundreds of pounds. They spent the winter there, spending Spanish gold like drunken, whoring pirates. Only a dozen years after that, the American Revolution broke out, and Nova Scotia—the hold-out, the fourteenth colony—was the key to what would one day be all of Canada. Had Nova Scotia joined the revolution, the Union Jack might have vanished from North America for ever. In 1776, when the rebels forced the British to abandon Boston, Halifax was the continent's last bastion of British power. The fleet and troops, along with an early invasion of Loyalists, descended by the thousands on the suffering settlement. Meanwhile, it spawned its own gang of seagoing buccaneers—privateers who captured enemy vessels as far away as Newfoundland and the West Indies and brought home dozens of prizes every year. Halifax was a busy spot. By 1783, when the war ended, it was feeding close to ten thousand Loyalist refugees on its little streets.

The Napoleonic Wars began in 1793, and Prince Edward, the cruel, stuffy, but dedicated soldier son of King George III, arrived in Halifax in 1794. He soon turned it into the strongest fortress in North America. Halifax privateers were once again marauding the Spanish Main, and in 1813 H.M.S. *Shannon* sailed out of Halifax to make history. In a fast and bloody skirmish, she captured the U.S. frigate *Chesapeake* just off Boston and brought her home to an ecstatic waterfront crowd. Coiled lines on her main deck were still thick with gore, and pieces of skin, fingers, and hair stuck to her sides. The young captain of the *Shannon*, now a hero, was Philip Broke. The young captain of the *Chesapeake*, now a corpse stretched out under The Stars and Stripes on her deck, was James Lawrence. While dying of his wounds, he'd earned immortality by shouting, "Don't give up the ship."

During the War of 1812, Halifax was the pivot for almost all of Britain's military power in North America, and it was there, in the town cemetery opposite Government House, that the

military buried one of their greatest heroes, General Robert
Ross. He was the commander of the British forces that in 1814
charged into Washington, chased President James Madison and
his cabinet out of town, and torched the White House. Three
weeks later, the audacious General Ross died while leading the
unsuccessful assault on Baltimore that inspired Francis Scott Key
to write "The Star-spangled Banner."

Describing Halifax during the royal visit of 1939, bluenose
novelist Thomas Raddall said, "Every handful of earth here was
crumbled history." It was to Halifax, in 1839, that Samuel
Cunard brought the first scheduled steamships that carried Her
Majesty's Mail to New York. It was in Halifax, in 1848, that the
first responsible government in the British Empire took office. It
was into Halifax, in 1864, that two Union cruisers chased the
Confederate raider *Tallahassee*. It was from Halifax, on a night as
black as the Earl of Hell's riding boots, that the *Tallahassee*, with
the help of a local pilot, sneaked past those Yankee warships and
out to the giddy freedom of the open sea. It was to Halifax that,
in 1867, French ships came in peace from Vera Cruz; they'd
been part of Napoleon III's futile intervention in the affairs of
Mexico. It was back home to Halifax, from England, in 1894,
that H.M.S. *Blenheim*—a crack cruiser, painted black for the
occasion—carried the body of Sir John Thompson, prime minister of Canada, dead at forty-nine. After being sworn into Her
Majesty's Privy Council, Thompson had collapsed over lunch at
Windsor Castle.

Sir Charles Tupper, another prime minister, and his arch-
rival, Joseph Howe, also lie in Halifax graveyards. So do
William Alexander Henry and Jonathan McCully, both Fathers
of Confederation. At Camp Hill cemetery the war heroes below
outnumber the joggers above. No city in Canada has such a concentration of downtown graveyards as Halifax has, and the in-
scriptions are keys to the social history of the city. Here lie
coopers, carpenters, gardeners, the goodly wives of honest
blacksmiths and bricklayers, a detective, a regimental shoe-
maker, a gate porter of Her Majesty's Naval Yard, men of the

Shannon, a merchant who lost a pistol duel in 1819, and an army officer murdered by two thieves in 1816. Here, too, lie the children struck down by waves of diphtheria, dysentery, and scarlet fever, and the victims of the typhus and cholera that came to town in the fetid holds of vessels from southern ports. Under the *kwawnk, kwawnk* of the squabbling ravens in the heights of elm and oak stand the headstones of lords and ladies, judges and assemblymen, premiers and mayors, shipping tycoons and merchant princes, captains of vessels and captains of industry, publishers, bankers, archdeacons, university presidents, and physicians. Their names mean little to Halifax now, except as labels for streets, buildings, and beer, but all of them had contributed to the life of the little port that seemed forever doomed to make big news.

It was in Halifax, in 1907, that Alexander Graham Bell, J.A.D. McCurdy, and Glenn Curtiss met with others to form one of the world's first flying clubs. It was out of Halifax, on April 15, 1912, that news of the *Titanic* disaster flowed around the world, and it was into Halifax that the S.S. *Mackay Bennett* sailed with a cargo of 190 of the *Titanic's* 1,503 drowned men, women, and children. It was in Halifax, in the spring of 1917, that Leon Trotsky, bound from New York to the Russian Revolution with questionable passports, was briefly incarcerated. It was in Halifax Harbour, on December 6, 1917, that a Belgian steamer struck a French munitions ship, causing a fire that set off the most horrible man-made explosion the world had ever known. It flattened much of the city, killed some two thousand Haligonians, and injured so many more that, even a half-century later, one of the city's distinctive features was the number of scarred and twisted faces on downtown streets. It was in the Halifax of World War One, and of the explosion, that novelist Hugh MacLennan set his *Barometer Rising*, a landmark in Canadian literary history.

Halifax bred native sons who fought with Nelson at Trafalgar and Wellington at Waterloo. Halifax was host to five princes who became kings, of authors William Cobbett, Captain

Marryat, Charles Dickens, and Richard Henry Dana, Jr.. Halifax heard Prime Minister Stanley Baldwin commend it as "this old British city on which the flag was never lowered"; and its mayor, in 1943, heard Prime Minister Winston Churchill, who'd just toured the city, say, "Now, sir, we know your city is something more than a shed on a wharf." I grew up in Toronto knowing that important things happened in Rudyard Kipling's "The Warden of the Honour of the North." After all, it was in Halifax that my father met, courted, and, in 1929, married my mother.

*   *   *

While living near the main library of Dalhousie University, I poked around in Special Collections, and there I discovered *Edna St. Vincent Millay*, written six decades ago by my mother, Gladys Agnes King. Daughter of a Nova Scotian lawyer who'd settled in Vancouver, she'd come east, at twenty-three, to study English at Dalhousie. The document I found, bound in red with a gold title, and typed in blue ink on dry onionskin, was her M.A. thesis. My father, twenty-two and working for a Halifax daily, had recently earned his B.A. at Mount Allison, where he'd been known as both a poet and a lover. In a farewell tribute, the college newspaper had said, "All too recent to be mentioned in anything but a spirit of awed respect are the swaths that Charlie has been cutting through the waves of femininity that have this year threatened to engulf him."

As a young reporter in Halifax, he cut a few more swaths. Just before he died in 1971, and only weeks after I'd immigrated from Ontario, I met a tall, striking woman in her sixties who walked with the help of a cane. She was Mrs. Mellish Lane, but in 1928 she'd still been Miss Marjorie Kennedy, one of a number of Halifax girls my father had known in the time of ukeleles and moonlit canoes on the Northwest Arm. "Ahh, Charlie," she smiled, looking back forty-three years. "We all loved him so. And then that Agnes King came in from Vancouver, and she stole him away from us!"

The Oxford Companion to English Literature says that Edna St. Vincent Millay had recently "established her persona as a reckless, romantic, cynical, 'naughty' New Woman." My mother was also something of a naughty New Woman. She was older than most Dalhousie girls, and for a while in Vancouver she'd earned a salary. She sometimes carried her own mickey of rye whiskey. Friends of Millay, my mother explained in her thesis, described her as "petite, blythe and winsome, with appealing, greenish-hazel eyes and wondrously lovely and long auburn hair, dainty, fascinating and adorable, radiating personality so delightful that her family and friends are proud almost to the point of idolatry." My mother had her own wondrously long and lovely auburn hair, and I've no doubt that Charles Tory Bruce held it in his hands and let it fall.

In the days of their courting, the whole neighbourhood south of the university—now a fancy residential district with a smug, long-established air about it—was a fine, wild forest for walking in a winter wonderland. The stone fence around the university enclosed a field. A cow grazed there in summer, and a brook tinkled and babbled its way across the little campus. Time destroyed the cow, and parking lots and new buildings destroyed field and stream. But the forty-two years between my parents' wedding and my own family's arrival in Nova Scotia drastically changed not only Dalhousie, and not only the face of Halifax, but also the whole purpose and character of the city.

"Halifax is no longer just a military town," Island industrialist Billy Rix told me in 1987. "The military are still a factor, sure, but they aren't as important as they were thirty years ago." The search for offshore oil, the container piers, the growth of universities, the pushy downtown developers, the research hospitals, the Bedford Institute of Oceanography, and the federal and provincial payrolls have at last made Halifax something more than an instrument of war. Moreover, the fact that defence commitments are now permanent, rather than just responses to threats as they arise, also gives the port a stability it has never before enjoyed. "Yeah, and it's the banking and commercial centre for Atlantic Canada, too," Rix added. "It's our Toronto. It's cosmopolitan. No doubt about it, Halifax has won."

When I accepted a job in Halifax in 1971, Toronto friends thought that, like a deranged Parisian banker who's joined the French Foreign Legion, I was fleeing some shameful personal crisis. But my father said, "You'll have a lot of fun down there." His voice was a shade forlorn; too much time and health had passed for him to return for good. He was right about the fun. I was thirty-six before I "found" Halifax, and like a convert who has at last found a religion, I celebrated it more blatantly than those who were born into it. I wrote a radio play about "this old, raw, bloody, greedy, devious, brave, beloved little city by the sea," and it ended with the narrator lurking by himself in Camp Hill cemetery. "Stand here with your feet in the spongy soil of this slightly sunken grave," he said, "and just listen to the poor, doomed, fleeting city in its glorious, headlong, impertinent celebration of its flicker in time."

I have lived not only in Toronto but also in New York, London, Ottawa, and assorted smaller places in Ontario, New Brunswick, and California, and all of them had their attractions. But not one had the peculiar chemistry of charm and romance— the formula of physical drama and social intimacy—that makes Halifax the best town I've ever known. Haligonians share a secret, and the secret is the sea. They don't think about the ocean all the time, but it shapes the city's character, keeps its pride of history fresh, and makes its people closer to one another than city folk usually are.

A man gave me a quarter because he saw me turning my pockets inside out after I'd parked beside a meter. He smiled, pressed the coin on me, kept right on walking. He was a classic Halifax man. He was formal but not stuffy, helpful but not pushy, friendly but never intrusive, a stranger but a fellow Haligonian. Halifax is full of people like that. If you were to walk down a sleepy Halifax street around breakfast-time in the golden mist of an October morning, and if your eyes met those of a man putting out garbage or a woman raking yellow leaves, it would be un-thinkable not to say, "Good morning." It's that kind of town. When I won a national award for a radio play I wrote, I got notes of congratulations not from other writers but from neighbours. When I first edited *Atlantic Insight* magazine, strangers stopped me in the street to say they liked it. When our boat drifted within talking distance of the backyards of the rich on the Northwest Arm, a woman came out of her house and down to the water's edge to tell me the same thing.

I *possessed* Halifax as I've possessed no other city. When I jogged there, I knew I was jogging in My Town. Every step of the way. On summer Sundays I ran past stately wooden rooming houses and the shaded stone mansions of the rich, and then, under skyscraping pines at the fingertip of Halifax peninsula, all the way around the oceanside perimeter of Point Pleasant Park. Yachts scooted out to sea, and when they tacked I heard the thunder and flutter of their sails. Seagulls glided and squawked, and, on my way inland again, a journalist, or a lawyer, or a dentist stuck his head out his car window and shouted, "Drive 'er, Harry, drive 'er." By the time I reached the Camp Hill graveyard, my torso glistened, my face looked like a baked tomato, and I was gasping like a dying horse. But not far from Joseph Howe's grave, a faucet stuck out of the ground, and a green watering can sat beside it. I filled up the can and dumped cold water on my head, four or five times. Delicious. Then I walked home, feeling fit and smug. My Town.

The walk took ten minutes. It was also a ten-minute walk from our house to the Waegwoltic Club, where our whole family swam and we kept our sailboat; to the wooden house where, in an office with an old and elegant fireplace, I edited *Atlantic Insight*; to the Dalhousie Library, which I mined for my freelance writing; the university track, where I did my most serious running; the faculty club, where I sometimes consorted with the urbane; and the Rebecca Cohn auditorium, which was not only home to a good film society and the Atlantic Symphony Orchestra but also the hall in which Penny and I witnessed performers from the sublime Luciano Pavarotti to the ridiculous Victor Borge. And then walked home on streets where the heavy branches of a soaking night hung so low the leaves brushed and sprinkled our heads. To walk right downtown, of course, was another matter. That took all of twenty minutes.

I was a recognizable frog in a medium-sized pond in Halifax, and so was almost everyone else. There are few ciphers among Haligonians; almost everyone is a *somebody*. The fact that Halifax is gossip-ridden is a tribute to its ceaseless fascination with all its somebodies. Haligonians don't limit their gossip to their separate professions and social enclaves. The talk ranges freely over what's doing in the arts, sports, courts, business, media, bureaucracies, and always, politics. It is proof of the city's life, and one's ability to share it. Nothing weaker than the magnetism of The Place could ever have induced me to leave Halifax; and once a month, Penny and I go back for a night or two, just to get our Halifax fix.

*　*　*

Could Canadian naval ratings of World War Two possibly have imagined a scene such as the one we witnessed on our last Hallowe'en on the streets of old Halifax? One reason why they ran amok in the infamous VE Day riots was that, for five tense years, many had found Halifax a mean, joyless place with a deadly shortage of good parties and legal bars. At war's end their bitterness exploded in a disgusting rampage of looting, burning, brawling, window-smashing, and liquor-store raiding. Soldiers, prostitutes, and civilian thugs joined the orgy.

For some, the riots of May 7 and 8, 1945, were like the modern Hallowe'en bashes: merely an excuse to get barrelhouse drunk. "You could see dozens of people going up Citadel Hill," a woman veteran recalled in Barry Broadfoot's *Six War Years*, "a long line of them, with beer and booze. I had thirteen mickeys of rye stashed around me, in my uniform. Even about four in my bloomers, in my jacket and shoulder purse. Thirteen, and wherever you looked on the hill there was people drinking. Two's, four's, eight's, big parties, and let me say, more than the usual quota of screwing. . . . The Halifax riot, to us girls in my quarters, was mostly about getting drunk. We were so young, eighteen, nineteen, or so. . . . We were in the army and it was pure excitement all the way."

For others, however, the riots were an excuse for revenge, muggings, thievery, and worse. The violence took a couple of lives and cost $5 million in property damages. An Ontario woman, once a teenage housewife in Halifax-Dartmouth, wrote to me in 1980 about things she'd seen on May 8, 1945, and wished she hadn't. Her husband had worked at the Halifax Dockyard, but they lived in Dartmouth, in an overpriced room with a creaky bed. Not knowing of the madness raging in Halifax that day, she took the ferry across the harbour to Water Street to meet him when he got off work:

> I arrived early, and while waiting, I was terrified. I remember I was wearing a yellow coat, and a sailor came up behind me and grabbed my shoulder. I thought it was my husband, so I turned around. He had a priest's collar on, and a dozen watches on each arm, and his hands were bloodied, and all I could see was the blood. Then a stationmaster, I believe it was, he came to me, and was I glad he did! . . . My husband arrived, and we took the ferry to Dartmouth. We wanted to get home quickly so we walked through a cemetery, and some of the sights there I will never forget. . . . Little children pulling wagons and baby carriages, all full of stolen groceries and clothes. . . . Girls being raped. . . . We went back over to Halifax the next day, and they'd smashed every store window from Spring Garden Road to the ferry, and there was smashed furniture on the street. They'd thrown it from the top floors of Eatons.

In the long pull of Halifax history, the shortage of drinking establishments in the middle decades of our own century was an aberration. For most of Halifax's 239 years, it has been a hard-drinking town. In the early 1760s—when it was still only a dozen years old, with a civilian population of two thousand—the armed forces, prostitutes, and booze had already given it a reputation as the most sinful port in North America. On Camp Hill and Citadel Hill, a few hundred yards west and up the slope from St. Paul's Church and Bulkeley's new house, as many as twelve thousand troops sometimes slept, ate, brawled, and worked up a mighty thirst. When a major fleet of the Royal Navy arrived, a few hundred yards east and down the slope, the disease-ridden waterfront swarmed with thousands upon thousands of sailors. Redcoats, jacktars, and desperately out-numbered townsmen had their choice of more than a hundred licensed drinking houses, and Halifax was barely a teenager.

A century later, a religious reformer complained in a pamphlet that no fewer than 340 Halifax booze-peddlers were doing the devil's work. The drunkenness of Halifax was woeful, "and the misery, wretchedness, degradation, and crime which it breeds baffle the power of language to describe." The wickedness was "more than sufficient to call down showers of fire and brimstone, such as once descended upon the Cities of the Plain." Announc-ing a new liquor law in 1887, the *Morning Herald* said, "Barroom drinking is suppressed. The number of licensed drinking places has been reduced from 184 to 54." But fifty-four bars in a town of forty thousand people was scarcely suppression of a severe kind, and as the paper conceded, "It is natural to suppose that the 54 will do three times the trade they did before."

As World War One began, Halifax boasted 150 liquor whole-salers and retailers. On July 1, 1916, Prohibition closed down every bar in the city. Blind pigs sprouted like crocuses in April. "We had about four bootleg joints right around here," Alex Nickerson told me, "and there were dozens and dozens all around the city." We were sitting in the Halifax *Herald* building, at Argyle and Sackville streets. Richard John Uniacke's town-house had once stood here, but Nickerson was telling me about a later time. A stocky, bald chap, with a faintly military air, he had kind eyes and a dark moustache. Half a century of working for Halifax newspapers had not worn him down. He was seventy-nine but looked sixty-five, and he was still cranking out pieces for the *Herald* papers. "One of the most famous places was only a block from here," Nickerson continued. "It was just known as Dauphinee's.

"This Dauphinee family were famous bootleggers. They ran booze in from Sambro and the mouth of the Northwest Arm, and there was a whole bunch of them. The place near here was an old frame house with iron or steel doors, and when you went in, you walked upstairs for your beer or a shot of rum. They were always being raided. They built a lookout. It projected from the front of the house, upstairs, and the fellow on duty could look up and down the street, and if he saw the police coming, he'd give a warning. By the time the law got through the metal doors, the rum was usually flushed down the toilet."

Some bootleggers had "ingenious hides" for liquor. While demolishing a wooden building on Water Street in the 1930s, a wrecking crew found a sink inside the front door. A hidden pipeline ran through the house, up a backyard slope and into another building on Hollis Street. "That's where the booze had been back in the twenties," Nickerson continued. "The bootlegger on Water Street could turn a tap on, and rum would come down the pipe from Hollis and into a pitcher in the sink. But he could also shut it off and turn another valve, and then out came only water. Just to tell you how smart they were."

Not only booze but also prostitutes infested Halifax from its very birth. Like seagulls over the wake of a ship, whores sailed into the settlement behind the first cursing, guzzling, brutish, and bellyaching British tommies. Harlots, hookers, courtesans, and call-girls have hung around Halifax ever since. As early as the mid-1750s, the Beach (Water Street) was a string of funky, ramshackle wooden lairs for whores and boozers. Up the hill toward the Citadel, "Barrack Street" (Brunswick Street) was no better. When the tars went up to Barrack Street with their cudgels, or the "lobsterbacks" came down to the Beach with their bayonets, blood flowed and bones broke, but life went on for the strumpets, and so did trade. Thus, two tart-infested slums flanked St. Paul's Church, the better part of town, and what is now the stage for the Hallowe'en blow-out.

If whoring thrived on warfare, so did Halifax. During forty-four of its first sixty-six years—from the time when Micmac allies of the French scalped Haligonians who strayed into the woods, till Napoleon's defeat at Waterloo—Britain was fighting the French, the Americans, or both at once. Whores and a handful of merchants who wheedled favours from successive governors had much in common: they sucked gold from every war. During the American rebellion, exiled Loyalists and bitter redcoats—troops the Yankees had driven out of Massachusetts—flooded Halifax. Rents and food prices soared, and, as Thomas Raddall wrote, "The merchants, the landlords, the brewers, the madams of the bawdy houses reaped the harvest; but the ordinary townsfolk, as so often in the story of Halifax, found themselves in open competition with a horde of strangers for a roof above their heads and the very food upon their plates."

* * *

If sailors and tommies resorted to brothels and floozies, the higher ranks had their own little amusements. Officers whiled away idle hours not only with drinking, duelling, fishing, hunting, cockfighting, and coursing hares with terriers but also with kept women. In 1776, when General William Howe, commander of British armies in the rebel colonies, withdrew to Halifax with his entire army and fleet, he brought along his wine cellar and mistress.

A decade later, Prince William, a son of George III, arrived in Halifax as commander of a Royal Navy frigate and promptly hurled himself not only into every brothel in town but also into the bed of the seductive, manipulative, and ambitious Mrs. John

Wentworth, wife of the former governor of New Hampshire and future lieutenant-governor of Nova Scotia. Prince William, a ruddy youngster with a pointed head, was the first royal visitor on what would one day be Canadian soil. Halifax was made for him; he was a lecher with a stupendous drinking capacity. At twenty-one, he was only half Mrs. Wentworth's age, but the generation gap apparently did not bother them.

When Prince Edward, William's brother, came to Halifax in 1794 for a six-year term as commander of the troops in Nova Scotia and New Brunswick, he set a somewhat better royal example for the *hoi polloi*. With him came Julie St. Laurent, a dark, petite Frenchwoman whose real name was Thérèse-Bernadine Mongenet, and he built them a lovenest far from the floggings and hangings that he thought were such a good idea downtown.

Six miles north of Halifax and overlooking Bedford Basin, Prince's Lodge was a two-storey wooden Italianate mansion with wings on either side, a series of waterfalls, a heart-shaped lake, shady paths that spelled out "Julie," replicas of Chinese temples with glass wind chimes and tiny bells, and down close to the water, a rotunda where the regimental band of the Royal Fusiliers entertained guests from Halifax.

Nearly two centuries after it was built, the rotunda still stands. It's near Prince's Lodge Esso on the Bedford Highway, and it's so familiar and so uncelebrated that thousands of commuters never notice it as they whiz by twice a day. During the two great wars of this century, this quaint round structure overlooked the formation of the mightiest convoys in naval history, while at the foot of what was once Edward and Julie's pretty playground, trains from central Canada carried doomed young Canadians down to the waiting whores and troopships.

When World War One broke out, local prostitutes still lurked in the neighbourhoods where trollops had operated for more than one hundred and sixty years—Water Street, and the old quarter above Argyle—but now they couldn't possibly satisfy the sudden and gigantic demand for their services. From 1915 to

1918, Canadian National Railways moved more than 800,000 soldiers from Montreal to Halifax for shipment overseas. Prostitutes, sniffing opportunity and led by a big contingent from Montreal, poured in from across Canada. They soon spread all over the city, and CNR's unintentionally appropriate code name for Halifax was "Uncalm."

By the Dirty Thirties the number of Halifax whores had declined as drastically as the economy, but streetwalkers were still noticeable. Like dowagers, matrons, movie stars, and virgins, they favoured the Princess Eugénie hat—a fancy little number with a jutting feather, named after a nineteenth-century empress of France—but at the outbreak of World War Two their most conspicuous trademark was white rubber overshoes. For a while, Halifax was full of stories that respectable south-end women, not knowing what signals their own white overshoes were sending out, endured gross propositions from drunken sailors on downtown streets. World War Two brought Halifax the biggest invasion of prostitutes in its history but, as Raddall reported, "vice was more dainty now—and more discreet. Doll Tearsheet of 1942 wore a fur coat and a smart dress, travelled in taxicabs, patronized the best shops and restaurants, let herself be seen at the best dances, exacted a high price for her favours, and bestowed them in snug flats and apartments, or in secluded cottages well outside the city."

This, however, was far from true of every prostitute in the 1940s. Some, for instance, worked downtown in a red-brick brothel at 51 Hollis Street, directly across from the back door of Government House. (The back door had once been the front door, but in response to the degeneration of Hollis Street, the main entrance had long since been moved up to the Barrington Street side of the mansion.) The boss at 51 Hollis was Germaine, and it was said that her wine cellar was superior to that of her vice-regal neighbour. Like many others who profited from Halifax harlotry, Germaine came to Halifax from Montreal, but she was originally from Paris. Before, during, and after World

War Two, she was Halifax's most notorious madam. Men lined up on the street to get inside 51 Hollis, and not all of them were drunken sailors. According to legend, a respectable south-end burgher died in the arms of one of Germaine's girls. The madam made a couple of discreet phone calls, and a pack of the man's friends picked up his corpse, took it a couple of blocks up Hollis Street, and dumped it on the steps of that venerable haven for the bluenose business élite, the Halifax Club. The press dutifully reported that he'd collapsed and died while entering not a harlot but the gentlemen's club he'd loved so long and well.

Germaine's successor as Halifax's most notorious madam was Ada McCallum. When Ada died in 1986, she was seventy-seven, and the *Globe and Mail* celebrated her career in an obituary under the heading "Woman a Halifax legend in four decades as madam." The paper said she'd "made a fortune operating call-girl services out of a succession of houses in Halifax and neighboring Dartmouth," having arrived in Halifax in 1946. In Alex Nickerson's memory, however, she was in the city before World War Two. The girlfriend of a well-known naval athlete, she was "a beautiful, socially accomplished woman." Even after becoming a madam, she attended at least one society ball, and charmingly hobnobbed with unsuspecting admirals, generals, and south-end snobs.

In her middle years, she had a hard-drinking editorial executive at the Halifax *Herald* newspapers as her beefy Romeo. After he died, she invited a randy, eccentric, gentleman of leisure from Iceland to live with her. He claimed to be both a graduate of the London School of Economics and a one-time concert pianist, and Ada bought a baby grand piano so he could perform for her friends.

One of her most successful establishments was on Morris Street near Barrington Street, and handy to the Nova Scotian Hotel. When two of my friends rolled into the Morris Lodge one night in the 1950s, Ada had only one girl "in residence." The men flipped a coin, and the winner got the whore. The loser, a college graduate, whiled away the time by listening to Ada's knowledgeable theories on the poetry of John Keats. Under more innocent circumstances in the early 1970s, she played poker with one of several boozer-playboys in the Liberal government of Premier Gerald Regan and lost much of her collection of Royal Doulton figurines. Ada often faced charges such as keeping a bawdy house, but she was seventy-four before she endured a heavy penalty, and even then it wasn't for peddling the services of whores. It was for hiding from the feds $65,000 in income from her call-girl service. She paid an $18,000 fine.

By the early 1980s, yuppies were restoring derelict houses near Morris and Hollis streets, moving into them, trying to make the neighbourhood respectable, and urging governments to purge it of squabbling hookers. This was understandable, but the new people were bucking a stubborn flow of street history.

* * *

One Saturday morning in April, I climbed on my white bike and glided downtown to meet Louis W. Collins. Fog smothered the city, and I couldn't see the tops of buildings. Wearing pith helmets and scarlet tunics, two girls with backs as straight as rake handles rode shiny black horses on Bell Road. The riders were members of the Junior Bengal Lancers, the supreme club for horsey little Haligonians. Lou Collins awaited me at the war memorial in Grand Parade, the small park that separates City Hall from St. Paul's Church, and he was immaculately turned out for his role as guide for my private walking tour of historic Halifax.

His hat, shirt, tie, sweater, sports jacket, and trench coat were a medley of browns, wools, and tweeds. He wore moccasin-style shoes and leather gloves and carried a black, rolled-up umbrella. His spiky black eyebrows, severe eyeglasses, and speckled beard reminded me of Aleksandr Solzhenitsyn. His eyes suggested that only fools failed to grasp that nothing in this whole wide world could possibly be more satisfying than simply walking around downtown Halifax on a foggy spring morning. Every city should have a Lou Collins.

It was he who led the mid-sixties fight to foil the politicians, bureaucrats, and developers who, while planning an expressway through the waterfront, aimed to smash down ironstone buildings whose very walls wept history. Remembering Lou as a strap-wielding school principal and as a Boy Scout leader with bony knees, Halifax writer Stephen Kimber said in 1971: "But there was another Lou Collins, one we didn't know or care about—the Lou Collins who had already begun the long and lonely struggle to preserve Halifax from the high-rise, tin-can developments that were so popular when I was growing up. To be against them, and be a member of such organizations as the Heritage Trust (as Lou Collins was and is), was at that time sort of a reflection on the virility of a man, and his name was sure to draw knowing nods when it came up in conversation."

Gradually, however, Haligonians began to see Lou not as a kook, but as a saviour. He was out to save the historical character of their own town, the evidence of a city's soul lingering in brick, stone, and wooden beam that went all the way back to the Napoleonic Wars. While others helped, it was Lou, more than anyone else, who stopped the expressway, saved the crumbling, tide-washed warehouses, and got them included in a National Historic Site. This was not a museum, like Fortress Louisbourg, but a busy commercial development tucked within renovated walls, and it was the first of its kind that the federal government had ever helped to create. For a dozen years Lou devoted every minute he could spare from his job as a high-school principal to his tedious, exhausting, and sometimes hated campaign for the preservation of mouldy stone hulks. He won, but the victory had its price: "My kids still regret the time I gave to it."

Though retired from the school system, Lou remains Honorary Civic Historian and keeps busy trooping gangs of visitors around town. He reminded me in the fog that the city removed the parking lot in front of St. Paul's in 1978, and that although this "eliminated a convenience for certain important men who liked to park there while drinking and chasing women," the new landscaping restored the Grand Parade connection between town government and historic church. "The design of this cenotaph," he told me, "is as close to the one in Whitehall as any I've seen in photographs from across Canada." He poked at two loose screws in the Cross of Sacrifice, as though they were his personal responsibility, and explained that the cross—with its centred initials for George, King, and Empire—was "one of the last relics of the British Empire."

We ambled down Duke Street to the northernmost block of Granville Street. Halifax boasts more Georgian architecture than any city in Canada, but what arose on Granville, after a fire destroyed its wooden shops in 1859, was a commercial strip of stone and brick buildings in an elegant Victorian style. The firm that supervised their design, William Thomas and Sons of Toronto in far-off Canada West, imported iron shopfronts from New York, but since assorted proprietors have been lathering them with paint for thirteen decades, you need a Lou Collins at your elbow to find that out. He pointed his umbrella at a tiny sign beneath the display windows of a shop selling trendy bamboo items, and I bent down to read "D.D. Badger & Co., N.Y." Lou said, "All these surrounds are metal. You can stick a magnet to them, but if I do that too often the men in white suits will come and get me."

Developers putting up the Barrington Inn in the mid-1970s hoped to bash down the west side of Granville to make room for shops, bars, restaurants, and the rear of the hotel. But William Thomas and Sons had designed the rows of buildings as foils for each other, and now, more than a century later, the federal government had recognized both sides as an architectural treasure. "The east side was more Italianate," Lou said, "and the west side simpler." By the time the west side was threatened, he could count among his allies some powerful Haligonians, including the bouncy mayor, Walter Fitzgerald. The developers soon discovered that to get all the property they needed they'd have to remove, number, and store not only every metal storefront but also every last stone on the face of the old Granville strip. Then, after they'd built the hotel and indoor shopping avenues, they'd be obliged to paste each ancient piece back into its proper place. "It cost them about $1.5 million," Lou chortled, "but it's the most striking example of facadism anywhere in Canada."

We strolled on to the Morse's Tea building, a gloomy warehouse at Hollis and Upper Water streets. It's made of slate from a quarry that once operated across the Northwest Arm from the city. Throughout the nineteenth century, this ironstone was what Haligonians used whenever they built something that they wanted to outlast Egyptian pyramids. If the enemies of historic buildings had triumphed back in the 1960s, wrecking crews would have had a sweaty time of it while trying to pull down the Morse's Tea building and its ironstone neighbours on the waterfront. Rain turns ironstone black and glistening, and on a wet night the tea building might be a secret lair for Sherlock Holmes's fiendish enemy, Moriarty. Even under full sunlight, ironstone has the forbidding cast of a penitentiary on a moor, but your true Haligonian sees a peculiar beauty in it.

Lou used to snoop all through these buildings, lurking among the smells, echoes, shadows, dust, and casually scattered relics of bygone commerce. In Simon's Office and Warehouse, built around the time of the Charge of the Light Brigade, he found portable, cylindrical oil-burning stoves, used to keep potatoes from freezing in the years when, late each fall, schooners brought loads of spuds from Prince Edward Island. In the Old Red Store on Collins' Wharf—Enos Collins, privateer, shipping tycoon, financier, and, when he died at ninety-seven, the richest man in Canada, was not a forebear of Lou Collins—he found huge ship's blocks from square-rigger days, presses that once squashed down cotton bales in the holds of ships, and the ads of long-gone steamship lines. "And in here," he said, poking Morse's Tea building with his brolly, "I stumbled on some glass grenades dating from the 1880s. They were called Harden's Hand Grenade Fire Extinguishers. They were glass bottles filled with a chemical mixture, and they broke when you threw them on a fire."

J.E. Morse and Company, tea merchants, bought the Jerusalem Warehouse in the early 1900s. The company had "a whole regiment of tea tasters," men who'd been trained on plantations in India. Indian carvings graced the windows in the ironstone walls. Tin cannisters of teas, each one numbered, lined the Blending Room, and in the Tasting Room, men sipped tea from small white porcelain cups with no handles, then spat it into brass cuspidors. "I took my wife's Girl Guide troop in there once," Lou chuckled, "and they were pretty shocked to see all these men swishing tea around in their mouths, and then squirting it into spittoons." But Morse's Tea no longer tasted and blended its own tea and coffee here in the neighbourhood Lou helped to save, and the cuspidors, cups, cannisters, scales, coffee mills, and assorted teapots have vanished from the building. Once more, it's a warehouse.

Lou led me south to the Dartmouth Ferry terminal. Ferries started to run to and from the Dartmouth side in 1752, and that, he asserted, meant this was "the oldest continuing salt-water ferry in North America." Horses on a treadmill once powered the ferry, "and we had not a steamship, but a *team*ship. Heh, heh." (Lou's little jokes reminded me he'd been a Boy Scout leader.) We continued south till we came upon a granite bollard, four feet high with a small cross carved on it. Weather had been smoothing the bollard for at least one hundred and fifty years. Lou patted it lovingly, as though it were a faithful hound, and said, "This is the only evidence of the distant past around here. It only became evident when they tore down some buildings. Please God, they don't take it away."

Right here, where the King's Wharf had once stood, the first royal visitor to North America had stepped ashore, and though the future King William IV was less interested in making Halifax history than in making Halifax women, it annoyed Lou that not so much as a plaque marked the scene of Silly Billy's arrival. Just inland, on Upper Water Street, O'Carroll's Restaurant and

Lounge occupied the exact spot where the Great Pontac had rocked to the revelry of the merry warriors at James Wolfe's dinner party.

Jim O'Carroll, a lean, suave, gray-haired gent from Donegal, is one of the more recent in the long procession of Irishmen who's enlivened Halifax. For decades he ran the finest restaurant in Glasgow, Scotland, and then, in 1982, he moved to Halifax and opened O'Carroll's. Twenty years ago, Lou told me, older Haligonians stayed away from downtown Halifax at night because it was often so deserted it seemed dangerous; but now that dozens of drinking joints thrive within a few hundred yards of one another, they stay away because the neighbourhood is often so *drunken* it seems dangerous. Street brawls and stabbings are on the rise. Many of the middle-aged folks who do brave the streets for a spot of night life avoid the raucous college-boy bars and head for O'Carroll's, where the atmosphere is as warm as a kitchen *ceilidh*, and Scottish and Irish performers serve up the good old songs.

Strolling through the Maritime Museum of the Atlantic, Lou and I paused before a glorious and garish ship's figurehead. She was bigger than any real woman and made Dolly Parton look like a flat-chested flapper. While showing her to proper ladies on his walking tours, Lou said, "I like to talk about keeping abreast of Halifax. Heh, heh." At Bishop and Hollis, across from the rear of Government House, he identified a vacant lot, surrounded by a low metal fence, as the spot where 51 Hollis Street had once stood, where Germaine had kept her complement of harlots. A historic site, if ever there was one.

We walked up Bishop to Barrington Street and around to the front driveway of Government House. The city owes this Georgian palace partly to Lady Wentworth, who insisted it be built—at horrendous expense in the Halifax of 1800—so she'd have a suitable place not only to entertain friends but also to snub ladies who'd once snubbed her for her dalliance with Prince William. "So Government House is really a monument to early feminism," Lou told me. A car pulled up beside us, and out stepped Rosemarie Abraham, wife of Lieutenant-Governor Alan Abraham, and their daughter Louise.

Across Barrington, in the cemetery where surly redcoats once guarded gravediggers and mourners from scalp-hungry Indians, lay the bones of the man who'd set the White House aflame. Next door to us, the spire of St. Matthew's soared above the church cellar that, back in the bad old days of the nineteenth century, a vintner had rented for the storage of booze. It was just about noon, and nearby traffic was getting busy on the most prettily named downtown street in Canada—Spring Garden Road—and Rosemarie and Louise and Lou and I, we all agreed that it was a fine thing to see the fog lifting and the sunlight falling.

*   *   *

By one of those coincidences that sometimes makes the Maritimes feel like the territory of one big clan, our daughter Annabel's first boyfriend turned out to be a grandson of the same Marjorie Kennedy Lane who'd dated my father half a century before. The boy's name was Phillip MacAulay, and his older brother, Callum, was in love with Annabel's close friend, Marlis Callow. When Marlis and Callum got married at St. Paul's Church, I was among the chattering tribes that awaited them at the reception in the clubhouse of the Armdale Yacht Club. The clubhouse was wooden, painted white and blue, and it sat above salt water, dozens of moored sloops, and a stone mast-shed that looked suitably grim for a property whose history as a prison for foreigners dated all the way back to the War of 1812.

"They're coming, they're coming," a girl squealed. I went outside just in time to see a black limousine, as sleek as a panther, crawl up toward the clubhouse. It crossed the little causeway, passed the grim shed, and crept up the hill toward me, and all the way it was led by a marching, gray-haired piper. He was the groom's father, Dr. Malcolm MacAulay, head of pathology at Dalhousie University and stalwart of the pipe band of the Halifax Police. He wore the kilt, in the MacAulay tartan.

Under the blazing sunlight that fell from a sky as blue as the taffeta dress of maid-of-honour Annabel Bruce, Dr. MacAulay's face was red, wet, and proud. He played "Scotland the Brave" and "Highland Wedding," and then the car stopped at the clubhouse door, and the bride and groom, shiny-eyed and impossibly attractive, joined the crowd, and everyone pushed inside to drink, eat, clap, cheer, shed a tear, and hear the toasts.

Not only Dr. MacAulay but his sons—Callum, Phillip, Alan, and Alexander—wore the kilt, in either the dress or hunting tartan of their clan. The best man, Lisbi Eaten, wore the Nova Scotia tartan. A youth of East Indian extraction, he delivered his toast with Highland panache, and all in all, this was a summer afternoon for laughter and formality, jokes and ceremony, families and lovers, Scots and yachts, history and expectation. Like God only knows how many Maritime couples before them, Callum and Marlis were about to move west. They were bound for Vancouver, and I remember their Halifax wedding as a quintessentially Down Home celebration.

11
HOME FOR CHRISTMAS

When my father was a boy, his sisters were schoolmarms at assorted villages and shores in Nova Scotia, and Christmas was the
only time in winter that he saw them together. He once wrote,
"I knew about a gentleman named Santa Claus. I may have sent
him an occasional postcard. But if I did it was only to be polite, a
kind of insurance just in case. He never took rank in importance
with Bess and Anna and Carrie and Zoe." Each came home with
a suitcase full of parcels, which she promptly locked away so
little Charlie couldn't get at them till the Big Day. The expectation of what would be in those packages, of hearing the laughter
of his sisters fill the house, of knowing that for a few precious
days the bedrooms would once again hold the girls who belonged
in them—these made the days before their arrival a time of
almost intolerable excitement for him.

On December 10, 1919, he used *The Shoreham Searchlight* to
remind Zoe to "DO YOUR XMAS SHOPPING EARLY" and to give
her a shopping assignment: "This *Searchlight* is all blots but I
can't help it. Find enclo. $1.00 part payment on presents for
Mama, Harold [MacIntosh, his chum from the farm next door,
and now my eighty-three-year-old neighbour], etc. I will send
more when I get my fur money. Just now, half-broke. 'Kid.'"

One or two of the girls might show up at The Place aboard the
mail-driver's sleigh on the weekend before Christmas, but Will
Bruce always made at least one trip to Boylston, five miles away,
to pick up a daughter who'd arrived by steamship from Mulgrave. He'd use the family sleigh, hauled by the skittish family
mare, Doll, and he'd cover his lap with the family buffalo-robe.
The boat had to steam up Chedabucto Bay to reach Boylston,
and from The Place you could see her moving inland. Once,
Sarah Bruce and little Charlie stood in the snow outside the
back porch and waved a red tablecloth at the vessel, just in case
Bess could see it from four miles out on the bay. Surely she'd be
looking in their direction.

All his life, my father carried memories of those Christmases,
of raisins, oranges, roast goose, red-and-green tissue-paper bells,
real bells that tolled over moonlit fields of snow, sleighbells at

the gate, frost on the windows, the far blink of a lighthouse, the hot kitchen where birch and maple crackled in the Waterloo range, and The Room. That was the dining room, and in there the light of a second fire flickered in an open Franklin stove and a tinselled fir brushed the ceiling. It was in The Room that Charlie stripped the wrapping from a red tin pig that ran when he wound it up, from a flashlight, a box of paints, and, above all, the Daisy air rifle he'd been dreaming about ever since he'd seen it in a summer catalogue. His stocking—boys wore long ones then, gartered above the knee—hung in the kitchen some years, and in The Room other years, but it was always "sure to bulge on Christmas morning, like something with mumps."

As Charlie grew older, he got more books as Christmas presents from his parents and the girls, but the book he most clearly remembered was a volume of poetry sent by someone in the States, not to him but to his mother. It was by George William Russell (1867–1935), the Irish intellectual who signed his works AE. Charlie was ten or twelve, and decades later he wrote, "I can still recall that tingling of the spine, discovering from the printed voice of that wonderful Irishman what men could do with words.

"The peacock twilight rays aloft
"Its plumes and blooms of shadowy fire."

If Christmas brought to The Place a book that fanned the flame of his ambition to write poetry, it also shone in his head in a way that cast later Christmases in shadow. He put up a good act during the Christmases of my boyhood in Toronto. He never let me and my brothers know that he found the jolly Yuletide season depressing. He hated its commercialism, the greed it aroused in us, the bills it dumped on his shoulders, and the way it disrupted work routines that normally made the world turn as it should. It also plunged him into memories of Christmases at The Place, Christmases he would never know again because he was no longer a boy, and Will was dead, and Sarah and the girls were scattered across the continent, and the old homestead had been rented to a fellow named Brown. My father died in Toronto in 1971, escaping his sixty-fifth Christmas by six days.

*　*　*

After Will Bruce died in 1934, Sarah lived for a while in the States with the families of Carrie and Zoe, but she ended up in Edmonton with her oldest daughter, Bess, a spinster. When Bess's long career as a schoolteacher was done, mother and daughter came back Down Home to live out their last years, and The Place was once again The Place of the Bruces. That was in 1953, but the summer visits had begun long before that. In July 1946, for instance, while Harry Brown and his wife Georgie were still renting The Place, a horde of folks with Bruce blood descended on them: Sarah and Bess from Edmonton; Zoe, and her son and daughter, from California; Carrie, and her daughter, from Detroit; and me, an eleven-year-old from Toronto. I got the small room over the kitchen that had once been my father's, but I can't imagine where everyone else slept. Bruce invasions occurred most summers, and I've a hunch no one along the shore looked forward to September as eagerly as the Browns did.

From 1953, Sarah and Bess lived in The Place year-round till Sarah died at ninety-nine in 1966, the year Canada, too, was ninety-nine. They'd shared a dozen quiet Christmases at The Place, but Bess soon began to close the home in November and to spend the winter at Anna's house in nearby Boylston. Anna and her husband, Robert MacKeen, had moved to Saskatchewan in 1928, and almost four decades later, just before his death, they, too, had resettled Down Home. So the spinster Bess and the widow Anna endured the winters together in Boylston, but each spring Bess went back along the road to The Place, and both sisters began to anticipate visits from Zoe in California and Carrie in Detroit. Even by the homecoming standards of ex-Maritimers, the returning record of these two frail, witty women is astounding. Zoe is ninety now, and Carrie ninety-three, but in the past twenty years they have failed to get home in the summer only a couple of times. They were here last summer. They'll be here next summer.

When Bess died—at ninety-four, in June 1986—our daughter Annabel sat with Carrie beside the open coffin at the funeral home in Guysborough. Men and women whose forebears Bruces knew in the nineteenth century flowed into the room to pay their respects, and Carrie, who was so deaf she could not have heard a bomb explode, simply watched the kindness in their faces and then murmured to her grandniece, "Mine own people." Much later, while rooting among crumbling, water-stained, and bug-ravished books at The Place, I found *Mine Own People* by Rudyard Kipling. On the front flyleaf, written in black ink in the neat, flowing hand of a conscientious schoolmarm, was "Miss Carrie Bruce. Xmas 1914." She was twenty-one when she unwrapped that book by the shining tree in The Room, and my father was eight. He was too old for the mechanical pig, and too young for the air rifle. Maybe that was the Christmas when he got the flashlight.

*   *   *

Penny and I still had an apartment in Halifax in December 1986, but our oldest son and his brood were coming back from Toronto for Christmas, and we decided that The Place was the place to be. Not for twenty years had the house been open in the winter, and cycles of freezing and thawing had buckled wallboards, left rooms reeking of mould and dampness, and spawned armies of sowbugs. But the beds were good, and we had enough of them. The oil furnace in the basement still worked. Where the old Waterloo had once stood in the kitchen, we had installed a new Resolute, a cute, pricey, and efficient air-tight stove. The previous summer, I had bought three cords of sixteen-inch birch and maple, and somehow I had managed to split it all without breaking a foot or losing a toe. If the power failed, we'd still be cosy. We had kerosene lanterns, too. We were ready for whatever winter might throw at us during the most historic Christmas our own little family had ever celebrated.

On December 18, Penny and I drove the 180 miles from Halifax to The Place, cut a little spruce, set it outside the front door and festooned it with lights. The house smelled like the inside of its own ancient Leonard refrigerator, but the oil furnace and a snapping fire in the trusty Resolute drove out the clamminess. We drank rum, wrapped gifts, and listened again to a record we've dragged out of one cupboard or another every Christmas for a quarter century: "Songs of Peace and Goodwill from the Welsh Mines" by the Rhos Male Voice Choir. The singing miners sounded more glorious than ever, and never before in our lives had we managed to wrap the bulk of the presents a full week before Christmas. We wanted everything to go right.

This would be the first Christmas that a real crowd of Bruces had spent at The Place in more than sixty years. Melinda and Jessica were coming from Toronto; they were four and two respectively, children of Alec and Vivien Cunningham Bruce. The last little kid to awaken in this house on Christmas Day in the morning had been their great-grandfather, darling Charlie, the Prince of The Place, who had turned four in 1910.

To round up our gang, I had to travel farther than Will did to pick up his daughters in Boylston. Decades have passed since the last ferry steamed up Chedabucto Bay with rail passengers from Mulgrave. Indeed, months may go by before we see *any* ship on the bay, though the Queensport lighthouse still offers its rhythmic glimmer. To meet my daughter Annabel and my son Max, both students at the University of King's College, Halifax, I drove twenty miles to a windswept stretch of the Trans-Canada Highway near the village of Monastery. I arrived just as a blue-and-silver Acadian Lines bus, jammed with homeward-bound Cape Breton Islanders, came arrowing east, pulled over to the shoulder, and released just two passengers, Annabel and Max. Annabel waved good-bye to the driver, and she and Max, grin-

ning like beautiful fools, walked toward me with their gift-filled
paper bags with handles, and the bus roared back onto the traffic
lanes, and the Tracadie River made its way through brown
eelgrass to the marching waves of St. Georges Bay, and how
come, at moments like this, I have always forgotten to bring
my camera?

My son Alec's job was with the *Globe and Mail* in the heart of
Toronto, where the atmosphere sometimes stank, and the moment he stepped outside Halifax Airport he said, "The air! I
can't get over it. It's so *clean*." His wife, Vivien, and their two
daughters had arrived before him, and I had picked them up at
her parent's house in town. Her father had made a superb teddy
bear, and her mother had bought another one, a supermarket
special. I happened to have bought an identical supermarket
special, and now we had three bears for two girls. With me and
Alec up front, and Vivien, Melinda, Jessica, and the wrapped
bears in the rear seat, and gift-stuffed luggage farther aft,
the little Toyota was tested, but the three-hour drive to Port
Shoreham went as smoothly as sailing on a broad reach in a
soft breeze.

Snow had dusted the fields, the sun was out, and as we swung
between the familiar dark hills, hundreds of millions of years
old, that flanked James River, the setting sun behind us filled the
flurries ahead with pink light, a light to make atheists believe in
angels. We arrived home as darkness fell on the shortest day of
the year, and when Alec got out of the car he said, "Boy, if I
could get a decent job down here, I'd be back in a flash." In the
spring of 1971 a Halifax businessman had told me, "We don't ask
to be rich. We aren't greedy. We just want the economy to be
healthy enough so our children won't have to keep on goin'
down the road, that's all."

* * *

Now we were all Down Home together. The term has many
meanings. If a Maritimer says "Down Home" while sitting in a
Toronto tavern, he could be talking about all the Maritimes, or

Prince Edward Island, or a valley, cove, county, village, or the house where he grew up. Down-homer, in its gently derogatory sense, is also relative. "The first time I ever heard the term down-homer was a bit more than thirty years ago," my father wrote in *Mayfair* in 1955. "It was used by Bill Fraser, a brakeman in Antigonish, to describe a freight-handler from Mulgrave. Now, Mulgrave is only forty-five railway miles down the line from Antigonish; and I suppose that whenever Bill swung down off a gondola a few miles farther west and talked about the way things were done in his home town, he too was a down-homer to the more cultivated citizens of New Glasgow and Truro."

But the most intimate use of "Down Home" I've ever heard came from the lips of Floyd Grady when he dropped over to give me a Yuletide bottle of navy rum. His childhood home was adjacent to The Place on the east, and his mother, Kay, still lived there. Floyd was off to Prince Edward Island to visit relatives. Jerking his head over his right shoulder, he explained that he would not be Down Home on Christmas Day. To him, Down Home was a few hundred feet away. Every house along the shore was a specific Down Home for a specific family. At the Down Home of Carl and Carol MacIntosh, our neighbours to the west, the house was brim-full. Grant, the oldest son, a bricklayer in Oshawa, Ontario, had driven his pickup truck nonstop for more than eleven hundred miles to get to his Down Home for Christmas. Stewart, the second MacIntosh child, had recently been crew aboard a 230-foot vessel that sailed across the Atlantic to the United Kingdom. London had not impressed him much. It was too tough. Nobody cared for you there. As his father said, "It's just been a city too long." It could never be a Down Home.

Down Home was the kind of neighbourhood where, when you went out to your highway letter-box on December 23, you found a bottle of homemade spiced grape jelly, and for your granddaughters, two candy canes, each with a little horse's head, made of red and green felt. They were from Jean Grady, widow of Floyd's uncle Oscar. She had never met Jessica and Melinda, but she knew they were at The Place. Down Home was also the kind of neighbourhood where, on December 24, the girls next door walked their pony around to your front door just to give two much tinier girls a Yuletide thrill. The visitors were Jennifer, Jane, and Sarah MacIntosh, and the pony was Fiona, a reddish-brown beastie with a straw-coloured mane, a barrel belly, and a fat, scarlet ribbon tied in a bow at her throat. Melinda had come from Queen Street in downtown Toronto, and when she saw Fiona strolling down our driveway, she squealed, "Yikes, get me outta' here. There's a *camel* coming!" Within five minutes, however, both she and Jessica were aboard Fiona's beamy back, as giant snowflakes fell.

Down Home was the kind of neighbourhood where, when your distant cousin Clayton Hart dropped in—he was the fellow who built our cottage—he brought a box of the world's best chocolate fudge, made by his wife, Rose. When Carl and Carol MacIntosh came over, trailing a couple of daughters, Carol handed us pillow-sized loaves of brown raisin bread, fresh out of the oven. When Grant showed up, he gave us oysters in the shell. When Stewart arrived, he produced English toffee. Grant and Stewart sat around till midnight on December 23, downing Mooseheads, talking, yarn-spinning, and dreaming out loud. We dubbed them the Two Wise Men. Grant thought he'd pull out on Boxing Day, heading south in his pickup truck for New Jersey. He had a friend down there, and the friend might fix him up with a job in Florida.

From before Christmas till a blizzard on New Year's Eve, the weather was God's gift to the Bruces. Most days, Christmas was green. After Carl MacIntosh delivered three cords of sixteen-inch firewood, Alec split some of it with a six-pound maul every day for a week, and he never once wore anything heavier than a shirt and sweater. (He split the whole pile, Vivien stacked it, and Penny and I were still burning it during the lonelier Christmas of 1987.) On Boxing Day, Alec and I dug out baseball gloves we hadn't used in years and played catch for an hour with a shiny, time-blackened hardball.

The weather sometimes staged shows, our own vast meteorological pantomimes. One morning, after midnight winds had roiled the floor of the sea and violent water had torn at the sandstone of Ragged Head, a pink stain split the cold blue of the bay, and even though the storm had long since passed and the air was still, big combers kept crashing ashore. Bahamians call this phenomenon a dry rage. While the dry rage continued— and we could hear it way up here at The Place—huge, soft snowflakes swirled around the house, and we felt we were inside a glass paperweight that chimed a carol. Through the fat flakes, we could see splashes of blue sky, and late in the afternoon the snow stopped falling, the waves quit crashing, and a swath of purple cloud sat on the stone hills across the bay. The rest of the sky was pure blue, and low sunlight slanted all across our sweet field of grass—yellow, russet, and blotched by snow.

Clayton Hart built a little box sleigh with steel runners, paint-ed it fire-engine red, and brought it over, and we dragged the little girls around on it whenever the snow was thick enough. One day, Annabel discovered a miraculously hard crust on top of the snow, and she climbed aboard Clayton's creation, and, whooping and screaming, she shot down our slope for a hundred yards. Dragging the sleigh by its yellow cord, she trudged up toward the house. Behind her, a curve of hairy evergreens on Bruce's Island stood out against the sheet of the bay, and some-thing in the way she laughed made me think the impossible was happening: we were all getting younger.

When she and Alec were small they were such pals they could read one another's minds, and they played for hours at a stretch in worlds they invented together. But long before Alec married Vivien—he was nineteen—the pull of different schools, ambitions, and sets of friends and enemies had destroyed that fine old closeness. In recent years, Annabel and Alec had scarcely even seen one another. During Christmas at The Place, however, she gave him Paul Simon's record "Graceland" (he brought the same record from Toronto for me and Penny), and in the evening they sat by the hot stove, wearing their parents' sweaters, and they listened to the driving rhythm of the music, drank beer, made jokes, and dredged up memories. They went for walks, too. They found their old skates in the shop where I store firewood, and defying all warnings about weak ice, skated on the long pond where James Christopher Bruce had launched his first trading schooner while David Livingstone was exploring Zambezi.

In 1970, when Alec was nine and Annabel seven, I had written about their skating together in a column for Maclean's. In the piece, I lay in bed in Ottawa on a Sunday morning. I was suffering from the kind of hangover that Dorothy Parker once said "ought to be in the Smithsonian Institute under glass." Thoughts tormented me, too, thoughts like pecking ravens. Environmental doomsayers had predicted that, thanks to population growth and industrial activity, there soon wouldn't be enough oxygen in the air for people to breathe. We were bound to run out of oxygen in only twenty or thirty years, and I just lay there, torturing my mind in my already-tortured head with hideous fantasies about what would happen to our children in the 1990s. The column ended with my edging my way downstairs for a cup of black coffee just as Alec and Annabel came bursting in the kitchen door: "They've still got their skates on, their faces are red, a gust of knifing Arctic air tears around the kitchen, we all start laughing and hollering and, sweet dying Jesus, they are beautiful children."

Now, sixteen years later at The Place, they burst into another kitchen, after another skate, and their cheeks were once again red, and a gust of Atlantic air tore around the room, and Annabel said, "God, we felt just like little kids out there." Later, each one got me aside to tell me how much the other loved The Place, and its fields, woods, streams, and bay. The Place was even growing on Max. The other two had childhood memories of our houses in Toronto, on Toronto Island, in Newcastle, Ontario, Ottawa, and Prospect, Nova Scotia, but since Max's infancy his only hometown had been Halifax. He loved the city, and even as a high-school student, he often lurked all night in the radio station at Dalhousie University. He detested the long drive to Port Shoreham. Being there bored him. It meant doing without video games, video music, movies, television, clubs, restaurants, street traffic, junk food, friends, and, aside from his parents, anyone even to look at, much less talk with. But with all of us together again, he liked The Place. With my old Pentax hanging from a shoulder, he took long walks by himself and took the best photographs anyone has ever taken of his ancestral home.

*　*　*

When Anna came over for Christmas dinner and to meet her great-grandnieces, four generations of Bruces sat down at two tables to gorge on roast turkey, cranberry sauce, gravy, mashed potatoes, carrots, cauliflower, plum pudding with hard sauce, and butterscotch pie with whipped cream. Jessica, Melinda, and Anna were the only teetotallers. The rest of us downed white wine. In the entire history of The Place it's doubtful if wine had ever graced a Christmas feast, but out of deference to Anna's principles and respect for the gentle ghosts of earlier teetotallers within these walls, we offered no raucous toasts to the fact that wine on the table was another "first." Later we opened the doors of the Resolute and installed a screen, and Anna sat in her father's rocking chair beside the flames. He'd been dead for fifty-two years, and she talked of times long gone.

She'd been told as a child that before the pioneers built schools here, male teachers had tutored children while boarding in the youngsters' houses. The only classes were for singing lessons, and a favourite song began, "Here we go to Miramichi, to get a load of sugar and tea." Maybe it was the chair, but something reminded Anna of the evening Bess vanished. She remembered that after Will's grocery store near Boston had failed, he and Sarah and the girls were living not here but at the home of Sarah's mother—the property now owned by sleigh-maker Hart—a little way inland on the McPherson Lake Road. With another little girl, Bess, who was eleven or twelve, went out to fetch cows. During the search, they met Will, who asked if they knew their way home. Bess said yes, but she was wrong. A search party scoured the woods till midnight, began again at dawn, and found the girls at midmorning. They'd spent the night under a tree, no doubt praying. "I can still see the men coming down over the hill with them," Anna said.

Before I drove her back to Boylston, she opened her purse and started to hand fifty-dollar bills to me and Penny, and twenty-dollar bills to Alec, Vivien, Annabel, and Max. We all protested. "Oh no, Anna, you mustn't do that. You really shouldn't."

"I certainly should," she said. "I'm the great-*great*-aunt of these little girls, not just the great-aunt. This is one Christmas in a hundred years."

And so it was.

"To a kid of four or five or six," my father wrote, "time is the Pool of Now." When you looked back later, the pool was still there, but it had become the Pool of Then, in which "people and events and places, laughter and tears and the words of songs — they drift and swirl and circle, far off and yet immeasurably close." The Christmas of 1986 has slipped into my own personal Pool of Then.

I remember Melinda and her aunt Annabel charging across our snowy field to greet one another, and Melinda "treating" her uncle Max with the toy doctor's kit she found under the tree. The best patient she'd ever have, he lay moaning on the chesterfield for much of Christmas afternoon. I remember Jessica, at two, dancing to "Graceland" in all the glory of her nakedness, and Annabel showing both her nieces how to make sugar cookies that looked like fish and teddy bears. I remember the friendly racket at midafternoon on Christmas Day when half a dozen MacIntoshes came into our kitchen. The room sounded like the corridors of Maple Leaf Gardens between periods of a hockey game in, say, 1946. That was the year I first saw The Place, and I gave swimming lessons to a sunny nine-year-old named Carl MacIntosh. Carl was a sunny forty-nine-year-old now, and he outweighed me by fifty pounds, and we sat by the stove, tossed back a rum or two, and swapped jokes.

A few days later, Alec and I explored our property lines, and he considered sites for the house he would build when the time was right for him to return for good. Neither of us knew whether that time would ever come. As Annabel pulled on her snow-boots before going back to Halifax, she said, "God, I hate to leave this place. I wish I could take it with me, on a key chain or something." She would graduate in journalism in the spring and head for Upper Canada. Alec and his family were about to fly back to Toronto, and Max would soon go to Montreal to study film production. As for Penny and me, we had lived in seventeen different apartments and houses since our marriage in 1955, and we knew we would never move again. But having found our home, we had lost our children.

Down Home, of course, there's nothing new in that.

ACKNOWLEDGMENTS

Because the shape of this book changed as I wrote it, I could not work into the text the material I got from several people who endured my interviews. The insight I gained from them increased my understanding of Maritimers and will influence other writing I do; I'd like to thank them here.

On Prince Edward Island, they were newspaper publisher Jim MacNeill; writer-broadcasters Kennedy Wells and Jim Cluett; and theatre director Ron Irving. In Fredericton, they were free-lance writer Colleen Thompson; Susan Montague, director of development, University of New Brunswick; and Alfred Goldsworthy Bailey, poet, historian, and essayist. In Saint John, they were Eric Teed, lawyer; Shirley J. Elliott, tourist officer, Saint John Visitor and Convention Bureau; David Goss, recreation supervisor for the city; Jack Shackleton, general manager, Market Square Corporation; Donald F. MacGowan, lawyer; and retired school principal Arthur Harrison.

Several Monctonians were helpful. These included newspaperman Michael LeBlanc, and ex-newspapermen Edward Larracey and J.E. (Ned) Belliveau. Belliveau drove me all around Moncton—whose people he had celebrated in two books—to give me history lessons on buildings, bridges, and neighbourhoods. Other Monctonians who helped me were Ned's son Peter Belliveau, of Moncton Industrial Development; Philippe Blandford, president of the University of Moncton; Paul-Emile Benoit of the university's public relations office; and CBC executive Claude Bourque. It was in Moncton, too, that Roger Doiron and Liane Roy, officers of the Society of Acadians of New Brunswick, allowed me to interview them.

In industrial Cape Breton, those who submitted to interviews included businessmen Ian Stott, S.A. (Sandy) Reeves, and Daniel White; freelance jounalist Parker Barss Donham; musician and stage performer Max MacDonald; historian R.J. Morgan, director of the Beaton Institute of Cape Breton Studies; ex-newspaper editor Ian MacNeil; ex-broadcaster Toby Halloran; ex-coal miner Robert Davis, of New Waterford; and Timothy Belliveau, another of Ned's sons and now director of public relations for the University College of Cape Breton. Tim gave me records of Cape Breton music that the university had issued and a dozen books of local history that it had published. Speaking of publications, I also thank Douglas Lochhead who, as director of the Centre for Canadian Studies, Mount Allison University, sent me lectures the centre had published.

With respect to print sources, I checked historical information by consulting such standard references as *The Canadian Encyclopedia* (Hurtig Publishers, Edmonton, 1985); *Encyclopedia Canadiana* (The Canadiana Company, Ottawa, 1963); *The Oxford Companion to Canadian History and Literature* (Oxford University Press, Toronto, 1967) by Norah Story; and *The New Columbia Encyclopedia* (Columbia University Press, New York, 1975).

I am grateful, too, to the Canada Council for financial assistance while I was researching and writing *Down Home*; and to Harry Flemming of Halifax, a highly knowledgeable Maritimer who read the page proofs.

I credited some print sources in the text, but for the sake of brevity and pace, did not provide full information about the books and articles I consulted and quoted. The following notes should fill in gaps for readers who might want to know the full story about my sources.

Chapter One
Won't You Come Back Home?

Figures and generalizations about the exodus from the Maritimes come mostly from demographic statistics in *Canada Year Book*;

from "Atlantic Region Population Dynamics, 1981–2001," a study prepared in 1979 by the Institute of Public Affairs, Dalhousie University, for the Atlantic Development Council; "The Golden Age and The Exodus: the Case of Canning, Kings County" (*Acadiensis*, Autumn 1981) by Alan A. Brookes; and "The Problem of Out-Migration from Atlantic Canada, 1871–1921: A New Look" (*Acadiensis*, Autumn 1985) by Patricia A. Thornton. Miriam Chapin's *Atlantic Canada* was published by The Ryerson Press, Toronto, in 1956. The first publisher of Charles Bruce's *The Mulgrave Road* was Macmillan of Canada, Toronto. My understanding of Acadian history and attitudes comes from *Chéticamp, History and Acadian Traditions* (Breakwater Books, St. John's, 1986) by Father Anselme Chiasson, translated by Jean Doris Le Blanc; *The Acadians of the Maritimes* (Centre for Acadian Studies, Moncton, 1982), edited by Jean Daigle; *Along the Shore of Saint Mary's Bay* (Université Ste. Anne, Church Point, N.S., 1977) by J. Alphonse Deveau; *Two Beginnings, A Brief Acadian History* (Lescarbot Press, Yarmouth, 1980) by J. Alphonse Deveau; *The Acadians: Creation of a People* (McGraw-Hill Ryerson, Toronto, 1973) by Naomi Griffiths; *Pélagie* (General Publishing, Toronto, 1983) by Antonine Maillet, translated by Philip Stratford; and *La Sagouine* (Simon & Pierre, Toronto, 1985) by Antonine Maillet, translated by Luis de Céspedes. The publisher of James Roy's *The Scot and Canada* was McClelland and Stewart, Toronto.

Chapter Two
Maritimers Are Like a Motorcycle Gang

Hugh MacLennan's story about the Halifax Customs inspector is from "Portrait of a City," an essay in his *Cross Country* (1949). The publisher of *Bluenose: A Portrait of Nova Scotia* was Harper and Brothers, New York; and the publisher of *My Island Pictures* (1980) was Ragweed Press, Charlottetown. With respect to "the spirit of wrangling and the vigour of parochialism," I relied heavily on *The Maritime Rights Movement, 1919–1927* (McGill-Queen's University Press, Montreal, 1979) by Ernest R. Forbes.

His "Maritime Rights" in *Horizon Canada* (Volume 8, number 92) was also useful. Arthur T. Doyle's *Front Benches and Back Rooms* (Green Tree Publishing, 1976) gave me insight into nineteenth-century religious squabbling in New Brunswick. The publisher of Donald Creighton's *Dominion of the North* was Macmillan of Canada, Toronto; the publisher of Charles W. Dunn's *Highland Settler* (1953) was the University of Toronto Press. My references to the International Railway come from G.R. Stevens's *Canadian National Railways* (Clarke, Irwin, Toronto, 1960.) A.W. Trueman described the teacher-hiring policy of the Saint John school board in his *A Second View of Things: A Memoir* (McClelland and Stewart, Toronto, 1982). The story about how two students viewed the Maritimes is in "Regional Identity: A Maritime Quest" (Centre for Canadian Studies, Mount Allison University, 1985), a lecture by William B. Hamilton. I found the quote about the scum rising to the top during the American Revolution in "The Loyalists: A Sympathetic View" (*Acadiensis*, Autumn 1976) by W.S. MacNutt. For this chapter, as well as others, my sources with respect to the Loyalists also included: "Understanding the Loyalists" (Centre for Canadian Studies, Mount Allison University, 1986), a series of lectures by J.M. Bumsted; *The Loyalist Governor* (Petheric Press, Halifax, 1983) by Brian C. Cuthbertson; "Loyalist Attitudes" by Margaret Ells, in *Historical Essays on the Atlantic Provinces* (McClelland and Stewart, Toronto, 1967) edited by George Rawlyk; *This Unfriendly Soil* (McGill-Queen's University Press, 1986) by Neil MacKinnon; *True Blue* (Collins, Toronto, 1985) by Walter Stewart; *The Loyalists of New Brunswick* (printed in Fredericton, 1955) by Esther Clark Wright; "Loyalist Souvenir," a pamphlet published by the New Brunswick Historical Society in 1933 to celebrate the 150th anniversary of the landing of the Loyalists at Saint John; and *Canada's First City, Saint John* (Lingley Printing, Saint John, 1962). A.C. Jost's description of the soldiers of the British foreign legion who settled near Guysborough, and their descendants, is from pages 154 and 155 of his *Guysborough Sketches and Essays* (Kentville Publishing, Kentville, N.S., undated). I first read the story of Jack Munroe in an unpublished manuscript by Donald Kerr, Halifax lawyer and former boxer.

Chapter Three
Confederation, Carpetbaggers, Come From Aways

Ernest R. Forbes discussed the impact on the Maritimes of the federal government's wartime policies in "Consolidating Disparity: The Maritimes and the Industrialization of Canada during the Second World War" (*Acadiensis*, Spring 1986). Part Two of my book *R.A.: The Story of R.A. Jodrey, Entrepreneur* (McClelland and Stewart, Toronto, 1979) describes the fall of DOSCO. William Y. Smith's rebuttal of Abraham Rotstein's opinion appeared in *Acadiensis* (Autumn 1976). J.M. Bumsted's analysis of how some historians have viewed Prince Edward Island's attitude toward Confederation may be found in *The Garden Transformed* (Ragweed Press, Charlottetown, 1982), a collection of essays edited by Verner Smitheram, David Milne, and Satadal Dasgupta. John G. Reid's review of nine books about Canadian history appeared in *Acadiensis* (Spring 1987). Carman Miller's remarks about editorial writers supporting "the Canadian option" are also from *Acadiensis* (Spring 1982). The *Chronicle-Herald's* opinion of the Meech Lake accord ran on July 31, 1987. "The Great Fundy Hot Air Project," which so enraged Premier Gerald A. Regan, appeared in *Saturday Night* in August 1971. The publisher of *Rambles Through the Maritime Provinces of Canada*, which I've quoted in later chapters as well, was Arthur H. Stockwell, London. The book is undated, but the author did his Down Home rambling in the late 1920s. Isabella Lucy Bird described her tea party with "Nancy Stuart of the Mountain" in *The English Woman in America*, published in 1856. Much of my information about Bloody Sunday and labour history in industrial Cape Breton comes from *The Company Store* (Doubleday, Toronto, 1983) by John Mellor.

Chapter Four
We're All in the Family

Though I got most of my information about Captain Joseph Salter from his great-grandson by phone, some of it came from *Chocolate River* by Edward W. Larracey (Lancelot Press, Hantsport, N.S. 1985). The publisher of *My Acadian Heritage* (1985) was also Lancelot. David MacDonald's story about nicknames among Nova Scotian Scots ran in the *Reader's Digest* in October 1980. I learned about Margaret Marshall Saunders in an article by Phyllis R. Blakeley in the *Nova Scotia Historical Quarterly* (September 1971). I owe the quotes from the letters of Rev. Norman McLeod to *Bulletin of the Public Archives of Nova Scotia* (Volume II, no. 1, 1939). The publisher of *Controlling Interest: Who Owns Canada?* was Macmillan of Canada. Peter C. Newman's remarks are from *The Acquisitors* (McClelland and Stewart, 1981). The publisher of *Debrett's Illustrated Guide to The Canadian Establishment* was Methuen. P.B. Waite's discussion of Robert Borden's letters appeared in *Acadiensis* (Autumn 1976). The publisher of the *South Shore Phrase Book* and *The Second South Shore Phrase Book* was Lancelot Press. My father's article in *Mayfair* ran in July 1955.

Chapter Five
The Land's Lousy—and Unforgettable

My chief source on the geological history of the Maritimes was *Geological Background and Physiography of Nova Scotia* by Albert E. Roland, printed in 1982 by Ford Publishing, Halifax, for the Nova Scotia Institute of Science. "The Physical Geography of the Atlantic Provinces," by Ian Brookes, also proved valuable. It is the first chapter of *Studies in Canadian Geography: The Atlantic Provinces.* I used "Geology Tour of Saint John" (New Brunswick Museum, 1978), the "Geological Highway Map of Nova Scotia," and the "Geological Highway Map of New Brunswick and Prince Edward Island." Both maps are provincially subsidized publications of the Atlantic Geoscience Society. I also consulted Franklin Russell's *The Atlantic Coast* (Natural Science of Canada, 1970). The publisher of *Searchers at the Gulf* (1970) was W.W. Norton, New York. *Rivers of Canada* was published by Macmillan of Canada. The publisher of *Atlantic Canada Today* was the Atlantic Provinces Economic Council. Jack Zinck tells the story of *Fantome* in *Shipwrecks of Nova Scotia, Volume 1* (Lancelot Press, 1975). Much of my information on the S.S.

Atlantic came from *Disasters at Sea* (1986), published and edited by Tony Cranston. *Jack in Port, Sailortowns of Eastern Canada* was published by the University of Toronto Press.

Chapter Six
In Search of *Moonshadow*

Marsden Hartley and Nova Scotia was published in 1987 by the Mount Saint Vincent University Art Gallery, Halifax, in association with The Press of the Nova Scotia College of Art and Design and the Art Gallery of Ontario. The editor was Gerald Ferguson, and the book includes essays by Ronald Paulson and Gail R. Scott.

Chapter Seven
Saint John: City of Turbulent Spirits

My chief source for historical background on Saint John was George W. Schuyler's *Saint John, Two Hundred Years Proud* (Windsor Publications, Burlington, Ontario). Ian Sclanders's description of King Street is from his "Streets of Canada: King," which *Maclean's* published on August 6, 1958. The quote from Rowse is from his *Memories of Men and Women* (The Quality Book Club, London, 1980), which I have also quoted in Chapter Eight on Fredericton. MacNutt's description of the brutish patriots is from "The Loyalists: A Sympathetic View" (*Acadiensis*, Autumn 1976). Babcock's comment on traditions of collective violence is from "The Saint John Street Railwaymen's Strike and Riot, 1914" (*Acadiensis*, Spring 1982). Statistics on the horrors of Partridge Island as a quarantine station in the 1840s may be found in Harold Wright's introduction to *The Diary of Nellie McGowan* (Partridge Island Research Project, 1984). Most of my material on the *Marco Polo* is from "The Fastest Ship in the World" (*The Atlantic Advocate*, July 1981) by Kathy Heighton-Bockus. I drew information on the opening of the railway bridge and the railway sod-turning festivities, both in 1853, from C.M. Wallace's "Saint John Boosters and the Railroads in

Mid-nineteenth Century" (*Acadiensis*, Autumn 1976). References to the pushy commercial character of Saint John in the 1860s are supported by the same source.

Chapter Eight
Fredericton: Pampered Pet of Old New Brunswick

I am most indebted to *History of Fredericton, The Last 200 Years* (City of Fredericton, 1980) by W. Austin Squires, edited by J.K. Chapman. I found Theodore Goodridge Roberts's descriptions of Bliss Carman's boyhood home and the "enchanted atmosphere" of Victorian Fredericton in "Bliss Carman and the Poetry of Mystery: A Defence of the Personal Fallacy," a lecture Malcolm Ross delivered at Mount Allison University on October 4, 1984. Quotes from Frank Risteen about "the Celestial girl" and "the Celestial citizen" are from his booklet *The Celestial City, Fredericton and the St. John River*, first published by the Fredericton Tourist Committee in 1897 and reissued in 1983 by Print 'n Press, St. Stephen, N.B. For information about Christ Church Cathedral, I relied on Robert L. Watson's *Christ Church Cathedral, Fredericton: A History* (published by the Bishop and Chapter of the cathedral, 1984). The lines by Fred Cogswell are taken from his "Ode to Fredericton," which was published in *The Blasted Pine*, edited by F. R. Scott and A.J.M. Smith (Toronto, Macmillan, 1967). Alden Nowlan's remarks about Fredericton's affection for its eccentrics are from his "Fredericton: It's for con-noisseurs of civility," in *Guide to Atlantic Canada* (Impact Publishing, Halifax, 1981). That's also the source of the quote that ends this chapter.

Chapter Nine
The Seductive Myth of the Perfect Island

I learned most of what I know about "the garden myth," its divergence from reality and effect on Island politics, from *The Garden Transformed: Prince Edward Island, 1945–1980* (Ragweed Press, Charlottetown, 1982), a book of essays edited by Verner

Smitheram, David Milne, and Satadal Dasgupta. David Weale's "'No Scope for Imagination,' Another Side of Anne of Green Gables" (*The Island Magazine*, Fall–Winter, 1986) was enlightening about aspects of Island life that both depressed Montgomery and inspired her to write fiction. I learned of Mayor Dawson's proposal to treat Charlottetown's drunkards in *Gaslights, Epidemics, and Vagabond Cows: Charlottetown in The Victorian Era* (Ragweed, 1987), a collection of historical essays edited by Douglas Baldwin and Thomas Spira. This book also tells the story of the city's refusing (though later accepting) help from the Grey Nun nurses. The source for my description of The Belfast Riot was H.T. Holman's "The Belfast Riot" (*The Island Magazine*, Fall–Winter, 1983). Some of my understanding of old attitudes toward absentee landlords comes from J.M. Bumsted's "The Origins of the Land Question on Prince Edward Island, 1767–1805" (*Acadiensis*, Autumn, 1982). I owe my quotes from Lucy Maud Montgomery's letters to "Lucy Maud's Island" (*The Island Magazine*, Fall–Winter, 1986) by F.W.P. Bolger. Marlene-Russell Clark described the 1966 by-election campaign in First Kings in *Canada's Smallest Province* (The Prince Edward Island 1973 Centennial Commission), a book of essays edited by F.W.P. Bolger. The publisher of *Trailing Pythagoras* (1987) was Methuen, Toronto. Moncrieff Williamson documented Robert Harris's affection for the Island and its capital in *Island Painter, The Life of Robert Harris (1849–1919)*, published by Ragweed in 1983. "Fiasco in Prince Edward Island: how to blow $10 million in a few easy steps" appeared in *The Star Weekly*, March 16, 1968.

Chapter Ten
Halifax: The Best Town I've Ever Known

My chief mine of historical information on Halifax was the revised (1971) edition of *Halifax, Warden of the North* (McClelland and Stewart, Toronto) by Thomas H. Raddall. It's the liveliest city history I've ever read. Here and there, I checked it against other sources. Another useful book was *In Halifax Town, On*

Going for a Walk in Halifax, Nova Scotia by Louis W. Collins. He had it privately printed by Halcraft Printing, Halifax, in 1975. For information on Collins himself, I went to Rosemary Bauchman's chapter on him in her book *Scotia Story Tellers* (Lancelot Press, Hantsport, N.S., 1983). The publisher of *Six War Years* was Doubleday, Toronto. The anonymous reformer who complained so violently about Halifax grogshops did so in *Halifax: "Its Sins and Sorrows,"* a booklet first published on April 9, 1862, and republished in more recent times by the Friends of the Old Town Clock. My information on troop movements to Halifax during World War One is from *Canada's National Railways and the War,* an undated booklet published by Canadian National Railways. For material on the Wentworths, I consulted Brian C. Cuthbertson's *The Loyalist Governor* (Petheric Press, Halifax, 1983).

Chapter Eleven
Home for Christmas

Charles Bruce described his memories of boyhood Christmases at The Place in "Tin Pigs and Raisins," published by *Canadian Homes and Gardens* in December 1954.